Hiking the Hawaiian Islands

Hiking the Hawaiian Islands

A Guide to 72 of the State's
Greatest Hiking Adventures

Suzanne Swedo

FALCONGUIDES

GUILFORD, CONNECTICUT
HELENA, MONTANA
AN IMPRINT OF THE GLOBE PEQUOT PRESS

For Keith

FALCONGUIDES®

Copyright © 2010 by Morris Book Publishing, LLC

Interior photos: Suzanne Swedo
Text design: Nancy Freeborn
Project manager: Julie Marsh
Layout artist: Maggie Peterson
Maps: Design Maps Inc. © Morris Book Publishing, LLC

Library of Congress Cataloging-in-Publication Data
Swedo, Suzanne, 1945-
  Hiking the Hawaiian Islands : a guide to 72 of the
State's greatest hiking adventures / Suzanne Swedo.
      p. cm.
  Includes bibliographical references and index.
  ISBN 978-0-7627-4347-6
  1. Hiking–Hawaii–Guidebooks. 2. Hawaii–Guidebooks.
I. Title.
  GV199.42.H3S94 2009
  919.6904'42–dc22
                                      2009022538

Printed in the United States of America
10 9 8 7 6 5 4 3 2 1

Contents

Acknowledgments xi
Introduction 1
    The Making of the Islands.. 2
    About Lava 3
    Flora and Fauna 4
    Threatened Hawai'i 9
    The People 9
    How to Speak Hawaiian 13
    A Few Words of Caution.. 15
    Zero Impact.. 18
How to Use This Guide... 19
Trail Finder... 23
Map Legend 28

The Hikes
Hawai'i: The Big Island 29
  1 Thurston Lava Tube 33
  2 Sulphur Bank Trail 35
  3 Sandalwood Trail... 37
  4 Kilauea Iki 42
  5 Kipuka Puaulu (Bird Park) 44
  6 Pu'uloa Petroglyphs... 47
  Trails on Mauna Loa (Hikes 7 to 11) 49
    7 Mauna Loa Trail to Red Hill.. 51
    8 Red Hill Cabin to North Pit Junction 55
    9 North Pit Junction to Mauna Loa Cabin...................... 59
   10 North Pit Junction to Mauna Loa Summit.................... 63
   11 Observatory Trail to North Pit Junction 65
 12 Pololu Valley.. 68
 13 Hawai'i Tropical Botanical Garden 71
 14 Akaka Falls State Park 74
 15 Kalopa Native Forest Trail 75
 16 Waipio Valley... 77
 17 Manuka Nature Trail.. 80
 18 Pu'uhonua o Honaunau (Place of Refuge)...................... 82

Hanalei

63   62   60

61

64-70   55-59   **KAUA'I**

71-72

Lihue

NIIHAU

Laie

53-54   51-52

O'AHU   37-38   50

40-45

39   46-49

Honolulu

PACIFIC

OCEAN

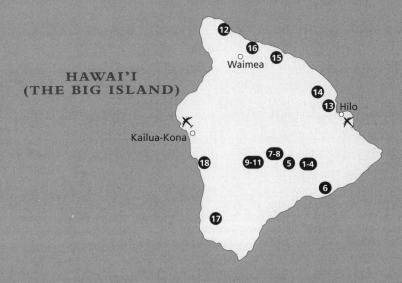

0   Kilometers   50

0   Miles   50

N

PACIFIC

OCEAN

MOLOKAI

○Hoolehua

Kapalua○

26

24-25

MAUI

23

27

28

LANAI

○Lanai
City

36

Kahului

29

30-32

19-22

Hana

33-34

35

KAHOOLAWE

12

16

15

Waimea○

HAWAI'I
(THE BIG ISLAND)

14

13 Hilo

Kailua-Kona○

18

9-11

7-8

5

1-4

6

17

Maui: The Valley Isle.. 85
  19 Hosmer Grove 87
  Trails on Haleakala (Hikes 20 to 22) 89
    20 Sliding Sands Trail to Kapala'oa Cabin 90
    21 Halemau'u Trail to Holua Cabin 94
    22 Holua Cabin to Paliku Cabin 98
  23 'Iao Needle 103
  24 Waihe'e Ridge Trail 104
  25 Waihe'e Valley (Swinging Bridges) 106
  26 Nakalele Blowhole 108
  27 Twin Falls 110
  28 Waikamoi Ridge Nature Trail 113
  29 Ke'anae Arboretum 115
  30 Sea Caves and Black Sand Beach 118
  31 Wai'anapanapa Coast Trail North 121
  32 Wai'anapanapa Coast Trail South to Hana 123
  33 'Ohe'o Gulch and the Seven Pools 126
  34 Pipiwai Trail 129
  35 La Perouse Bay (Hoapili Trail) 132
  36 Olowalu Petroglyphs 135

O'ahu: The Capital Isle 139
  37 Waimano Loop 141
  38 'Aiea Loop 144
  39 Diamond Head 147
  40 Manoa Falls 149
  41 'Aihualama Trail 152
  42 Pu'u Pia 154
  43 Manoa Cliff Trail 156
  44 Makiki Valley Loop 159
  45 Judd–Jackass Ginger Pool 162
  46 Kuli'ou'ou Valley Trail 164
  47 Kuli'ou'ou Ridge Trail 167
  48 Koko Crater Botanical Garden 169
  49 Ka Iwi (Makapu'u Point) 171
  50 Maunawili Falls 174
  51 Hau'ula Loop Trail 178
  52 Ma'akua Ridge Trail 181
  53 Ka'ena Point North 183
  54 Ka'ena Point South 186

Kaua'i: The Garden Island... 189
55 Nounou Mountain (Sleeping Giant) East 192
56 Nounou Mountain (Sleeping Giant) West.............................. 196
57 Kuamo'o–Nounou Trail.. 198
58 Kuilau Ridge 200
59 Moalepe Trail.. 203
60 Kilauea Lighthouse 205
61 Hanalei–Okolehao Trail 207
62 Limahuli Garden and Preserve.. 210
63 Hanakapi'ai Beach 212
64 Na Pali Coast (Kalalau Trail).. 215
65 Awa'awapuhi Trail.. 221
66 Nu'alolo Trail.. 224
67 Pu'uka'ohelo–Berry Flat Trail... 227
68 Canyon Trail–Black Pipe Trail Loop 232
69 Kawaikoi Stream.. 236
70 Pihea Trail to the Alaka'i Swamp 239
71 Iliau Nature Trail... 243
72 Kukui Trail and Waimea Canyon 246

Bibliography.. 249
Index.. 250
About the Author 252

Acknowledgments

Thanks to everyone with the National Park Service for helping and for caring deeply about their islands, especially Judy Edwards and Kiera Strom-Herman-Lyons at Haleakala National Park on Maui, Mardie Lane and Jim Gale at Hawai'i Volcanoes National Park on the Big Island, and George Enuton at Pu'ukohola Heiau National Historic Site on Hawai'i.

Thanks also to Peter Van Dyke, manager of the Amy B. H. Greenwell Ethnobotanical Garden on Hawai'i. The Na Ala Hele trails and access specialists for the Division of Forestry and Wildlife for the state of Hawai'i, especially Aaron Lowe on O'ahu, and Irv Kawashima on Hawai'i, were great sources of information. Wade Holmes of the Hawai'i Nature Center on Maui and Jennie Peterson of the Hawai'i Nature Center on O'ahu were especially generous with their time in volunteering help and answering questions, as was Nancy Merrill at Limahuli Garden and Preserve and Paulette Burtner at the Koke'e Museum on Kaua'i.

For help and company along the trail, for moral support, and for technical assistance, thank you to Joellyn Acree, Alix Benson, Karen Cassimatis, Eugene DeMine, Jim DiMora, Melinda Goodwater, Lois Hall, Chris Haun, Jim Johnson, Pat Medley, Fay Metz, and Michael Perry.

◀ *Young Cook Pines on the Hau'ula Loop (Hike 51)*

Introduction

Twenty-five hundred miles away from anywhere, remote, tropical, with crashing surf and steaming volcanoes, Hawai'i is as exotic a place as you can imagine, and it's one of our own fifty states. The landscape is different; the people a golden mix of races and cultures with their own special foods, expressions, and customs. It's like traveling to some distant land but you don't need a passport, shots, or language lessons. Heart-stopping beauty, waterfalls, rainbows, flowers; Hawai'i is truly paradise, and it doesn't even have snakes! No wonder its most important product is tourism.

While so many think of these islands as places to lie beneath a palm tree and sip a drink with an umbrella in it, there are miles and miles of hiking trails and lots of wilderness for more active travelers to explore. There are beach strolls, treks to swimming holes, hikes to archeological sites, hikes through forests, deserts, swamps, and high mountains, hikes from sea level to almost 14,000 feet. There are two national parks with great trail systems, and Na Ala Hele, the state of Hawaii's Trails and Access Program under the Division of Forestry and Wildlife, manages many more. There are vigorous and enthusiastic local hikers and hiking groups on all the islands that help to promote open space and maintain trails. At the same time, a survey conducted by Hawaii's Department of Land and Natural Resources found that 78 percent of people who use these trails are visitors from the mainland.

There's a whole lot more to hiking in Hawai'i than scenery and exercise. It is one of the most exciting places on the face of the earth for anyone interested in the world of nature, a place where new land is in the process of creation, where you can witness geologic forces at work on a global scale. There is a profusion of flowers and birds and reptiles and bugs, offering people so much to learn about how plants and animals colonize a new environment, how they spread and flourish, and unfortunately, how easily they can be destroyed. Hawai'i has the dubious distinction of being named the extinction capital of the world by the Hawai'i Biological Survey. Walking Hawaii's trails is the best way to see some rare and beautiful life forms before they are gone forever, and perhaps to motivate you to help to preserve them.

It would take more than a lifetime to explore all the wild corners of these islands, so the hikes chosen for this book are the crème de la crème. They are the most scenic and the most varied, and all are relatively easy to access by visitors with an ordinary passenger car. Hikes not included are those that are logistically difficult to reach and without enough else to recommend them, such as those that require a car shuttle of more than a half-day or driving on steep, slippery, dangerous four-wheel-drive roads. Also excluded are trails that are officially closed because they are unsafe or those that cross or end on private property whose owners have not granted right of way.

◀ *Pu'u O'o eruption, creating new land*

If you are a resident you might find some new adventures close to home, and if you are a visitor, you will discover a Hawai'i much richer and more exciting than anything a sedentary tourist who does not venture beyond Waikiki could ever dream of. Aloha.

The Making of the Islands

The Hawaiian Islands are the most isolated bits of land in the world. They are the farthest from any continent, 2,500 miles out in the Pacific Ocean. What are they doing out there?

They are volcanoes, but are nowhere near any tectonic plate boundaries, where volcanoes are usually found. They are not part of the Pacific Ring of Fire, a volcanic zone that runs from the tip of South America, up along the west coasts of South, Central, and North America, across to the Aleutian Islands, and down along Japan, the Philippines, Indonesia, and beyond. Instead, they are the products of a hot spot, a place beneath the earth's crust where the magma is so hot it melts its way upward through the crust to erupt, in Hawaii's case, through the ocean floor, depositing layer upon layer of lava, building a mountain that eventually rises above the ocean's surface to make new land. There are between forty and fifty such spots scattered over the surface of the globe—Yellowstone and the Galapagos Islands are others—and why they occur at all is still a matter of conjecture and controversy among geologists. The hot spots do not move, but the plates that the ocean floor and the continents ride upon do. As the plate glides over the hot spot, a volcano erupts and builds a new island that grows, cools, dies, and begins to erode away as the plate moves on, leaving the hot spot behind.

At the moment, the Big Island of Hawai'i, home of Mauna Loa, largest volcano in the world, is directly above the hot spot. Both Kilauea and Mauna Loa, two of the five volcanoes that make up the Big Island, are erupting, building new land right before your eyes. To the north Haleakala on the island of Maui is moving on, dormant but by no means extinct. North of Maui, O'ahu, Kaua'i, and the smaller nearby islands have cooled and are slowly eroding away.

That is not all there is to Hawai'i however. A map of the Pacific shows smaller remnants of the Hawaiian hot spot, the Leeward Islands, extending northward, trending slightly west and continuing on for 1,500 miles, ending in the tiny specks of Kure and Midway Island. All that's left of most of these former mountains are circular or crescent-shaped atolls built by corals that have established colonies along the rims of now-submerged volcanic craters.

But the story does not end there, either. The island chain makes a dogleg to the north and continues under the sea in the form of the Emperor Seamounts, remnants of still older islands, which extend for another thousand miles, almost to the Aleutians. To the south of the island of Hawai'i, a new island, Loihi, is building, but so far is still 3,000 feet beneath the surface of the ocean. Don't expect it to emerge for another 100,000 years.

About Lava

Since these islands are volcanic, you as a hiker will become intimately acquainted with lava in its myriad forms and textures. The nature of the lava beneath your feet has a great deal to do with the ease or difficulty, the safety or danger, of every hike in the Hawaiian Islands. After a few weeks of experience, you will be able to tell from the ground beneath you, without looking beyond your toes, what island you are on. Two terms are used by geologists around the world to describe the two kinds of lava, and they will appear over and over again in trail descriptions in this book, so you will need to know what they mean. The terms originated in Hawai'i, but are so universally used that they will not be italicized here.

Pahoehoe is hot, more liquid, and flows more freely over the ground. It cools into a smooth, more ropy surface, something like cake batter. It is much easier to walk on than . . .

A'a, which is slightly cooler in temperature. It is denser, more sluggish as it advances, and piles up in lumps and clumps that often have very sharp edges.

Trails try to avoid a'a whenever possible, but sometimes you have to cross an expanse of it to get to your destination. If you fall on it, you can get a nasty cut. It will shred even sturdy boots in short order, and will consume cheap running shoes in about a week.

Chunky textured a'a lava

The younger islands of Hawai'i and Maui, which have not been subjected to erosion for long, have not yet developed the red clay soil you must deal with on the older islands of O'ahu and Kaua'i. When it is dry, walking on the clay is effortless, but when it is wet—and it is often wet—it turns to slippery slime, coating tree roots and rocks and you in red goo.

Flora and Fauna

The Hawaiian Islands are the most isolated landforms in the world, so it should be no surprise that they are home to some of the rarest and most unusual plants and animals anywhere.

Any creature living on these islands that was not brought by human beings had to be able to swim or to fly. Birds and insects could arrive on air currents or ocean flotsam, as could Hawaii's only terrestrial mammal, the Hawaiian hoary bat, but the only other mammals here are the aquatic ones; dolphins, whales, and seals. You are not likely to get a close look at one of Hawaii's bats, but you can sometimes spot Hawaiian monk seals basking on rocky beaches off Ka'ena Point on O'ahu or Kilauea Point on Kaua'i.

Humpback whales arrive from the Arctic in late December or January. Some cruise on to Mexico and Japan, but many hang out in Hawai'i until April. Some of the best spots to look for them from shore are off Ka'ena and Makena Points on Oahu, and Kilauea Point on Kaua'i. Whale-watching boats do a big business between Lahaina on Maui and the island of Lanai during the season. Spinner dolphins can

Sea turtle

often be seen from shore as well, and sometimes they put on a show for kayakers in protected bays like Kealakekua on the Big Island, shooting out of the water in great exuberant arcs, twirling their bodies like figure skaters.

Green sea turtles (named for their flesh, not their shells) can also be seen from Hawaiian shoreline trails, basking on beaches or swimming offshore. They are vegetarians that can weigh as much as 400 pounds and live as long as eighty years. They breed on the mostly uninhabited atolls to the north nowadays, though once they bred on the main islands. They are endangered now, not only because many of their traditional breeding beaches have been "developed" but because they were a prized source of fresh meat and eggs for the crews of thousands of sailing ships in the days of long ocean voyages.

Hawaii's native land birds are another story altogether. While only an occasional bird managed to find these remote islands over a period of seventy million years (it is estimated that no more than fifteen species made their way here and survived during all that time), when they got here they found dozens of unoccupied environmental niches with no local residents to compete with and no predators. By the time humans came along to count them, 140 native Hawaiian species, had evolved, 85 to 90 percent of them endemic (that is, found nowhere else in the world).

The most famous of these are the Hawaiian honeycreepers. One single introduction, a (probably) lonely, pregnant female finch, produced offspring that eventually evolved into fifty different species and subspecies.

In the higher-elevation forests and scrublands you can still see Hawaiian honeycreepers along the trail, mostly small birds, usually brightly colored in yellows and

Feral pig

reds. Some have short strong bills for cracking seeds; others have small pointed bills for catching insects, scimitar-shaped bills for foraging under bark, or long curved bills to precisely fit into long, curved Hawaiian flowers to reach their nectar. Even amateur birders have a chance to see some very rare and unusual species like i'iwis, apapanes, amakihis, and 'elepaios. There are several small, pocket-size books available to help you identify them.

It is a great tragedy that fully half of Hawaii's native birds are extinct. Forty species of large, ground-dwelling birds whose remains have only recently been discovered disappeared before explorer Captain James Cook's time. Their forest habitat was cleared for agriculture, and they were easy prey for the original Polynesian settlers, their dogs, rats, and pigs. Many were killed by mosquito-borne diseases brought by whalers. Mosquitoes are not native to Hawai'i but were accidentally introduced in 1826 by a whaling ship whose water casks, filled in Mexico, harbored larvae. They carried avian malaria and pox to which the Hawaiian birds had no immunity. Some of the native forest birds still survive at higher elevations where the climate is too cold for mosquitoes, such as in the Alaka'i Swamp on Kaua'i and in forests on Maui and Hawai'i (though this may be changing as our atmosphere warms.) The activities of sugar planters, ranchers, developers, and tourists also have contributed to the disappearance of dozens more, and many of those remaining are threatened or endangered.

Many of the seabirds, while not limited to Hawai'i, are marvelous to watch from shoreline trails. Enormous albatrosses, shearwaters, and petrels spend most of their lives over the open sea, coming to land here only to breed. Magnificent frigate birds (that's their real name, not just a description) are black with long forked tails and look

Nene goose

like holdovers from the Jurassic period. They make their living stealing fish caught by other birds, snatching them away in midair. Graceful white-tailed and red-tailed tropic birds, with tail streamers longer than their bodies, float along the dark green cliffs, following the valleys deep into the interiors of the islands.

Then there is Hawaii's pride and joy, its state bird and everybody's favorite goose, the nene. They have recently been brought back from the brink of extinction and are both beautiful and ridiculously tame. They have already mastered the art of panhandling from tourists, sidling up close and staring at your sandwich with pitiful, longing eyes. Do not give in! There is plenty of food in their natural environment and yours is bad for them.

Beach Naupaka flower

Lots of exotic species have been introduced as well. You might be surprised to see bright red northern cardinals from North America, along with two other kinds of cardinals, both of them striking gray and white birds with flame-red heads, one with a crest, the other without. Several species were brought here for hunting: ring-necked pheasants, chukars and Kalij pheasants from Asia, California quail, and even turkeys. A few birds have been introduced for their beautiful songs, including the shama thrush (or white-rumped shama) from Malaysia. It's a slender forest bird with a black head and back, chestnut belly, and a white rump and outer tail feathers. Its clear, liquid song echoing through the forest will stop you in your tracks to listen every time. The first birds you'll see when you step off the plane, and the ones you will see (and hear) the most anywhere in Hawai'i, except at the very highest elevations, are the mynahs. They are bold and noisy, yellow-legged and yellow-billed brown and black birds with yellow patches around their eyes. Their wings show flashes of white when they fly. Their original home is India.

Hawai'i plant life is also unique, partly because of the islands' remoteness, partly because their location in the tropics whose abundance of sun and rain plants love. In fact, Hawai'i has the only tropical rainforest in the United States. It also has a tremendous range of elevations. You can bask on the shore, sweat along leeward desert trails, or get soaked hiking the wet windward forests. You can even ski on 13,796-foot Mauna Kea. Besides this incredible variety of habitats, there are rich volcanic soils in all stages of development, from fresh, bare lava on the younger islands to deep valley soils on the older ones.

The original landscaping of the Hawaiian Islands occurred a little faster than the establishment of its birdlife. It is estimated that one new plant arrived (and survived) every 20,000 to 30,000 years. Some of these came by seed carried on the wind, and some of the coastal species arrived by sea, but most of them were transported in the digestive systems or feathers of birds. There are 1,000 species of native Hawaiian flowering plants on these small islands, more than 90 percent of them endemic—the largest percentage of endemic plants found anywhere in the world.

The most common native Hawaiian plants you are likely to see are the koa *(Acacia koa)*, a forest giant up to 100 feet tall and 6 feet in diameter with scimitar-shaped leaves (that aren't really leaves at all) and small rounded yellowish balls of tiny flowers. The other is the almost ubiquitous ohia lehua *(Metrosideros polymorpha)*, a small tree that occurs at just about every elevation up to timberline, and is the first to colonize new lava flows. Its bright red powder puff flowers are unmistakable.

It may surprise you to learn that most of the flora you see around you, especially the showy, colorful blossoms of the gingers and orchids, come from somewhere else. The original Polynesian settlers brought more than thirty species, including taro, breadfruit, bananas, paper mulberry, ti, yams, sugarcane, and even coconut palms. Since then, at least a thousand other plants have become fully naturalized, including eucalyptus from Australia, mesquite from the Americas, flame trees from Africa, and everything from sugi cedars to lotus flowers from Asia.

The native Hawaiian flowers are relatively drab, small, and odorless, but that's because they did not need to compete among themselves to attract pollinators like plants in temperate regions do. They had no natural enemies, so they did not need to develop fragrances or spines or stickers or poisons or stinging hairs. Hawaiian mints have no smell, berry bushes have no thorns, Hawaiian nettles don't sting, and you'll never find poison ivy or poison oak along a Hawaiian trail.

Threatened Hawai'i

Some organizations, like Hawai'i's Biological Survey, say the state has been more heavily affected by the degradation of the environment than any other site on the planet.

The most obvious reason for this is habitat destruction. Before the arrival of humans, Hawaii's forests reached from timberline to the shore, but by Captain Cook's time, the original Polynesians had cleared almost every patch of ground between sea level and 2,000 feet for agriculture. European planters, developers, and tourists have cleared most of what remained for sugarcane, pineapples, cattle, hotels, and highways.

Among the most destructive agents in undeveloped areas are feral goats and pigs. The goats were brought by Europeans specifically for hunting, and whenever you see great swaths of denuded, eroded red mud hillsides, you can be sure goats are present. Feral pigs especially love the roots and young shoots of native forest plants, and big muddy gouges are common where they have been rooting. Both goats and pigs are hunted, but there are no efforts to eradicate them altogether since hunting is a time-honored Hawaiian tradition. Government agencies have installed miles of fencing around national parks and other sensitive areas to keep pigs and goats out, and these have been successful, but of course, they are extremely expensive to install and maintain.

One of Hawaii's best known, if least successful, battles against harmful introduced species is that of the mongoose and the rat. Rats are not only a threat to birds, but to agricultural crops, especially sugarcane. Somebody who knew the reputation of the scrappy little mongoose, the same animal that will take on a cobra, thought that if they were introduced to Hawai'i, they would make short work of the rats, and the sugar would be saved. Nobody remembered that while mongoose are diurnal animals, active during the day, rats are nocturnal, active at night, so the two rarely confront one another. Now Hawaiian crops and birds have round-the-clock enemies, rats and mongoose.

Backcountry travelers should always remember that only a few tiny protected slivers of original unspoiled Hawai'i remain. Some of these are so rare and fragile they are off-limits to human travel altogether, but many others offer the finest hiking on the islands. Please handle with care.

The People

The first people to find and colonize the islands are believed to have come from the Marquesas Islands, over 2,000 miles to the southeast. They came in double-hulled sailing canoes, perhaps as long ago as A.D. 400. Nobody knows for sure why they left their original home, how they found these remote islands, or how they survived such a long journey over open ocean. They brought with them pigs, dogs, and chickens, along with taro, bananas, coconuts, and other plants many visitors mistakenly assume to be native to Hawai'i. Obviously, they intended to stay.

By the time Captain Cook arrived, the native population had grown to more than 250,000 people who had developed an agricultural system, culture, and religion distinctly their own. They had built an extensive network of fields, terraces, and irrigation ditches where they grew taro, sweet potatoes, yams, coconuts, sugar, and bananas for food. They planted paper mulberry trees for cloth, gourds for containers, plants for medicine, and of course, cultivated a recreational drug. In addition to the animals they brought from their homeland to furnish protein, they harvested the ocean and even raised fish in hatcheries.

Orchids at Hawai'i Tropical Botanical Garden (Hike 13)

Their society had become highly stratified by the time Europeans arrived. The commoners fished and farmed, made tools and clothing, and paid taxes to the ali'i or chiefs, who owned the land. A chief might control all or part of an island. He (in the early days it was always a he) had subchiefs to apportion land, work among the commoners, and collect the taxes. The ali'i were descended from the gods, and could recite their genealogies many generations back to prove it. They had so much mana or divine power that an ordinary person could not touch any object belonging to the chief, had to prostrate himself in the chief's presence, and could not even allow his shadow to fall over that of an ali'i. This system of kapu or prohibitions was enforced by the priestly caste of kahuna. Division of labor and relations between the sexes were governed by kapu as well. Men and women could not eat together, and women were prohibited certain foods such as pork and bananas.

The Hawaiians were no exception to the rule that when societies develop agriculture to a point where permanent settlements are established and populations grow, territorial disputes arise that sooner or later lead to war. By the time Europeans landed in the islands, the ongoing competition among chiefs for land and power had become especially fierce. The cult of the war god Ku was strong and demanded that ever more elaborate heiaus, or temples, be built to his glory, dedicated by hulas, chants, and human sacrifice. The commoners went along with all this, since they owed their safety and prosperity to their ali'i's connection and influence with his divine ancestors.

Captain Cook

In 1779, Captain James Cook sailed from England to seek the Northwest Passage, the navigable connection between the Pacific and Atlantic Oceans. He first landed at Kaua'i and found the people there friendly and willing to trade. He re-supplied his two ships and made another fruitless voyage north, after which he returned to Hawai'i and landed at Kealakekua Bay on the Big Island. There, a series of unhappy events occurred, including several incidents of theft by the Hawaiians, who would do anything to acquire iron tools including diving beneath a ship to pull out the nails. On top of it all, Cook's arrival coincided with a religious ritual celebrated each year in which a fertility god called Lono was expected to return to the people from the sea on some sort of seagoing tree. Captain Cook's approach in his wooden ships at first seemed to fulfill the prophecy. During a melee on the beach in which Cook's sailors attempted to take an ali'i hostage until a stolen boat was returned, stones were hurled, shots were fired, and Cook was clubbed to death. His monument is a white obelisk on the shore of Kealakekua Bay.

Before the arrival of Europeans, territorial battles among the Hawaiians had been limited in scope, partly because the only weapons available were spears and stone clubs. Captain Cook would not trade firearms with the locals, but fur traders, now stopping off at the newly "discovered" islands to rest and resupply on their long sea voyages, had no qualms about selling guns to warring chiefs.

By 1795, a young upstart (according to some) named Kamehameha, with the help of a newly acquired arsenal and technical support by some English and Yankee traders, conquered all the other islands except Kaua'i in a celebrated battle on O'ahu. A few years later he acquired Kaua'i too, after a series of negotiations with its chief. All of the islands were united for the first time as the Kingdom of Hawai'i, and Kamehameha became Kamehameha the Great.

Kamehameha maintained the kapu system, but welcomed traders and foreign influence in the islands, and when he died in 1819, big changes were on the way. His son and successor Liholiho, known as Kamehameha II, lacked the confidence and drive of his father and was drunk most of the time anyway. Kamehameha the Great's widow, Ka'ahumanu, however, was willing to step in. She persuaded Liholiho to break the old kapu by eating in the presence of women. She herself ate forbidden pork and bananas and did not suffer so much as a bellyache. She insisted that her husband had transferred his mana to her before he died and intended her to help rule the islands. She got away with it and changed the status of Hawaiian women forever.

The system was about to break down anyway, though. In 1820 a group of Calvinist missionaries sailed from Boston to convert the heathen. Their progress was slow but sure, and in exchange for their destruction of a culture, they created a Hawaiian alphabet and gave the islands a written language. Ka'ahumanu and Liholiho themselves converted to Christianity, donned western clothes, sailed off to England in 1825 to meet the Queen, caught measles there, and died.

Between 1820 and 1840 Hawaii, especially Lahaina on Maui, became a center for the whaling industry. The whalers, of course, did their best to counteract the influence of the missionaries, further spreading the venereal disease already rampant since the time of the first English sailors. Hawai'i was becoming part of the greater world, and in 1840 even adopted a parliamentary form of government, though the monarchy survived for many more years.

The descendents of the missionaries realized how much money there was to made in sugar. The problem was that the ali'i still owned all the land. The haoles (whites) introduced the concept of land ownership based upon deeds and legalities to the chiefs, who had never before had any need or knowledge of such things. The haole's argument was that now the chiefs could legally buy and sell land, and with the profits buy western luxuries that could only be obtained by cash. Of course the haoles ended up owning almost everything, and the Hawaiians very little, a situation that persists to this day.

Now that they had almost unlimited land to grow sugar, they needed workers to cultivate and harvest it. The native Hawaiians, whose numbers by this time had decreased dramatically due to disease, were not interested, so the planters imported Chinese workers, many of whom stayed in Hawai'i after their contracts expired to become merchants. The planters tried Portuguese workers as well, who, as Europeans, expected to be paid a reasonable wage and be treated with more respect than they actually got, so most did not stay, but the Portuguese influence is still present in the islands. The Japanese came next, and while they too expected better treatment from the planters than what they got, they did stay and ultimately became the most powerful political presence in Hawaii, as they still are. The Filipinos constituted the last wave of plantation workers, and many remained to become stirred into the Hawaiian melting pot.

The last Hawaiian monarch was Queen Liliuokalani, who was forcefully deposed by a powerful coalition of planters in 1850, and in 1898 Hawai'i was annexed by the United States and became an American territory. For years Hawai'i sustained a colonial atmosphere, with immigrant laborers under the thumbs of corporations that originated with the sugar planters and grew to control processing, transportation, retailing, and just about everything to do with daily life. Pineapples became an important crop, too.

American activities in the Philippines during the Spanish-American War made Hawai'i a valuable naval base, and military spending became a more important part of the economy, eventually surpassing even sugar and pineapples. The bombing of the U.S. naval base at Pearl Harbor in 1941 brought an end to what was left of Hawaii's isolation.

Statehood came at last in 1959, and in the 1960s commercial jet service made travel to Hawai'i so fast and easy that tourists began to pour in. The original sugar planters, along with many foreign investors, began to develop resorts and other tourist facilities, and now, of course, tourism dwarfs every other source of income for the islands. Pineapple growing has become unprofitable and has moved elsewhere. Sugar plantations are closing one after another, though they might be gearing back up very soon, growing sugar this time for ethanol.

The most interesting recent development in Hawai'i is a nationalist movement by native Hawaiians, who are once more taking pride in their culture, celebrating traditional arts, language, and customs. The United States government has made an official apology to native Hawaiians for overthrowing the monarchy in the nineteenth century, but is not likely to grant independence to the islands in the foreseeable future.

How to Speak Hawaiian

It looks so difficult in print, a confusing series of vowels broken up by apostrophes, but pronunciation of Hawaiian words is really very easy with just a very little attention and practice.

The Hawaiian language has only twelve letters: the vowels a, e, i, o, and u; and the consonants h, k, l, m, n, p, and w. It also has a diacritical mark, the glottal stop, indicated by an apostrophe, that tells you how to separate the syllables. The apostrophe gives spoken Hawaiian its distinctive sound and rhythm. The glottal stop means you simply stop the sound of the letter. For example Koke'e is not pronounced "ko-key," it's pronounced "ko-keh-eh." One of the two kinds of lava, a'a, is not pronounced "aah," but "ah-ah." The word Hawai'i itself has a glottal stop, and you probably already know how to say it: "Hawai-ee." If the two vowels are not separated by a glottal stop, they are pronounced together, like the ai in Hawai'i. There's another mark—the macron, a horizontal line over a letter that indicates stress—but since that almost always falls on the next-to-last syllable it is not used here. Some maps and books use one or the other, some use both, some use neither.

This is how the individual vowels are pronounced:
A = aah
E = eh
I = ee
O = oh
U = oo

Here are a few of the words you will hear and see over and over in Hawai'i, and that are used in this book. Many refer to physical features of the land and help interpret the names of significant landmarks.

pu'u = hill
mauna = mountain
a'a = rough, chunky lava
pahoehoe = smooth, ropy lava
mauka = toward the mountain
makai = toward the sea
loa = long
kea = white (Now you know what Mauna Loa and Mauna Kea mean.)
pali = cliff
lua = hole or pit; also means toilet
kokua = please or help
wahine = woman
kane = man
keiki = child
haole = white person, foreigner
heiau = holy place
ali'i = chief
kahuna = priest
pau = finished; or at a restaurant: "We're out of it."
ohana = family (You'll see this on lots of businesses and restaurants.)
Mahalo is used constantly: It means thank you.

Kapu is very important to know for your own safety. It's related to "taboo" and means forbidden, keep out.

Of course, you know that *aloha* means hello, good-bye, or love.

For emphasis, a word may be repeated, or two of the same word put together. If you have flown into Honolulu, you will have seen the wikiwiki shuttle bus. Wiki means hurry, quick. Wikiwiki means very quick (which the shuttle bus really isn't, but you get the idea).

Note: The "hang loose" gesture with thumb and little finger extended, the others folded, is a friendly gesture, a greeting, also meaning OK or thanks. It is not just a tourist thing. Hawaiians use it all the time. If you decide to adopt it yourself, make sure you are using the correct fingers.

A Few Words of Caution

Weather Patterns

Weather in Hawai'i is usually lovely, with temperatures between 70 and 80 degrees year-round. There are essentially two seasons. Summer (May through October) is only slightly warmer than winter. The trade winds blowing from the northeast usually keep even the warmer days pleasant. Rainfall is lighter and of shorter duration in summer than in winter. Rainfall in winter is more frequent, heavier, and lasts longer, but is not likely to spoil most hikes unless there is a Kona storm. These occur when for some reason or other the trade winds fail. Kona storms come from the opposite direction, from the southwest instead of the northeast, and can pour down buckets for days on end.

More important than the season is the side of the island you are on. All the islands are mountainous, and all the islands have windward (wetter) sides and leeward (dryer) sides because the mountains block the moisture carried by the trades. The bigger the island, the more pronounced the difference. Elevation is important too. Hikes at sea level on the leeward side of any island can be miserably hot and are best done early in the day or in winter. It is almost always cool and comfortable at 4,000 feet, and it can be downright cold, even below freezing, on Haleakala on Maui and Mauna Loa and Mauna Kea on Hawai'i.

For hiking in Hawai'i, pack plenty of layers, some of them synthetic rather than cotton for fast drying and wicking moisture away from your skin. A windbreaker and rain gear are essential items to carry in your day pack.

Make sure you have a brimmed hat and lots of sunscreen, too. The sun is directly overhead close to the equator.

Drinking Water

All free-flowing water on the islands must be treated before drinking. In Hawai'i, leptospirosis is the most significant waterborne disease-causing organism. It is spread primarily by rats, mice, and mongooses. It is a bacterium that can cause flulike symptoms including fever, diarrhea, nausea, muscle pain, chills, headache, and weakness, and if not treated with antibiotics can lead to very serious problems like heart or kidney failure.

Chemical treatment or boiling will take care of drinking water, but you can get leptospirosis by swimming in contaminated water as well as by drinking it. You are advised not to swim in fresh water if you have a cut or broken skin, and not to put your head underwater. That said, swimming and splashing in Hawaii's streams and pools is one of the most popular pastimes in the islands, and nobody appears to be overly concerned, but just so you know . . . .

Stream Crossings

Speaking of water, it rains a lot in Hawai'i and there are few hikes that do not involve stream crossings. Some are shallow enough to rock-hop, though rocks are usually rounded and slick and wading is safer. If it has been raining long and hard, streams may be too high and fast to ford safely. Unexpected flash floods are especially danger-ous and have killed lots of people. Many of Hawaii's streams flow down almost per-pendicular cliffs, and floods may originate high up in the rainy mountains, offering no sign of their approach as you stroll along the coast under sunny skies. If a stream appears muddy, or if you can hear rocks rolling along the streambed, turn around! Tropical vegetation often releases tannins into the water, making it dark in color and hard to see through even under ordinary conditions, but swirling mud is serious.

Waves, Currents, and Riptides

The seas around the islands have weird patterns. There are lovely quiet coves perfect for snorkeling and big regular waves for surfing, but in some places riptides can pull you off your feet and sweep you out to sea in an instant. Never turn your back on the sea when exploring tide pools or walking along sea cliffs. A rogue wave can sneak up on you any time. Beaches where it is not safe to swim are almost always clearly marked with warning signs, and they mean business! Hawai'i has experienced tsu-namis or tidal waves that killed many at rare intervals in its history. You will probably notice yellow civil defense warning sirens on posts along windward coastlines. If these begin to blow, get to higher ground immediately.

Losing the Trail

Forest cover off established trails is usually so dense you couldn't get through it any-way, but sometimes animals make their own paths. Where more than one path exists, the clearest, most defined trail is usually the right one. Sometimes trails become so badly eroded by people going their separate ways to avoid mud puddles or deep holes that they create new mud puddles and deep holes, and a whole network of false paths. Stay alert and look beyond the worn spots to find where the trail picks up again. If you are uncertain about which path to take, try one for a short distance. If it seems to lead nowhere, turn around and go back to where you knew where you were, then start over. Don't compound a mistake by plunging farther and farther into the unknown.

In Hawai'i it is especially important to stay on trails, maybe more so than in other places. On the Big Island in particular, the volcanic ground is still cooling. The crust is often thin and a step off the trail could mean a scalding from escaping steam. Even a completely cooled surface may be hollow underneath and thin enough to punch through. A shallow crack may be enough to cause a sprained ankle, but there is always the possibility of a large cave only a few inches below. Thick undergrowth can also mask deep cracks or overhangs.

Many routes skirt or cross private property whose owners have granted hikers the right of way, so please stay on the trail. Dense forest vegetation can obscure the boundaries of private property. A KAPU sign means no trespassing.

Pig and goat hunting are time-honored pastimes in the islands. At present, hunting is permitted in certain areas on weekends and holidays, but the schedule does change. Trailheads in areas where hunting is allowed will usually have a sign saying so. If you stay on the trail and wear bright clothing, there is very little danger from hunters.

Sticking to the trail will also help you respect cultural traditions by steering you away from religious sites and cemeteries.

Trailhead Vandalism

This is the most distressing, even if not life-threatening, experience most hikers ever face. For the most part, Hawaiians are friendly, helpful, and kind. Unfortunately, there is some poverty and resentment here (as everywhere), and tourists are easy marks.

If you are about to pull into a parking space at a remote trailhead and see broken glass on the ground, be warned. Leave absolutely nothing in your car, not even in the trunk. You might consider leaving the doors unlocked to avoid having a window broken, although even that doesn't always work. Rental cars are usually obvious, and tourists are apt to leave all sorts of belongings in their cars when they go off for a hike.

Thin crust and escaping steam are just two hazards of wandering off the trail.

Isolated trailheads where no one will hear breaking glass are the worst places for potential break-ins. Usually busy trailheads with people coming and going all day are safer, as are trailheads in national parks. Overnight parking at trailheads is risky anywhere near a big population center, not just in Hawai'i. At especially notorious spots, like the Kalalau trailhead on Kaua'i, nearby businesses offer shuttle service to the trailhead and a safe place to leave your car.

There is no need to spoil your visit by worrying about your car. The odds against any problems are in your favor, but you can greatly improve them by taking a few precautions.

Zero Impact

As we venture into the outdoors, we have a responsibility to protect our wild places. So please, do what you can. The following will help you understand better what it means to "do what you can" while still making the most of your hiking experience. Anyone can take a hike, but hiking safely and well is an art requiring preparation and proper equipment.

Zero impact. Always leave an area just like you found it—if not better than you found it. Pack out all your trash and extra food. Bury human waste at least 100 feet from water sources under 6 to 8 inches of topsoil. Don't bathe with soap in a lake or stream—use prepackaged moistened towels to wipe off sweat and dirt, or bathe in the water without soap.

Stay on the trail. Paths serve an important purpose; they limit impact on natural areas. Straying from a designated trail may seem innocent but it can cause damage to sensitive areas—damage that may take years to recover from, if it can recover at all. Even simple shortcuts can be destructive. Please stay on the trail.

Leave no weeds. Noxious weeds tend to overtake other plants, which in turn affects animals and birds that depend on them for food. To minimize the spread of noxious weeds, hikers should regularly clean their boots, tents, packs, and hiking poles of mud and seeds. Also, brush your dog to remove any weed seeds before heading off into a new area.

Keep your dog under control. Always obey leash laws and be sure to bury your dog's waste or pack it out in resealable plastic bags.

Respect other trail users. You're not the only one on the trail. With the rise in popularity of multiuse trails, you'll have to learn a new kind of respect, beyond the nod and "hello" approach you may be used to. First, investigate whether you're on a multiuse trail and take the appropriate precautions. You're not likely to hear mountain bikers coming, so be prepared and know ahead of time whether you share the trail with them. Cyclists should always yield to hikers, but that's little comfort to the hiker. Be aware. When you approach horses on the trail, always step quietly off the path, preferably on the downhill side, and let them pass. If you're wearing a large backpack, it's often a good idea to sit down. To some animals, a hiker wearing a large backpack might appear threatening. Make sure your dog doesn't harass these animals.

How to Use This Guide

The purpose of this guide is to help you choose and plan a day hike or backpack in Hawai'i best suited to your time, energy, experience, and personal preferences. It offers a preview of what you are likely to see and experience along your chosen route: volcanic features, historical and archaeological sites, tropical trees, flowers, birds, waterfalls, and beaches.

Trail descriptions are intended to be used along with U.S. Geological Survey topographic maps. These are not easy to find in Hawai'i, but are available through the USGS at P.O. Box 25286, Federal Center, Denver, CO 80225; (800) USA-MAPS (800-872-6277); or online at www.mapping.usgs.gov. These maps may not be necessary for shorter hikes, and other, less detailed hiking maps are available for each island. These are described in the introduction to each island. Each trail description begins with a summary of the hike. A statistical section follows for quick reference to more specific characteristics of the hike.

Start: Describes the starting location of the trailhead.

Distance is described in miles. The mileage is one-way for a loop in which you return to the place where you started without retracing your steps. Round-trip mileage is provided for an out-and-back hike in which you return to the trailhead the same way you came.

Elevation change: This is often the most important factor in determining a hike's difficulty. Numbers given here reflect the major ups and downs of the trail, not just the net distance between lowest and highest points on the trail.

The **Difficulty** rating is bound to be interpreted differently by hikers in varying degrees of physical condition. In general, "easy" trails are less than 5 miles long with less than 500 feet of elevation change. Most easy trails here in fact involve less than 3 miles of distance. "Moderate" trails may challenge those who are not accustomed to much physical activity. They range in distance from 4 to 6 miles with less than 1,500 feet elevation change, though usually much less. "Strenuous" hikes are for experienced hikers who are physically fit and prepared to negotiate challenging terrain. Some of these are less than 3 miles in distance, but involve very steep ascents and/or descents; a few, such as hikes on Mauna Loa, involve more than 10 miles of travel at elevations above 10,000 feet.

If the distance of a hike appears to fall into the easy category, but is rated as moderate or strenuous, it is because the route is challenging in some other way—such as difficult footing or extreme temperatures—and will be qualified here or in the hike summary.

Approximate hiking time: The times given here cover a range since everyone hikes at a different pace. They cover actual travel time and do not include stops for swimming, sightseeing, or photography.

Trail surface: The trail surfaces in Hawai'i range all the way from asphalt or concrete sidewalks to sandy beaches, through mud puddles and slippery clay, and all the way to uneven lava boulders with sharp edges and tricky cracks. These have almost as much to do with the degree of difficulty and the hiking time involved in hikes on Hawai'i as do distance and elevation change.

Seasons: Most hikes in Hawai'i are accessible year-round, but some may not be as pleasant during the winter because of rain or sometimes even snow and ice.

Other trail users: This will alert you to watch out for equestrians or bicycles on the trail.

Canine compatibility: Hawaii's state parks and all national parks do not allow dogs on trails. Other jurisdictions welcome dogs on a leash. Hunting is permitted on many of Hawaii's public lands, however, and you may encounter unleashed hunting dogs in these areas. They are no danger to hikers but dog/dog territorial confrontations are possible.

Land status: This section lists the landowner, usually a government agency, that manages the land on which the hike lies.

Nearest town: The closest town to the hike with at least a gas station and some basic supplies is listed here.

Fees and permits: National parks charge an entrance fee by car or by individual for seven days. Annual passes are also available that allow multiple entrances. Other governing agencies may not charge any fee. Permits are required for overnight camping.

Maps: The overview map of each island indicates major access roads to each trailhead and possibly more important, the relative locations of hikes to one another to help you plan a whole day of hiking in one vicinity.

The route map is your primary guide to each hike. It shows all accessible roads and trails, points of interest, water, landmarks, and geographical features. It also distinguishes trails from roads. The selected route is highlighted, and directional arrows point the way. These maps are not intended to replace more detailed agency maps, road maps, state atlases, and topographic maps, but they do indicate the general lay of the trail to help you visualize and navigate its course.

Trail contacts: This listing provides the address, phone number, and e-mail address of the land manager for the specific hiking trail. Usually it's a state park, national park, or city park.

Finding the trailhead: This section provides detailed directions to the trailhead. With a basic current state highway map, you can easily locate the starting point from the directions. Distances may vary with different car odometers, so be sure to keep an eye open for specific signs, junctions and landmarks mentioned in the directions.

All of this guide's hikes have trailheads that can be reached by an ordinary passenger car. None requires a four-wheel-drive vehicle because the majority of hikers

Ohe Naupaka in Swamp, Hike 70 ▶

come from off-island and are using rental vehicles which most rental agencies do not allow off-road.

The Hike: All the hikes in this guide can be easily done by people in good physical condition, and most of the time, trails are obvious and easy to follow. If there are ambiguous places, the hike description will help you stay on track.

Miles and Directions: To help you stay on course, a detailed route finder sets forth mileages between significant landmarks or junctions along the trail. Some hikes follow discrete paths or are short enough that Miles and Directions are not needed. The GPS coordinates for the trailhead are provided here. If there are none, the GPS coordinates for the trailhead are given at the end of Finding the trailhead.

Trail Finder (By Island)

Hawai'i

Easy
1. Thurston Lava Tube
2. Sulphur Bank Trail
3. Sandalwood Trail
5. Kipuka Puaulu (Bird Park)
6. Pu'uloa Petroglyphs
13. Hawai'i Tropical Botanical Garden
14. Akaka Falls State Park
15. Kalopa Native Forest Trail
17. Manuka Nature Trail
18. Pu'uhonua o Honaunau (Place of Refuge)

Moderate
4. Kilauea Iki
12. Pololu Valley
16. Waipio Valley

Strenuous
7. Mauna Loa Trail to Red Hill
8. Red Hill Cabin to North Pit Junction
9. North Pit Junction to Mauna Loa Cabin
10. North Pit Junction to Mauna Loa Summit
11. Observatory Trail to North Pit Junction

Maui

Easy
19. Hosmer Grove
23. 'Iao Needle
25. Waihe'e Valley (Swinging Bridges)
26. Nakalele Blowhole
27. Twin Falls
28. Waikamoi Ridge Nature Trail
29. Ke'anae Arboretum
30. Sea Caves and Black Sand
33. 'Ohe'o Gulch and the Seven Pools
36. Olowalu Petroglyphs

Moderate
24. Waihe'e Ridge Trail
31. Wai'anapanapa Coast Trail North
32. Wai'anapanapa Coast Trail South to Hana
34. Pipiwai Trail
35. La Perouse Bay (Hoapili Trail)

Strenuous
20. Sliding Sands Trail to Kapala'oa Cabin
21. Halemau'u Trail to Holua Cabin
22. Holua Cabin to Paliku Cabin

O'ahu

Easy
37. Waimano Loop
39. Diamond Head
40. Manoa Falls
42. Pu'u Pia
43. Manoa Cliff Trail
45. Judd-Jackass Ginger Pool
46. Kuli'ou'ou Valley Trail
48. Koko Crater Botanical Garden
49. Ka Iwi (Makapu'u Point)
53. Ka'ena Point North
54. Ka'ena Point South

Moderate
38. 'Aiea Loop
41. 'Aihualama Trail
44. Makiki Valley Loop
47. Kuli'ou'ou Ridge Trail
50. Maunawili Falls
51. Hau'ula Loop Trail
52. Ma'akua Ridge Trail

Kaua'i

Easy
57. Kuamo'o-Nounou Trail
58. Kuilau Ridge
59. Moalepe Trail
60. Kilauea Lighthouse
62. Limahuli Garden
67. Pu'uka'ohelo-Berry Flat Trail
71. Iliau Nature Trail

Moderate
55. Nounou Mountain (Sleeping Giant) East
56. Nounou Mountain (Sleeping Giant) West
63. Hanakapi'ai Beach
65. Awa'awapuhi Trail
68. Canyon Trail–Black Pipe Trail Loop
69. Kawaikoi Stream
70. Pihea Trail to the Alaka'i Swamp

Strenuous
61. Hanalei–Okolehao Trail
64. Na Pali Coast (Kalalau Trail)
66. Nu'alolo Trail
72. Kukui Trail and Waimea Canyon

Hawai'i Trail Finder Chart

Number	Hike	Best Hikes for Backpackers	Best Hikes for Birds and Wildlife	Best Hikes for Waterfalls	Best Hikes for Beaches and Shorelines
3	Sandalwood Trail		●		
4	Kilauea Iki		●		
5	Kipuka Puaulu (Bird Park)		●		
7	Mauna Loa Trail to Red Hill	●			
8	Red Hill Cabin to North Pit Junction	●			
9	North Pit Junction to Mauna Loa Cabin	●			
10	North Pit Junction to Mauna Loa Summit	●			
11	Observatory Trail to North Pit Junction	●			
12	Pololu Valley				●
13	Hawai'i Tropical Botanical Garden		●	●	●
14	Akaka Falls State Park			●	
16	Waipio Valley			●	●
18	Pu'uhonua o Honaunau (Place of Refuge)		●		●

Maui Trail Finder Chart

Number	Hike	Best Hikes for Backpackers	Best Hikes for Birds and Wildlife	Best Hikes for Waterfalls	Best Hikes for Beaches and Shorelines
19	Hosmer Grove		•		
20	Sliding Sands Trail to Kapala'oa Cabin	•			
21	Halemau'u Trail to Holua Cabin	•			
22	Holua Cabin to Paliku Cabin	•	•		
23	'Iao Needle			•	
24	Waihe'e Ridge Trail			•	
25	Waihe'e Valley (Swinging Bridges)			•	
26	Nakalele Blowhole				•
27	Twin Falls			•	
30	Sea Caves and Black Sand Beach				•
31	Wai'anapanapa Coast Trail North				•
32	Wai'anapanapa Coast Trail South to Hana		•		•
33	'Ohe'o Gulch and the Seven Pools		•	•	•
34	Pipiwai Trail			•	
35	La Perouse Bay (Hoapili Trail)				•
36	Olowalu Petroglyphs				•

O'ahu Trail Finder Chart

Number	Hike	Best Hikes for Backpackers	Best Hikes for Birds and Wildlife	Best Hikes for Waterfalls	Best Hikes for Beaches and Shorelines
40	Manoa Falls			●	
41	'Aihualama Trail			●	
49	Ka Iwi (Makapu'u Point)		●		●
50	Maunawili Falls			●	
53	Ka'ena Point North		●		●
54	Ka'ena Point South		●		●

Kaua'i Trail Finder Chart

Number	Hike	Best Hikes for Backpackers	Best Hikes for Birds and Wildlife	Best Hikes for Waterfalls	Best Hikes for Beaches and Shorelines
60	Kilauea Lighthouse		●		●
61	Hanalei–Okolehao Trail			●	
63	Hanakapi'ai Beach	●			●
64	Na Pali Coast (Kalalau Trail)	●		●	●
65	Awa'awapuhi Trail		●		
68	Canyon Trail–Black Pipe Trail Loop			●	
69	Kawaikoi Stream	●	●		
70	Pihea Trail to the Alaka'i Swamp		●		
72	Kukui Trail and Waimea Canyon	●		●	

Map Legend

Transportation

Interstate Highway	═══(H1)═══
State Road	══(19)══
Dirt Road	═ ═ ═ ═ ═
Featured Trail	■-■-■-■-■
Other Trail	- - - - -

Hydrology

Lake/Reservoir	
River/Creek	～
Marsh/Swamp	
Waterfall	

Land Use

National Park	
State Park	

Symbols

Visitor Center	?
Campground	▲
Point of Interest	■
Mountain/Peak	▲
Parking	P
Picnic Area	🛆
City/Town	○
Trailhead (Start)	5
Bridge	≍
Gate	•—•
Viewpoint	
Lighthouse	
Cavern	∧
Airport	✕

	Kilometer	
0		1
Scale	Mile	
0		1

Hawai'i: The Big Island

The Big Island really is. It's bigger than all the other Hawaiian Islands put together, not only because it is geologically the youngest, and is increasing in size faster than it can be eroded away, but because it is made up of five distinct volcanoes that have coalesced into one landmass. Kilauea, the newest, most active volcano, is the current home of Madame Pele, the volcano goddess herself, but Mauna Loa, only slightly older, still rumbles, steams, and occasionally erupts. Mauna Loa is also the largest volcano in the world, measured from its base on the seafloor. Mauna Kea, now dormant, rises 13,796 feet above sea level, the highest point in Hawai'i. Kohala in the north is also dormant, but Hualalai in the western part of the island is still in the process of falling asleep.

Because of its size and its mountainous topography, the Big Island has the best variety of hikes anywhere in the state, and there are many miles of trails, from paved paths accessible to everybody to some truly challenging expeditions. Most are maintained by the National Park Service and by Na Ala Hele, the trail and access system operated by the state of Hawai'i.

The mountains block the trade winds as they blow from northeast to southwest, bringing plenty of rain to the eastern coast, carving deep river valleys, creating waterfalls, and nourishing green tropical forests. Hilo is the biggest population center on this side of the island, a fun and funky little town with a wonderful old-time Hawai'i atmosphere. It's the most convenient base for hikes along the Hamakua coast, and it is also the cheapest place to stay in Hawai'i, with several hostels and inexpensive motels.

The leeward (Kona) side can be very hot and very dry because the trades are blocked by the mountains, but the beaches are breezy and beautiful, and there are many historical and cultural sites to explore on foot, as long as you avoid Kailua-Kona, its main population center. Kona consists of a string of beachfront resorts with golf courses, sunburned tourists, and traffic.

The most exciting and extensive hiking of all is in Hawai'i Volcanoes National Park, where you can wander from forest to a true alpine environment, and where in some places you can find real solitude. You must be prepared to change your travel

Big Island Overview

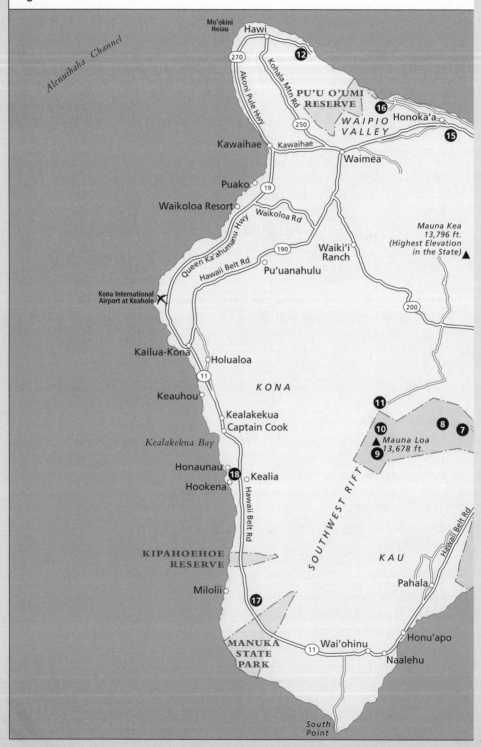

Alenuihaha Channel

Mo'okini Heiau

Hawi

270

12

Akoni Pule Hwy

Kohala Mtn Rd

PU'U O'UMI RESERVE

16

250

WAIPIO VALLEY

Honoka'a

15

Kawaihae

Kawaihae

Waimea

Puako

19

Waikoloa Resort

Waikoloa Rd

Queen Ka'ahumanu Hwy

190

Waiki'i Ranch

Mauna Kea
13,796 ft.
(Highest Elevation
in the State) ▲

Hawaii Belt Rd

Pu'uanahulu

Kona International
Airport at Keahole ✈

200

Kailua-Kona

Holualoa

KONA

Keauhou

Kealakekua
Captain Cook

11

Kealakekua Bay

Honaunau

18

Kealia

Hookena

Hawaii Belt Rd

11

10

8

7

Mauna Loa
13,678 ft. ▲

9

SOUTHWEST RIFT

KIPAHOEHOE
RESERVE

KAU

Pahala

Hawaii Belt Rd

Milolii

17

MANUKA
STATE
PARK

Wai'ohinu

11

Honu'apo

Naalehu

South
Point

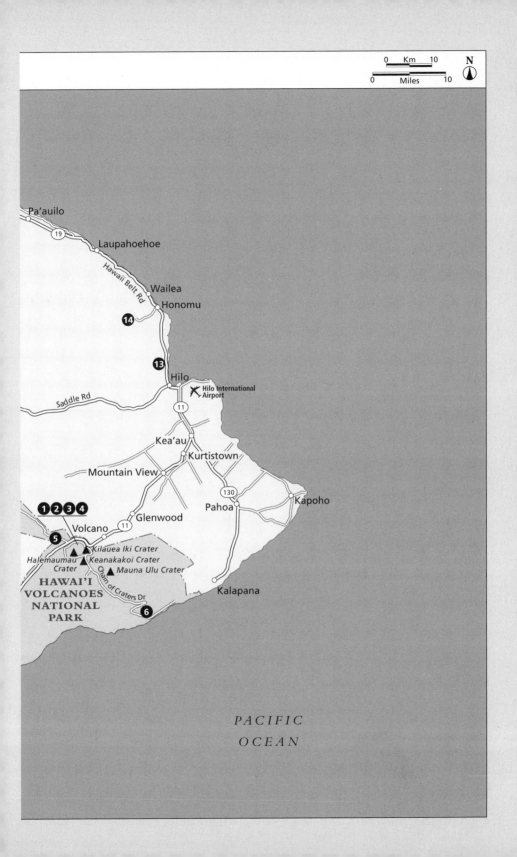

0 Km 10

0 Miles 10

N

Pa'auilo

19

Laupahoehoe

Hawaii Belt Rd

Wailea

Honomu

14

13

Hilo

Hilo International
Airport

Saddle Rd

11

Kea'au

Kurtistown

Mountain View

130

Pahoa

Kapoho

1 **2** **3** **4**

Glenwood

11

Volcano

5

▲ Kilauea Iki Crater

Keanakakoi Crater

Halemaumau
Crater

▲ Mauna Ulu Crater

Chain of Craters Dr

**HAWAI'I
VOLCANOES
NATIONAL
PARK**

Kalapana

6

PACIFIC

OCEAN

plans at short notice if Pele throws an unexpected tantrum, though. Since 1983, Kilauea has been pouring lava down the southeast slope of the island to the sea, burying the Royal Gardens housing development near Kalapana along with the national park's coastal visitor center. This has put a few favorite hikes off-limits. Since March 2008 Halema'uma'u pit, inside Kilauea Caldera, has blown a new vent in its wall and is belching out an enormous plume of noxious gasses, so hikes to Halema'uma'u are also prohibited until further notice.

Don't let any of this discourage you from visiting Volcanoes Park! It's a big place and there are lots of hikes that are perfectly safe. Just make sure to check on current conditions at the visitor center before you go. They can change without notice: On one occasion since the latest eruption began, the trade winds failed, or at least temporarily shifted direction, and the entire park shut down for about thirty-six hours. For several days the whole island of Hawai'i choked under an ugly layer of vog, volcanic gas and fog, that even affected air quality on neighboring islands.

Volcanoes National Park is a good place to save money on lodging. If you are not backpacking, there are rustic cabins and a campground near the visitor center, convenient to dozens of trails.

Two airports serve the Big Island, one at Hilo, the other at Kona. All the car rental companies have offices at both, and you will need to rent a car if you aren't a resident. There is no useful public transportation for hikers. The best map for finding your way around Hawai'i island is the one published by the University of Hawai'i Press, available in bookstores, visitor centers, and sometimes at airports.

1 Thurston Lava Tube

This is a very popular (and safe) way to explore a potentially dangerous volcanic phenomenon. A lava tube forms when hot liquid rock is flowing at just the right rate of speed beneath the surface to allow the crust to cool while the still molten lava river continues to rush underground. When the molten material drains away, it leaves a hollow tunnel. This one is in a beautiful setting in a forest of tree ferns, and is dimly lit so you can find your way. You even have an opportunity to explore an unlit portion of the tube on your own. (You'll need a good flashlight.)

Start: Thurston Lava Tube Trailhead on Crater Rim Drive
Distance: 0.5-mile loop
Elevation change: 50 feet
Difficulty: Easy
Approximate hiking time: 30 to 45 minutes
Trail surface: Paved
Seasons: Year-round

Other trail users: None
Canine compatibility: Dogs not permitted
Land status: Hawai'i Volcanoes National Park
Nearest town: Volcano Village
Fees and permits: Park entrance fee
Map: *USGS Volcanoes,* but no map is needed
Trail contact: Kilauea Visitor Center; (808) 985-6000; www.nps.gov/havo

Finding the trailhead: From the Hilo International Airport turn left (south) onto HI 11 and follow it 28 miles to the entrance of Hawai'i Volcanoes National Park, on your left (west). Drive through the entrance kiosk and immediately turn left (south) onto Crater Rim Drive. The busy parking area is about 2 miles ahead. There are toilets and water near the trailhead. There is no gas in the park. **GPS:** N19 24.49' / W155 14.19'

Lava tube entrance

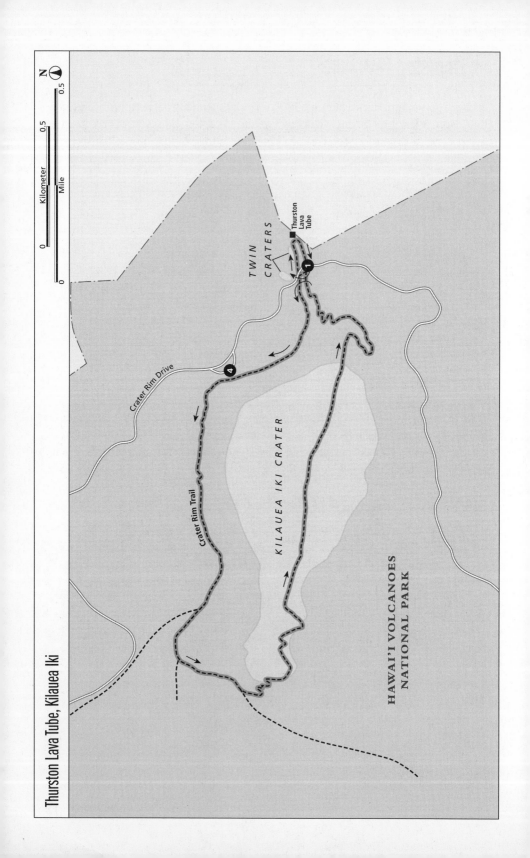

Thurston Lava Tube, Kilauea Iki

N

Kilometer
0   0.5

0   0.5
Mile

TWIN
CRATERS

Thurston
Lava
Tube

Crater Rim Drive

Crater Rim Trail

KILAUEA IKI CRATER

HAWAI'I VOLCANOES
NATIONAL PARK

The Hike

Stop for a look over the railing at the start of the trail down onto a dense tree fern forest, where interpretive panels provide information about rain forests and birdlife. Another panel to the right of the trail shows how a lava tube is formed. Start walking to the right (counterclockwise) downhill into the forest, where you might almost expect to see a velociraptor peeking out from behind one of the trunks. Unless you have gotten an early start, when you reach the mouth of the lava tube you'll probably have to wait a minute while tourists take each others' pictures at the entrance.

Entering the tube you drop into the dripping semidarkness, where rain filtering through the rock overhead leaves shallow pools on the floor. The stringy material dangling from the ceiling is made up of roots of trees on the surface. At the far end of the tunnel is a gate leading to a less-developed section of the cave that is not lit at all. The floor is rough and the ceiling is low, so you'll need a good flashlight if you want to explore a bit farther. From the gate you ascend steps to complete the loop through the forest, a beautiful stroll in itself, even without the added attraction of the lava tube.

2 Sulphur Bank Trail

Stroll through an eerie, evil-smelling landscape of barren boulders where minerals from steaming volcanic vents have deposited exquisite yellow crystals among the nooks and crannies. Even in a place like Volcanoes Park, with all its geologic activity, there is no place anywhere else quite like this. The hike starts conveniently right from the visitor center, so don't miss it. Stay away if you have respiratory problems, though.

Start: Kilauea Visitor Center
Distance: 0.7 mile out and back
Elevation change: Negligible
Difficulty: Easy
Approximate hiking time: 30 minutes
Trail surface: Asphalt and boardwalk
Seasons: Year-round
Other trail users: None

Canine compatibility: Dogs not permitted
Land status: Hawai'i Volcanoes National Park
Nearest town: Volcano Village
Fees and permits: Park entrance fee
Maps: *USGS Kilauea Crater,* though the map you receive as you enter the park is all you need
Trail contact: Kilauea Visitor Center; (808) 985-6000; www.nps.gov/havo

Finding the trailhead: From the Hilo International Airport turn left (south) onto HI 11 and follow it 28 miles to the entrance of Hawai'i Volcanoes National Park on the left (west). Drive through the entrance kiosk, keep right, and almost immediately you'll see the Kilauea Visitor Center on your right. The trail begins at the far (west) end of the parking lot in a grassy area in front of the Volcano Art Center Gallery. **GPS:** N19 25.46' / W155 15.30'

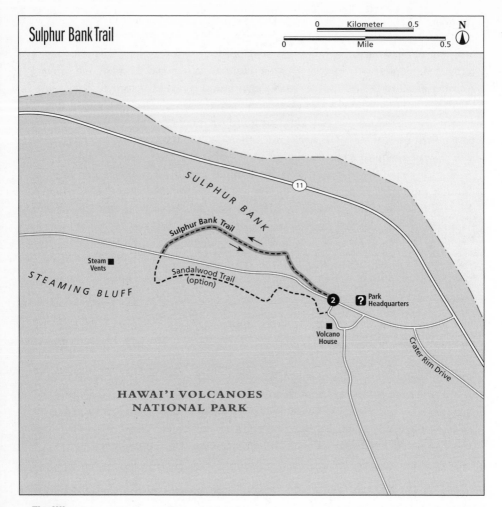

The Hike

Begin at a set of interpretive signs with a map of trails in the area, overlooked by a massive, somewhat abstract sculpture of Pele. The direction to the Sulphur Bank is marked and the path parallels the highway along the edge of a grassy park with ohia and koa trees. The raised stone platform surrounded by ti plants is for hula performances. Turn right and pass a few steam vents in a little patch of forest dense with *uluhe* (false staghorn fern), ginger, and roses, then emerge into a wasteland of gray and yellow.

The noxious steam escaping from the vents tucked into the rockpiles has deposited crystals of sulphur around their mouths that sparkle like jewels. A wooden walkway keeps you safely above the places where the crust is fragile. Don't bypass the interpretive panels without a glance. The story of how and why this spot exists just here, and how the scattered plant life manages to survive in such inhospitable surroundings, is fascinating. You can turn around at the farthest vent and return the way you came, or you can continue along the asphalt path to where it crosses the Chain of Craters Road. Across the road and to the right are the steam vents at the edge of Kilauea Caldera. If you turn left instead, you can pick up the Sandalwood Trail and follow it back to Volcano House, and from there, cross the road back to the visitor center, making a short loop.

3 Sandalwood Trail

There isn't a lot of sandalwood left here, but there is a wonderful variety of lacy ferns, a very good chance to get a look at some native Hawaiian birds, and opportunities to peek right down into some steaming, sulphur-smelling volcanic vents. On some older maps it may be called the Iliahi Trail, the Hawaiian word for sandalwood. It's a short jaunt within easy reach of the visitor center and Volcano House. You can hike the loop in either direction, but it is described clockwise here so the slightly steeper part is downhill.

Start: Halema'uma'u Overlook outside the back door of Volcano House
Distance: 1.1-mile loop
Elevation change: 100 feet
Difficulty: Easy
Approximate hiking time: 30 minutes to 1 hour
Trail surface: Asphalt, lava, packed dirt
Seasons: Year-round
Other trail users: None
Canine compatibility: Dogs not permitted
Land status: Hawai'i Volcanoes National Park
Nearest town: Volcano Village, about 1 mile outside the park entrance
Fees and permits: Park entrance fee
Maps: USGS Kilauea Crater, but the free one you'll receive when you enter the park is all you need
Trail contact: Kilauea Visitor Center; (808) 985-6000; www.nps.gov/havo
Special considerations: If you suffer from asthma or any other respiratory problems, or are traveling with an infant, avoid this hike. The volcanic vents you will be walking alongside, and sometimes right over, emit wisps of steam that are not dangerous, but the irritating, possibly lethal sulphur dioxide spewing from nearby Halema'uma'u could mean big trouble. Even if you have no breathing difficulties, stay on the trail. You don't want to disappear down one of those apparently bottomless cracks in the earth, many of which are hidden by vegetation.

Finding the trailhead: From the Hilo International Airport turn left (south) onto HI 11 and follow it 28 miles to the entrance of Hawai'i Volcanoes National Park, on your left (west). Drive through the entrance kiosk, keep right, and almost immediately you'll see the Kilauea Visitor Center on your right. Park here. Follow the signs across the street and along a grassy path to the historic Volcano House hotel. Go through the front door, past Uncle George's Lounge, and out the back door to the overlook.

The Hike

Begin at the jaw-dropping overlook right on the rim of Kilauea Caldera, home to Pele, goddess of the volcano, where the pit of Halema'uma'u began puffing out a plume of sulphur dioxide-laden smoke in March 2008. Turn right (facing the caldera) on the asphalt trail and walk a few yards to a big trail sign. You are on the Crater Rim Trail, a 12-mile route that circles the entire crater, part of which may be closed due to volcanic activity.

Tree fern

Go down a short series of stone steps and turn left (southwest) onto the Halema'uma'u Trail. You enter a Hawaiian forest of ohia trees with bright red powder-puff blossoms and several kinds of ferns, some of them up to 30 feet tall. Slender naked purplish fiddleheads look like some kind of garden sculpture, but are the young stalks of uluhe or false staghorn ferns. In spring and summer there are splashy colorful ginger flowers too, along with purple and white bamboo orchids.

Walk downhill alongside a deep trench on your left. The trail swings right at a bench and slips through a narrow mossy crack, then drops down some steep steps to a junction at 0.3 mile. This is the beginning of the Sandalwood Trail, which soon makes a tight turn to the right. Follow the edge of Kilauea Crater along a section of its wall that has collapsed and become covered in deep forest. This might be one of the best birding spots around. You can look down upon and across the forest canopy where brilliant red i'iwis, apapanes, and yellow amakihis, all rare Hawaiian natives, flash among the foliage. You're sure to hear their songs whether you see them or not.

As you begin a gradual climb, you will feel the air become warm and damp and your glasses will begin to fog. Cross several little bridges, beneath which are steaming volcanic crevasses where rainwater seeping into cracks in the lava is heated by the still cooling magma underground. About halfway around the loop, look out over a clearing for fabulous views of Kilauea Caldera and Halema'uma'u in the distance, also releasing clouds of steam. The view here is actually better than the one from Volcano House. The building on the cliff across the way is the Jaggar Museum and Hawaiian Volcano Observatory, well worth a visit.

The moisture rising around you becomes thicker as you pass open patches of grass and ferns. The ground below this area is too hot for tree roots. The trail nears Crater Rim Drive, where a big interpretive panel provides information about nearby Steaming Bluff. You can make a short detour here, turning left (west) and wandering another 0.5 mile past more steaming trenches if you haven't had enough fumes, or you can cross the road and return to the starting point via the Sulphur Bank Trail.

At mile 0.7 you rejoin the Crater Rim Trail and turn right (east). Notice how the ohia trees here are covered with lichen from the steam. Alongside the pits and trenches you might see objects wrapped in ti leaves said to be offerings to Pele. Do not disturb them.

The trail parallels the road for a short time now, and the occasional sandalwood tree appears. They are hard to pick out in the rest of the greenery and there are very few of them left. Swing right again and find yourself at the original junction with the Halema'uma'u Trail at 1.0 mile. Keep left and climb the few steps back up to Volcano House.

Miles and Directions

0.0 Start by turning right down stone steps (N19 25.43' / W155 15.30')

0.1 Halema'uma'u Trail; turn left (southwest). You'll come back to this junction.

0.3 Sandalwood Trail; turn right (west)

THE SANDALWOOD TRADE

Sandalwood *(Santalum* spp.) is a small tree or large shrub once common on all the major Hawaiian Islands, as well as in other parts of the Pacific. It is not spectacular in appearance, but is prized all over the world for its fragrance. It has beautiful, fine-grained heartwood that can be made into cabinets, carvings, and coffins, and it is often burned for incense. The native Hawaiians powdered the wood and sprinkled it on their tapa cloth to make it smell good and to repel insects. It was especially prized by the Chinese, who were willing to pay exorbitant prices for it. The Yankee traders who stopped in Hawai'i on their long sea voyages knew about the Chinese market and soon learned that Hawaiian forests had lots of sandalwood. They promised the chiefs (who still owned all the land and its products) plenty of cash for all they could supply. By this time (around 1810) the ali'i had developed a taste for European and American luxuries and were happy to comply. The commoners were put to work cutting sandalwood and hauling it to the shore where it could be shipped to China. The profits were so good that the ali'i began to demand greater and greater quantities from their subjects, who were forced to abandon their families and fields to collect it. By 1840 the people were hungry and the sandalwood was almost completely eradicated from the islands.

You can still find plenty of sandalwood in Hawai'i, but you won't be able to identify it by its smell. Most of the aromatic ones are gone forever. It is shrubby with small, opposite, waxy leaves; small red, white, or greenish four-lobed flowers; and fleshy white to red fruits. It is a partial root parasite on other plants.

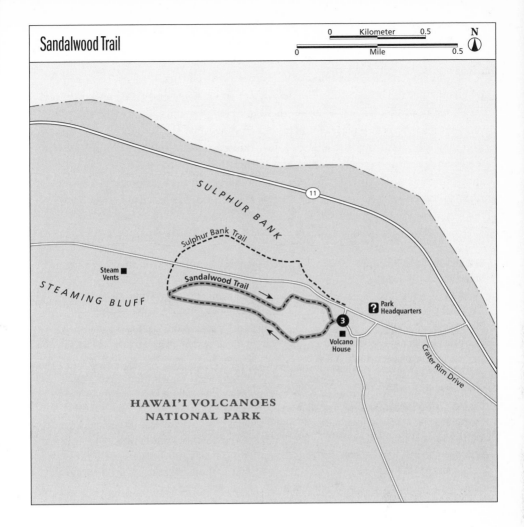

0.7 Rejoin the Crater Rim Trail and turn right (northeast). The Sulphur Bank Trail connects here. (N19 45.49' / W155 15.57')

1.0 Rejoin the Halema'uma'u Trail and keep left

1.1 Return to Volcano House

Option: You can extend this loop by continuing straight ahead on the Sulphur Bank Trail at mile 0.7, crossing the road and heading eastward back to the visitor center, from where you cross the road again and return to Volcano House. This adds about 0.5 mile to your walk.

4 Kilauea Iki

If you only have time for one hike at Volcanoes National Park, this is the one. On this hike you enter the home of the Goddess of Volcanoes, Pele herself. The trail takes you across the floor of a live caldera, still smelling of sulphur and hissing with steam. You can peer into the vent where a fountain of lava shot 1,900 feet into the air and turned the ground beneath you into a lake of fiery molten rock. In the background you can see Halema'uma'u, a pit inside the larger Kilauea Crater to the west, spewing out ash and volcanic gasses. Until March 2008 you could hike across the floor of Kilauea itself right to the edge of Halema'uma'u. Today, Kilauea Iki (Little Kilauea) is as close to the action as you can get.

See map on page 34.
Start: Kilauea Iki Overlook
Distance: 4.1-mile loop
Elevation change: 400 feet
Difficulty: Moderate
Approximate hiking time: 2 to 3 hours
Trail surface: Asphalt and lava
Seasons: Year-round
Other trail users: None
Canine compatibility: Dogs not permitted
Land status: Hawai'i Volcanoes National Park
Nearest town: Volcano Village
Fees and permits: Park entrance fee. No permit needed for a day hike.
Maps: USGS *Kilauea Crater*, but the free one you receive when you enter the park is all you need
Trail contact: Kilauea Visitor Center; (808) 985-6000; www.nps.gov/havo
Special considerations: You *definitely* need to check in with the park service to find out whether air quality is healthy enough for a hike here. Normally the trade winds blow noxious gasses like sulphur dioxide away from the popular visitor areas of the park, but if the trades should fail, as they do now and then, the vog (volcanic gasses mixed with moisture in the air) settles over the island and some areas of the park are off-limits. Occasionally, the whole park shuts down.

Finding the trailhead: From the Hilo International Airport turn left (south) onto HI 11 and follow it 28 miles to the entrance of Hawai'i Volcanoes National Park, on your left (west). Drive through the entrance kiosk and immediately turn left to Crater Rim Drive. In about 1 mile you will come to a parking area at the Kilauea Iki Overlook. You might notice a trail sign that says Kilauea Iki Trail is 0.7 mile away, but this is the best place to start because it is less crowded and the distance is the same.

The Hike

Before you start hiking, take a long look over the railing down into the crater. You should be able to see the trail and perhaps other hikers crossing the caldera. The big red hill on the far side is Pu'u Pua'i, source of the spectacular fountain of fire and lake of lava that filled this crater in 1959. In the background Halema'uma'u is puffing out clouds of steam, stealing the scene in a big way since early 2008.

Facing Kilauea Iki, turn right (west) and descend, first on asphalt stair steps, then on trail, along the crater rim, through a deep forest of ohia lehua, tree ferns, and ginger. You will hike the loop in a counterclockwise direction. At 0.7 mile the trail continues straight ahead (west), while the Crater Rim Trail heads uphill to the right (north) toward Volcano House. Continue downhill and keep left (south) on the trail marked KILAUEA IKI at the next junction; the right-hand fork leads to the Byron Ledge Trail. At a second Byron Ledge cutoff, the trail switchbacks steeply downhill to the left (southeast), where you suddenly emerge from the forest out on to the shadeless floor of the caldera, desolate and black with wisps of steam rising from cracks.

Notice you have to step down a few terraces of lava to reach the crater floor. This is a sort of "bathtub ring" marking the highest level the lava lake reached during the last eruption. The trail is fairly distinct, but you do have to pay attention. If you're uncertain at any point, keep watch for ahus (cairns) that mark the way. (For some reason, the ahus in this caldera all seem to be collapsing. Still, they are obvious rock mounds, not stones strewn at random.)

The trail stays near the southern wall at first. Passing close to Pu'u Pua'i you can get a good look at the mostly filled-in vent at its base, which shot a spectacular fountain of lava into the air in 1959. The vent is not at the center of the hill because the vent created the hill; the wind, blowing toward the south at the time of the eruption, deposited ash and cinders on that side of the opening.

Continue across the caldera floor, stepping up and down over slabs of lava that heaved upwards, cracked, and sank back down again as the rock cooled. When you

Floor of Kilauea Iki crater

reach the far end of the crater, reenter the forest and begin climbing back toward the rim. The grade is much gentler at this end than where you entered the caldera, taking you upward on easy switchbacks. You emerge from the forest at the Thurston Lava Tube parking area on the Crater Rim Trail. It's usually a mob scene here, with lots of traffic and tour busses, which is why it's better to start your hike at the overlook. Follow the parking area to the west (to the right as you face the caldera) and pick up the Crater Rim Trail again, ducking back into the more peaceful forest for a last 0.5 mile before closing the loop at the Kilauea Iki Overlook.

Miles and Directions

0.0   Kilauea Iki Overlook (N19 24.59' / W159 15.22')

0.7   Kilauea Iki/Crater Rim Trail junction; go straight ahead (west)

0.9   Byron Ledge Trail cutoff; keep left (south)

1.1   Second Byron Ledge Trail cutoff; turn left, heading steeply downhill (southeast) (N19 24.56' / W155 15.22')

1.2   Crater floor (N19 24.54' / W155 15.19')

2.4   Far end of crater (N19 24.44' / W155 14.34')

3.6   Thurston Lava Tube parking area (N19 24.49' / W155 14.20')

4.1   Return to overlook

5 Kipuka Puaulu (Bird Park)

This one is for the birds. A kipuka is an island of vegetation in a sea of lava. When an eruption poured lava down this hillside 400 years ago, it missed this section of forest, so the species of plants and animals that live here have been isolated for at least 2,000 years, when an even older flow covered the land. Human activities, introduced animals, and repeated eruptions elsewhere in the park make unspoiled kipukas like this hard to find now. This one has been protected by a pig- and goat-proof fence. The hike is an easy loop among koa, ohia, and other trees favored by a variety of native and introduced birds. Come early or late in the day and bring your binoculars. Even if you're not a birder, this is a very pretty walk.

Start: Kipuka Puaulu Trailhead
Distance: 1-mile loop
Elevation change: 100 feet
Difficulty: Easy
Approximate hiking time: 45 minutes to 1 hour
Trail surface: Gravel and forest duff
Seasons: Year-round
Other trail users: None

Canine compatibility: Dogs not permitted
Land status: Hawai'i Volcanoes National Park
Nearest town: Volcano Village
Fees and permits: Park entrance fee
Maps: USGS Kilauea Crater, but a map is not necessary
Trail contact: Kilauea Visitor Center; (808) 985-0600; www.nps.gov/havo

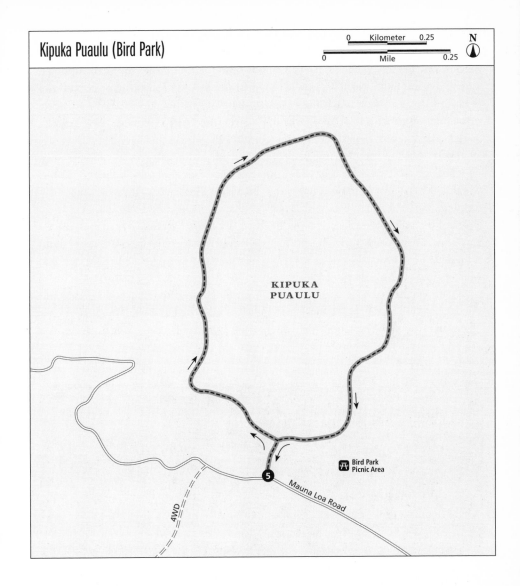

0   Kilometer   0.25

N

0   Mile   0.25

KIPUKA
PUAULU

Bird Park
Picnic Area

5

Mauna Loa Road

4WD

Finding the trailhead: From the Hilo International Airport turn left (south) onto HI 11 and follow it for 30 miles, passing the turnoff to the national park entrance. About 2 miles beyond the park entrance watch for Mauna Loa Road on the right (north). Turn right on Mauna Loa Road and go 1.5 miles to the parking area and turnaround loop. **GPS:** N19 26.15' / W155 18.11'

The Hike

Pick up a guide to the Kipuka Puaulu Nature Trail at the Kilauea Visitor Center before you start (if there are any available; they often run out). The trail begins at a panel with pictures of the birds that live in the kipuka. The route is described here in a clockwise direction, but you may walk either way.

You stroll among some very big old koa trees whose extraordinary leaves deserve a close examination. If you find a young tree, you'll see two different kinds of leaves on the same branch. When leaves first sprout from their buds they are small and pinnately divided, rather fernlike, but as they mature, the tiny leaves disappear and the petioles (the stems that attach the leaves to the twig) flatten and expand to a sickle shape that looks like a leaf. All the mature "leaves" are really modified stems. Perhaps it is an adaptation to help the tree conserve moisture.

There are also some very big, shaggy ohia trees, with bright red powder-puff–like bunches of flowers that are a favorite source of nectar for birds. Look for the famous mamaki, or Hawaiian stingless nettle, too. These are shrubs or small trees with finely toothed, light-colored leaves with small inconspicuous greenish clusters of flowers attached directly to the stems. In the treetops, watch for red i'iwis, apapanes, yellow amakihis, and 'elepaios, tiny birds with cocked tails. You are almost certain to see Kalij pheasants, an introduced species from Nepal, much too tame for their own good, as well as showy red northern cardinals.

The trail climbs a little at the beginning, drops a little at the end, but is gentle and smooth so you can enjoy the forest and the birds without having to watch your feet. There are even some benches to encourage you to relax and take your time.

Kalij pheasant

6 Pu'uloa Petroglyphs

The early Hawaiians left incised geometric designs and stylized human figures in the lava in groupings scattered all over the islands. The drawings are surely religious, but their exact meanings are unknown. Some, like circles with a dot in the center, are said to be receptacles for the umbilical cords of newborns that would help to protect the child. This lonely site overlooking the sea has one of the biggest and oldest collections of these petroglyphs, and is easy to reach by a short walk.

Start: Pu'uloa Petroglyphs Trailhead on Chain of Craters Road
Distance: 1.4 miles out and back
Elevation change: Negligible
Difficulty: Easy
Approximate hiking time: 1 to 1.5 hours
Trail surface: Fairly smooth pahoehoe lava
Seasons: Year-round
Other trail users: None
Canine compatibility: Dogs not permitted
Land status: Hawai'i Volcanoes National Park

Fees and permits: Park entrance fee
Maps: USGS *Makaopuhi* and *Kalapana*, though the map you receive as you enter the park is all you need
Trail contact: Kilauea Visitor Center; (808) 985-6000; www.nps.gov/havo
Special considerations: Travel with a full tank as there is no gas in the park. Try to leave nothing in your car at all, but anything you do leave should be out of sight in the trunk.

Finding the trailhead: From the Hilo International Airport turn left (south) onto HI 11 and follow it 28 miles to the entrance of Hawai'i Volcanoes National Park, on your left (west). Drive through the entrance kiosk and immediately turn left (southeast) onto Crater Rim Drive. In about 3 miles, turn left again (south) on Chain of Craters Road, and follow it 20 miles steeply downhill, almost all the way to the ocean, to the signed trailhead on the left (south).

The Hike

The walk is shadeless and windy, leading you to wonder why such a desolate spot as this was chosen for a petroglyph site. There is very little vegetation except at the very beginning of the hike, where there are a few scraggly noni bushes. Beyond these, nothing but the intricate patterns of swirling pahoehoe lava underfoot distracts you until you reach the petroglyphs. A raised boardwalk around the most concentrated set of designs protects them, and several interpretive panels offer information about early Hawaiian history. Retrace your steps to the trailhead when you

Pu'uloa petroglyphs

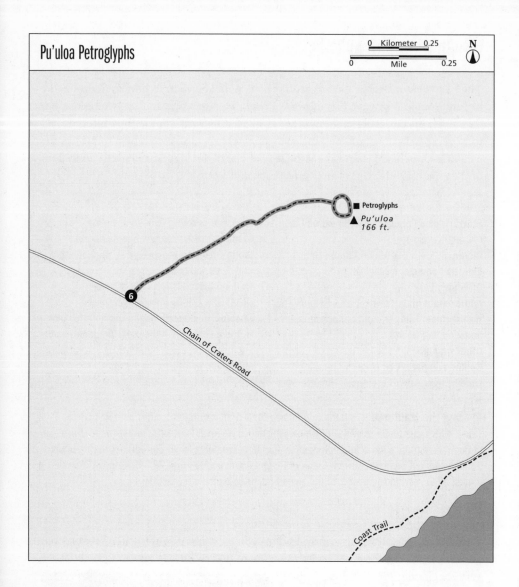

have seen enough. You might want to continue a few miles farther along the Chain of Craters Road to have a look at the Holei Sea Arch and to see where the most recent lava flow has permanently closed the highway.

Miles and Directions

0.0 Start (N19 17.21' / W155 07.48')

0.7 Petroglyphs (N19 17.33' / W155 07.17')

1.4 Return to the trailhead

Trails on Mauna Loa (Hikes 7 to 11)

Hikes on Mauna Loa need a special introduction. Mauna Loa is the largest mountain in the world. The part you can see, the part above sea level, is big enough at 13,677 feet, but from the base on the sea floor, the mountain is even taller than Mount Everest. It is also one of the world's most active volcanoes. As if that weren't enough reason to visit, it is strikingly, starkly, weirdly beautiful. The rock comes in an infinite variety of shapes and textures, from jagged, knifelike ridges to sculptures with Henry Moore–like curves, drippy blobs, braided ropes, pearl-sized droplets called Pele's tears, and spun-sugar strings called Pele's hair. Colors range from black to yellows, oranges, reds, and purples, and there are stretches of sand that look like gold dust. Here and there wisps of steam escape from cracks and cones.

You can sample the mountain in smaller tastes on day hikes, or swallow it whole (at least the part above sea level) on a backpack trip of three days or more. Even the lower legs of the hike involve lots of elevation gain, though, and you must be in good physical condition and be well prepared with proper clothing and lots of water to hike any of it.

If you plan to hike the entire mountain, from the Mauna Loa Trailhead to the summit, you will be climbing 19 miles and 6,000 feet one way. Hikes 7 through 11 break that distance down into sections so that you can put together your own itinerary. Snapshots of the hike segments are provided here:

7   Mauna Loa Trailhead to Red Hill: 15 miles out and back; 3,393-foot elevation change; can be done as a very strenuous day hike, an overnight backpack, or the first stop on the way to the top.

8   Red Hill Cabin to North Pit Junction: 9.5 miles one way; 3,000-foot elevation gain; you can camp here then return to the trailhead, or continue on to either the Mauna Loa Cabin or the summit.

9   North Pit Junction to Summit Cabin: 2.1 miles one way; 230-foot elevation gain.

10 North Pit Junction to Mauna Loa Summit: 2.6 miles one way; 650-foot elevation gain.

11 Observatory Trail to North Pit Junction: 7.6 miles up and back; 2,000-foot elevation change; can be done as a strenuous round-trip day hike or the first section on the way to the top.

Overnight Trips on Mauna Loa: You *must* check in at the Kilauea Visitor Center to get a permit. You will be asked about your camping equipment and level of experience, and will be updated on conditions on the mountain including weather and availability of water. Rangers have maps and literature on regulations and on hiking safety on the mountain. There is also good information on how to prepare for Mauna Loa on the Hawai'i Volcanoes National Park Web site: www.nps.gov/archive/havo/visitor/ml.htm.

Important advice includes carrying very warm clothing: several layers, including rain gear. This may be Hawai'i, but nights at elevations above 10,000 feet anywhere in the world can be very cold, often below freezing. Mountains make their own weather and you can expect a storm at any time, even if it's sunny elsewhere. Carry at least twice the water you think you will need. The air is extremely dry, and it can be hot when sun reflects off the dark lava. Carry and use lots of sunscreen too.

The footing is rough and uneven, guaranteed to chew ordinary running shoes to shreds in a very few days, and ankle support is helpful, so good boots are recommended. Stay on trails, following ahus (cairns) where the path is obscure. Occasionally clouds roll in and you can't see more than a few feet in front of you, and there are spots where the crust is thin and fragile.

The most common problems are hypothermia and acute mountain sickness (AMS). The first can be prevented by bringing proper clothing and drinking plenty of water. Acute mountain sickness is difficult to prevent in Hawai'i because there is nowhere to spend a day or two acclimating at high altitude. The best you can do is take your time and recognize the symptoms if they occur. Symptoms include headache, nausea and vomiting, fatigue, insomnia, dizziness, and loss of balance. If rest and aspirin don't help, head back downhill.

Spatter cone on the Mauna Loa Trail

Less common but more serious conditions are high altitude pulmonary edema (HAPE) and high altitude cerebral anemia (HACE). HAPE begins with symptoms like those of AMS, but if they are accompanied by a cough or gurgling sounds in the chest, racing pulse, and mental confusion, *immediately* head to lower elevation. The condition can be fatal. The symptoms of HACE can begin in the same way, but if there is severe headache that does not respond to aspirin, loss of coordination, confusion, inability to speak, or finally, coma, evacuate *immediately*. This condition is fatal if not treated at once.

7 Mauna Loa Trail to Red Hill

The hike to Red Hill Cabin is the first leg on the journey to the top of Mauna Loa, though it's well worth the effort as a final destination in itself. There are great views out over Kilauea and Halema'uma'u Craters all the way to the sea, where Pu'u O'o shoots a jet of steam over the coast like a boiling teapot. Photographers will love the sunrise and sunset shots of Mauna Kea floating above the clouds just across the valley. Pu'u Ula'ula (Red Hill) is your only source of shelter and of water (usually) on the whole mountain until you reach the summit cabin. Very strong hikers can do this as a day hike, but be warned: It will take longer than you think.

Start: Mauna Loa Trailhead
Distance: 15 miles out and back
Elevation change: 3,393 feet
Difficulty: Strenuous
Approximate hiking time: 8 to 12 hours
Trail surface: Rough lava
Seasons: Spring, summer, and fall. Expect ice and snow in winter.
Other trail users: None
Canine compatibility: Dogs not permitted
Land status: Hawai'i Volcanoes National Park
Nearest town: Volcano Village, about 1 mile outside the park entrance
Fees and permits: Park entrance fee. A free wilderness permit is required and is available at the Kilauea Visitor Center. You must show up in person, no sooner than one day in advance, so rangers can give you up-to-date information

about volcanic activity, weather conditions, and water availability. Cabins are available on a first-come, first-served basis, but you must get a permit whether you are staying in a cabin or camping. You must check back in with the park service after you have finished your hike.
Maps: USGS *Kipuka Pakeke* and *Pu'u Ula'ula*, or *National Geographic Trails Illustrated Hawai'i Volcanoes National Park* map. You can also buy a 1:200,000 scale topographic map of Volcanoes National Park at the visitor center, though it's somewhat dated.
Trail contact: Kilauea Visitor Center; (808) 985-6000; www.nps.gov/havo
Special considerations: Stay on the trail. This is an active volcano, still steaming hot just under the crust. The trail follows the most stable route over the safest lava.

Finding the trailhead: From Hilo International Airport, turn left (south) onto HI 11 and follow it 28 miles to the entrance of Hawai'i Volcanoes National Park on the left (west). Drive to the entrance kiosk, pay the fee, then keep right on Crater Rim Drive. The Kilauea Visitor Center is on your right. Pick up your permit here, then go back out past the park entrance to HI 11 again and turn left (west). Drive 2.5 miles to Mauna Loa Road. Turn right (northwest) and drive the narrow winding lane 11 miles to its end at a parking lot. The road is paved but only one lane wide for most of its length, often too narrow for two cars to pass. Take your time. The trailhead has a covered shelter with a picnic table, a pit toilet, and an emergency telephone. There is *no* water.

The Hike

The trailhead is located at 6,660 feet in a koa forest. There may be a few friendly nenes (Hawaiian geese) around to see you off on your hike. Do not feed them.

Set out to the east, leaving the big old koa trees behind almost immediately. Enter a zone of shorter, bright red flowered ohia lehua trees and the usual Hawaiian mountain flora: ohelo berries, a'ali'i (hops), red and white pukiawe berries, and the shiny black berries of kukae nene (translation: goose doo doo). In about 0.5 mile go through a gate, making sure to close it behind you to keep destructive introduced animals out of the native vegetation. This first section of the trail is the most difficult because it's winding and easy to lose among the shrubbery. Make sure you can see the next ahu (cairn) before you leave the last one.

In about 1 mile you'll reach the 7,000-FOOT sign, still in relatively abundant vegetation. Be sure to glance behind you now and then, back toward the southeastern coast. If it's clear you can look down into Kilauea Caldera where Halema'uma'u is pouring out steam, and even farther on to the coastline where the pointed cone of Pu'u O'o is erupting too. By the 8,000-foot sign the shrubbery has become stunted and sparse.

As the gently curving summit of Mauna Loa comes into view, the trail swings left, (west) straight toward the mountain, and the grade levels out for a while. At mile 3, the last tree worthy of the name that is within reach of the trail

▶ Start early so you don't get caught in the dark. Even if you are a very strong hiker you cannot maintain a steady pace over constantly changing, difficult footing and at such high elevations. Since you cannot camp at the trailhead, you will be climbing from sea level (or at most, from 4,000 feet) to above 10,000 feet in one day. Unless you have very recently been hiking or climbing at altitudes like these, you are going to be affected.

Take warm clothing, lots of water, and lots of sunscreen. It can be very cold at 10,000 feet, especially if you are wet, and if it rains there is no shelter until you reach the cabin. On the other hand, if it is clear the dark lava absorbs sunshine and radiates it back at you. This, along with the thin air and almost constant breezes, can suck the moisture out of your body at an alarming rate. There is usually water (that must be treated) at the cabin, but in drought conditions, the tank might be dry.

appears, a good-sized ohia in a protected gully. Feast your eyes, and stop for a snack beneath it. It's the last shade you'll see for awhile, especially if you're heading all the way to the summit.

Not far past "the tree" the climb resumes, and you hit a patch of rough a'a lava walking, just enough to make you grateful when you're back on smoother pahoehoe. The rock takes on more interesting shapes and colors, with collapsed lava tubes and bridges and what seem to be bottomless pits. It's sometimes a deep burgundy color splattered with little nuggets of golden olivine that sparkle in the sun. After a steeper than usual stretch you top a ridge and catch sight of Pu'u Ula'ula (Red Hill) for the first time. There's no mistaking which one it is. The high-tech looking structures you might glimpse off to the right belong to the Kulani Radio Facility. Do not disturb.

The trail becomes smoother and easier to follow above 9,000 feet, undulating across the bottom of a shallow bowl and causing you to lose a few feet of hard-won elevation. Negotiate a particularly nasty patch of jagged a'a and pass through another gate, closing it behind you. Finally, toil up a crumbly slope of coarse cinders and top a rise to see the trail winding up the side of the spatter cone of Red Hill just ahead. The cinders underfoot become finer and redder at every step. At last you pass through a gap between two signs announcing your arrival at Pu'u Ula'ula (10,035 feet).

The cabin lies below you in a sheltered dip. It has eight bunks with mattresses, a picnic table, a pit toilet, and a tank to catch rainwater. It's a bit dilapidated (especially the toilet) but serves its purpose, keeping out the wind and rain. Please leave it cleaner than you found it, and leave nothing behind.

Red Hill Cabin with Mauna Kea in the background

Mauna Loa Trail to Red Hill, Red Hill Cabin to North Pit Junction

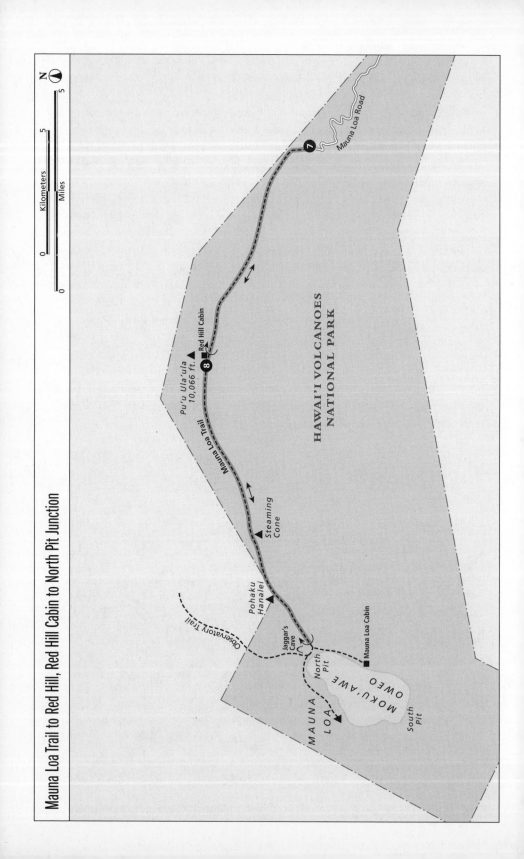

The stars here are closer and more numerous than anyplace you've ever been. That's why there are dozens of observatories on Mauna Kea, the next mountain over. Some people prefer to sleep outside the cabin to enjoy the night sky and there are several flat sleeping spots with rocks piled up around them for wind protection. You also can climb to the summit behind the cabin where there is a marker pointing out various features of the Big Island.

If you do not plan to continue on to the summit of Mauna Loa, return the way you came.

▶ The island has an inversion layer in which rising warm, moist air is held down by a layer of colder, drier air, so most of Hawaii's precipitation occurs below 8,000 feet. It's too dry for much of anything to grow higher up on the mountain.

Miles and Directions

0.0 Start at the Mauna Loa Trailhead (N19 29.34' / W155 23.07')
1.0 Reach 7,000 feet
2.5 Reach 8,000 feet
3.2 The last tree
4.8 Climb a rise for the first view of Red Hill
5.1 Reach 9,000 feet
7.5 Red Hill Cabin (N19 31.49' / W155 27.52')
15.0 Return to Mauna Loa Trailhead

8 Red Hill Cabin to North Pit Junction

This is the second leg of the Mauna Loa Trail, leading to a campsite at a major trail junction. From the junction you can continue on in one direction to the Mauna Loa cabin (2.1 miles; 13,250 feet) or head off in the opposite direction to the official summit of the mountain (2.6 miles; 13,677 feet). If you want to see both, the best plan is to head to the cabin, spend two nights there, and day hike to the summit and back without a pack. That said, you have already seen the best of the mountain on your way to North Pit. The trails to both the cabin and the summit are more of the same, but with rougher footing, so many hikers go to North Pit, count it as the top, and turn around.

See map on page 54.

Start: Red Hill Cabin on Mauna Loa

Distance: 9.5 miles one way from Red Hill; 17.0 miles one way from Mauna Loa Trailhead

Elevation change: 3,000 feet from Red Hill; 6,300 feet from Mauna Loa Trailhead

Difficulty: Strenuous

Approximate hiking time: 8 to 10 hours

Trail surface: Rough lava

Seasons: Spring, summer, and fall. Expect ice and snow in winter.

Other trail users: None

Canine compatibility: Dogs not permitted

Land status: Hawai'i Volcanoes National Park

Nearest town: Volcano Village, about 1 mile outside the park entrance

Fees and permits: Park entrance fee. A free wilderness permit is required and available at the Kilauea Visitor Center. You must show up in person, no sooner than one day in advance, so that rangers can give you up-to-date information about volcanic activity, weather conditions, and water availability. Cabins are available on a first-come, first-served basis, but you must get a permit whether you are staying in a cabin or camping. You must check back in with the park service after you have finished your hike.

Maps: USGS Pu'u Ula'ula, Koko'olau, and Mauna Loa, or National Geographic Trails Illustrated Hawai'i Volcanoes National Park map. You can also buy a 1:200,000 scale topographic map of Volcanoes National Park at the visitor center, though it's somewhat dated.

Trail contact: Kilauea Visitor Center; (808) 985-6000; www.nps.gov/havo

Special considerations: Stay on the trail. This is an active volcano, still steaming hot just under the crust. The trail follows the most stable route over the safest lava.

Finding the trailhead: From Hilo International Airport, turn left (south) onto HI 11 and follow it 28 miles to the entrance of Hawai'i Volcanoes National Park on the left (west). Inside the park keep right on Crater Rim Drive; the Kilauea Visitor Center is on your right. Pick up your permit then go back out to HI 11 and turn left (west). Drive 2.5 miles to Mauna Loa Road. Turn right (northwest) and drive the narrow winding lane 11 miles to its end at a parking lot. Follow the Mauna Loa Trail for 7.5 miles to Red Hill Cabin.

The Hike

The trail leaves Red Hill Cabin through a dip in the west rim of the little crater. There is a trail sign, but it's out of date since the 1984 eruption. You must add 0.3 mile to all the numbers given on the sign, so it's 9.5 miles to the Summit Trail at North Pit.

The first mile of trail is mostly over crumbly a'a, but the footing eventually becomes easier. Wind your way around multicolored spatter cones whose shapes seem to become more and more grotesque with every step. There are collapsed lava tubes, many of whose insides are even more brilliantly colored than the cones. Patches of lava glitter and glisten with gold sparkles of olivine. If the weather is clear, you'll want to stop and take photos every few steps, especially with Mauna Kea across the saddle as a backdrop.

After a mile or so, if clouds don't interfere, you can look northward, to the left of Mauna Kea, to spot Haleakala Volcano on Maui. By the second mile you enter a big patch of mustardy olivine ash. If you squat in one of the cindery patches you can find the most exquisite lacy golden and opalescent little jewels, along with tiny polished teardrops called Pele's tears. Run your fingers through them and marvel, but leave them where they are. Pele is said to inflict terrible curses on anyone who takes away pieces of her mountain.

At mile 2.7 you enter a darker pahoehoe flow, a rolling sea of lava that dates from the 1984 eruption. The trail had to be rerouted here and doesn't quite match the topo map. After meeting the 11,000-FOOT sign, skirt a big cone known as Pakauahi and follow ahus over alternating smooth and rough footing as you make a wide arc to the right (north) toward Dewey Cone. It's big, but rather drab brown in color and not very exciting. It was part of an eruption that occurred in July 1899, a short time after the Battle of Manila, when Admiral George Dewey was commander of the U.S. naval fleet. After you have passed it, the trail again becomes paved with gold. There's a flat spot with a low rock wall around it that makes a good rest and snack stop out of the wind. You could camp here too, if you have water. Just beyond are two more low cones, startlingly bright salmon in color.

▶ Start early so you don't get caught in the dark. Even if you are a very strong hiker, it's nearly impossible to maintain a steady pace over constantly changing, difficult footing and at such high elevations. Unless you have very recently been hiking or climbing at altitudes like these, you are going to be affected by altitude.

Take warm clothing, lots of water, and lots of sunscreen. It can be very cold at these elevations, especially if you are wet. If it is clear the dark lava absorbs sunshine and radiates it back at you. This, along with the thin air and almost constant breezes, can suck the moisture out of your body at an alarming rate. Be sure to carry all the water you will need.

Climb close alongside a deep trench, path of the lava that poured out of Steaming Cone just ahead. Eventually you drop down into, then up out of, this trench, heading around the base of the cone. Don't miss the sharp right-hand turn the trail takes at a big ahu or you will find yourself stumbling through some crumbly lava crust. The area around Steaming Cone (which doesn't steam much anymore) is one of the most striking and unearthly places you've ever seen. As you pass Steaming Cone you enter another novel and utterly bizarre landscape. Deep mustardy-green sand, dotted with sharp, misshapen black boulders, stretches away before you, the scene dominated by bright red Steaming Cone in the center. The colors are not like anything else you have ever seen on Earth.

Beyond Steaming Cone the rock becomes more solid and the trail climbs to the 12,000-foot sign. There is a water hole/ice cave just below this, but it's not easy to find and is not a reliable water source. It's hard going over a'a as you pass a dark black cone, then follow a gully coming from Pohaku Hanalei, the next cone at mile 7. This cone was cut right in half by the 1984 eruption. Continue west, then south, then west again toward a wall you will veer away from to the right. You can see the huge ahus that mark North Pit ahead. Hop a fabulously colored and textured trench, then a few minutes of hiking deposits you at a junction.

The left fork takes you to Mauna Loa Cabin, the right to a three-way junction with the Observatory Trail and the Summit Trail. Both begin to the north. Near the junction is a very tall ahu, and just beyond it, Jaggars Cave, which is not a cave at all, but a flat-bottomed pit with rock walls built around the edges to block the wind. You can sleep in Jaggar's Cave, though you'll need a tent if it rains and you'll have to have plenty of water. There is a collapsed lava tube nearby where you can sometimes chip a bit of ice from rainwater that has pooled at the bottom then frozen, but it is not at all reliable. For that matter, the tank at Mauna Loa cabin may be dry, and there is no water at the summit either.

There's a pit toilet about 0.1 mile along the Observatory Trail. Even if you don't need it, you should walk toward it. The setting is gorgeous. While we're on the subject, please carry a plastic bag and pack out your toilet paper.

Miles and Directions

0.0 Red Hill Cabin (Pu'u Ula'ula; 7.5 miles from Mauna Loa Trailhead) (N19 29.34' / W155 27.52')

2.9 11,000-FOOT sign (10.4 miles from Mauna Loa Trailhead)

4.2 Dewey Cone (11.7 miles from Mauna Loa Trailhead) (N19 31.09' / W155 30.56')

5.5 Steaming Cone (13.0 miles from Mauna Loa Trailhead)

6.2 12,000-FOOT sign (13.7 miles from Mauna Loa Trailhead)

7.0 Pohaku Hanalei Cone (14.5 miles from Mauna Loa Trailhead)

9.4 Junction with Mauna Loa Cabin Trail (16.9 miles from Mauna Loa Trailhead)

9.5 North Pit Junction (17.0 miles from Mauna Loa Trailhead) (N19 29.36' / W155 34.38')

⑨ North Pit Junction to Mauna Loa Cabin

If you decide to push on past North Pit, you can spend the night in a comfortable (if Spartan) cabin, or camp under the stars at the rim of Moku'aweoweo crater at the top of the world's biggest volcano. This is the only place near the summit of the mountain with shelter and (sometimes) water. It's only 2.1 miles from North Pit and only 5.9 miles from the Observatory Trailhead, but it will seem longer. Read the entries in the logbook at the cabin if you think you're the only person to ever have felt this tired . . . and triumphant. If you have the time (and adequate water) this is a good place to settle in for two nights and make the 8.4-mile round-trip trek to the actual summit and back as a day hike.

◀ *Jaggar's Cave at North Pit*

Start: North Pit Junction on Mauna Loa

Distance: 2.1 miles one way from North Pit

Elevation change: 230 feet according to the signs (it's probably at least 100 feet more)

Difficulty: Strenuous

Approximate hiking time: 1.5 to 2.5 hours one way

Trail surface: Rough lava

Seasons: Spring, summer, and fall. Expect ice and snow in winter.

Other trail users: None

Canine compatibility: Dogs not permitted

Land status: Hawai'i Volcanoes National Park

Nearest town: Volcano Village, about 1 mile outside the park entrance

Fees and permits: Park entrance fee. A free wilderness permit is required and available at the Kilauea Visitor Center. You must show up in person, no sooner than one day in advance, so that rangers can give you up-to-date information about volcanic activity, weather conditions, and water availability. Cabins are available on a first-come, first-served basis, but you must get a permit whether you are staying in a cabin or camping. You must check back in with the park service after you have finished your hike.

Maps: USGS *Pu'u Ula'ula, Koko'olau,* and *Mauna Loa,* or *National Geographic Trails Illustrated Hawai'i Volcanoes National Park* map. You can also buy a 1:200,000 scale topographic map of Volcanoes national park at the visitor center, though it's somewhat dated.

Trail contact: Kilauea Visitor Center; (808) 985-6000; www.nps.gov/havo

Special considerations: Stay on the trail. This is an active volcano, still steaming hot just under the crust. The trail follows the most stable route over the safest lava.

Finding the trailhead: From Hilo International Airport, turn left (south) onto HI 11 and follow it 28 miles to the entrance of Hawai'i Volcanoes National Park on the left (west). Inside the park keep right on Crater Rim Drive; the Kilauea Visitor Center is on your right. Pick up your permit then go back out to HI 11 and turn left (west). Drive 2.5 miles to Mauna Loa Road. Turn right (northwest) and drive the narrow winding lane 11 miles to its end at a parking lot. Follow the Mauna Loa Trail for 17 miles to North Pit Junction.

The Hike

From the three-way junction at North Pit, head left (south) on the Mauna Loa Trail to a sign directing you toward the cabin. Drop to the right, down into North Pit, and follow ahus straight across the crater floor, over great bulbous globs of lava from the 1984 eruption. Climb out of North Pit and pass Lua Poholo, a big, scary crater that will draw you toward its rim to see just how deep it goes. Resist the temptation to go closer because nasty fissures all around the edge look as though they could break loose and tumble into the crater at the slightest touch. From here on, the trail deteriorates. With the exception of a few short sections of pahoehoe, the footing is over big, sharp chunks of a'a, skirting or hopping deep fissures and ankle-grabbing holes. You climb gradually but steadily toward the rim of Moku'aweoweo Caldera, but won't be able to see in until you're almost at the cabin. At a sign that says simply TRAIL swing right and keep watch ahead for the cabin roof to appear on the horizon. After another long, frustrating 0.5 mile the first sign of civilization you will reach is the pit toilet. Regardless of need, do pause to enjoy the magnificent view out over the caldera. You might also wish to contemplate the mystery of why hikers who have come this way before you have desecrated this magical place by stuffing used toilet paper into rock crevices all over the mountain.

Just beyond lies the cabin. A sign on its side says the elevation is 13,250 feet, but it's probably at least 100 feet higher. The cabin was remodeled in 1979 and is light and airy with cheerful curtains at the windows. It has twelve bunks with mattresses, a water tank (sometimes empty), a table and chairs, and a log book in which you can read comments by previous visitors, such as: "Two point one miles, my ass!" If you prefer to sleep outside, there are several flat spaces surrounded by windbreaks, but expect freezing temperatures most nights.

▶ The hike features constantly changing, difficult footing and high elevations. Unless you have very recently been hiking or climbing at altitudes like these, you are going to be affected by altitude.

Take warm clothing, lots of water, and lots of sunscreen. It can be very cold at these elevations, especially if you are wet. If it is clear the dark lava absorbs sunshine and radiates it back at you. This, along with the thin air and almost constant breezes, can suck the moisture out of your body at an alarming rate. Be sure to carry all the water you will need.

Outside your front door lies Moku'aweoweo, an enormous caldera 2.7 miles by 1.6 miles across and 600 feet deep. It was formed by the collapse of Mauna Loa's summit when molten material ceased to erupt and the magma chamber below emptied. Moku'aweoweo most recently erupted in 1984, shooting up a curtain of fire along cracks in the caldera floor that lasted two hours and added several feet of fresh lava to

Summit cabin at Mauna Loa

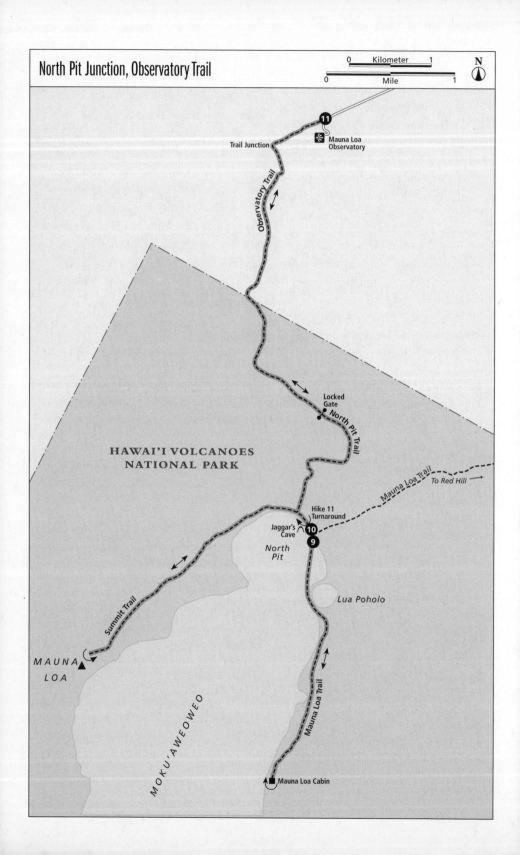

North Pit Junction, Observatory Trail

0   Kilometer   1

0   Mile   1

N

11   Mauna Loa Observatory

Trail Junction

Observatory Trail

Locked Gate

North Pit Trail

HAWAI'I VOLCANOES NATIONAL PARK

Mauna Loa Trail   To Red Hill →

Hike 11 Turnaround

Jaggar's Cave   10   9

North Pit

Lua Poholo

Summit Trail

MAUNA LOA

MOKU'AWEOWEO

Mauna Loa Trail

Mauna Loa Cabin

the mountain. The lava continued to flow, first underground, then rising to the surface below Red Hill and creeping almost to Hilo before it stopped. It's still plenty hot under there, as you can see from the escaping steam. The actual summit of Mauna Loa is on the far side of the crater, but you won't be able to identify it from where you are.

Miles and Directions

0.0 Start at the junction at North Pit (17 miles from Mauna Loa Trailhead) (N19 29.36' / W155 34.38')

0.1 Junction with Mauna Loa Cabin Trail; turn right, down into North Pit

1.3 Trail sign; curve right

2.1 Mauna Loa Cabin (19.1 miles from Mauna Loa Trailhead). GPS is N19 27.59' / W155 34.54'

10 North Pit Junction to Mauna Loa Summit

There isn't much more to see from the summit than there is from the cabin across Moku'aweoweo crater, but you do get the satisfaction of standing on top of the biggest volcano in the world. You will probably want to make the trip a day hike either from North Pit if you are camped there, or from the summit cabin. You could probably get there and back from the Observatory Trailhead in one day if you are a very strong hiker and very well acclimatized to the altitude, but it's a grueling trek.

See map on page 62.
Start: North Pit Junction on Mauna Loa
Distance: 2.6 miles one way from North Pit Junction; 19.6 miles from Mauna Loa Trailhead
Elevation change: 650 feet
Difficulty: Strenuous
Approximate hiking time: 1.5 to 2.5 hours one way from North Pit
Trail surface: Rough lava
Seasons: Spring, summer, and fall. Expect ice and snow in winter.
Other trail users: None
Canine compatibility: Dogs not permitted
Land status: Hawai'i Volcanoes National Park
Nearest town: Volcano Village, about 1 mile outside the park entrance
Fees and permits: Park entrance fee. A free wilderness permit is required and available at the Kilauea Visitor Center. You must show up in person, no sooner than one day in advance, so

that rangers can give you up-to-date information about volcanic activity, weather conditions, and water availability. Cabins are available on a first-come, first-served basis, but you must get a permit whether you are staying in a cabin or camping. You must check back in with the park service after you have finished your hike.
Maps: USGS *Pu'u Ula'ula, Koko'olau,* and *Mauna Loa,* or *National Geographic Trails Illustrated Hawai'i Volcanoes National Park* map. You can also buy a 1:200,000 scale topographic map of Volcanoes national park at the visitor center, though it's somewhat dated.
Trail contact: Kilauea Visitor Center; (808) 985-6000; www.nps.gov/havo
Special considerations: Stay on the trail. This is an active volcano, still steaming hot just under the crust. The trail follows the most stable route over the safest lava.

Finding the trailhead: From Hilo International Airport, turn left (south) onto HI 11 and follow it 28 miles to the entrance of Hawai'i Volcanoes National Park on the left (west). Inside the park keep right on Crater Rim Drive; the Kilauea Visitor Center is on your right. Pick up your permit then go back out to HI 11 and turn left (west). Drive 2.5 miles to Mauna Loa Road. Turn right (northwest) and drive the narrow winding lane 11 miles to its end at a parking lot. Follow the Mauna Loa Trail for 17 miles to North Pit Junction.

The Hike

▶ The hike features constantly changing, difficult footing and high elevations. Unless you have very recently been hiking or climbing at altitudes like these, you are going to be affected by altitude.

Take warm clothing, lots of water, and lots of sunscreen. It can be very cold at these elevations, especially if you are wet. If it is clear the dark lava absorbs sunshine and radiates it back at you. This, along with the thin air and almost constant breezes, can suck the moisture out of your body at an alarming rate. Be sure to carry all the water you will need.

It's an easier walk to the summit from North Pit than to the cabin, even though it's a little longer. From the three-way junction at Jaggar's Cave, head northwest around the rim of North Pit, passing another ice cave and crossing a colorful crack. In about a 0.5 mile pass a junction where the old Observatory Trail used to join this one. Keep left (west). Struggle across an expanse of a'a lava, veering gradually southwest until you reach rim of Moku'aweoweo crater. It's not long now to the summit at 13,677 feet, marked by an ahu that doesn't look all that different from the other ahus.

The crater is impressive, broad and black and steaming. It is 2.7 miles long by 1.6 miles across and 600 feet deep. Mauna Loa's summit collapsed and formed the crater when an eruption stopped and the magma chamber below emptied. Moku'aweoweo most recently erupted in 1984, first shooting up a curtain of fire along cracks in the caldera floor that lasted two hours and adding several feet of fresh lava to the mountain. The lava continued to flow, first underground, then rising to the surface below Red Hill and creeping almost to Hilo before it stopped. It's still plenty hot under there as you can see from the escaping steam. Have your picture taken and return the way you came.

Look across Maku'aweoweo crater to Mauna Loa summit

Miles and Directions

0.0 Start at the junction at North Pit (17.0 miles from Mauna Loa Trailhead) (N19 29.36' / W155 34.38')

2.6 Mauna Loa summit (N19 28.46' / W155 36.09')

11 Observatory Trail to North Pit Junction

This is the shortest, fastest route to Mauna Loa's North Pit; from there you can continue to the Mauna Loa cabin at 13,250 feet, or to the summit of the mountain at 13,677 feet. You can spend the night at North Pit and go on to either the summit or the cabin the next day, or you can do the whole trip as an out-and-back day hike. Once you have reached North Pit, you have really seen the best the mountain has to offer. Special considerations: The trail covers desolate and surprisingly beautiful country. There is not a blade of grass or a molecule of chlorophyll anywhere, but the lava comes in such a range of colors and textures that you won't miss the green.

See map on page 62.
Start: Mauna Loa Weather Observatory Trailhead
Distance: 7.6 miles out and back
Elevation change: 2,000 feet
Difficulty: Strenuous
Approximate hiking time: 6 to 8 hours
Trail surface: Rough lava. The trail is sometimes obscure; watch for ahus (cairns).
Seasons: Spring, summer, and fall. Count on ice and snow from November to April.
Other trail users: None
Canine compatibility: Dogs not permitted
Land status: Hawai'i Volcanoes National Park
Nearest town: Hilo
Fees and permits: Park entrance fee. A free wilderness permit is required if you plan to stay overnight and is available at the Kilauea Visitor Center. You must show up in person, no sooner than one day in advance, so that rangers can give you up-to-date information about volcanic activity and weather conditions. You do not need a wilderness permit for a day hike, but you should stop by the visitor center anyway to check on current conditions.
Maps: USGS *Koko'olau* and *Mauna Loa,* or the *National Geographic Trails Illustrated Hawai'i Volcanoes National Park* map. You can also buy a 1:200,000 scale topographic map of Volcanoes national park at the visitor center. It's somewhat dated, but accurate enough to get you there and back.
Trail contact: Kilauea Visitor Center; (808) 985-6000; www.nps.gov/havo.
Special Considerations: You must be in excellent condition and well acclimated to elevations above 11,000 feet, which is where this hike begins. Otherwise acute mountain sickness (AMS) is practically guaranteed. You will need to carry all your water, and if you decide to camp, you will need a tent.

Finding the trailhead: From the airport in Hilo turn right (north) onto HI 11 for less than 1 mile to Kamehameha Avenue. Turn left (north) on Kamehameha Avenue. There is a signal. Drive through Old Hilo Town for about 1 mile to Waianuenue Avenue, also at a signal, and turn left (southwest). In another mile the road forks. Take the left fork onto Kaumana Drive. This passes through suburbs and turns into HI 200, also known as Saddle Road. Drive to mile 28 on the Saddle Road, watching for an obvious timbered hill on the left (south) surrounded by bare lava. Turn left (south) onto the unmarked road (Mauna Loa Observatory Road) just before you get to the hill. If you see a Hunters Checkpoint Station on the left (west) side of the hill, you have gone too far. Drive the narrow, winding road 19 miles to where it is blocked by a gate just below the weather observatory. The road is paved all the way and fine for ordinary passenger cars, but it is very narrow and has steep hills and deep dips that limit your visibility. Take it slowly. Keep in mind that rental car companies do not like you to drive their cars on Saddle Road at all. If you get stuck, you're on your own. No gas, water, or facilities of any kind are available once you have left Hilo.

The Hike

Park in the little square of asphalt marked PUBLIC PARKING below the observatory. The observatory is not open to the public. The trail (the combined North Pit and Observatory Trail) begins at the gate that blocks the road where the pavement ends at 11,000 feet. The trailhead sign says that the summit and Mauna Loa cabin are 5.9 and 6.0 miles respectively, and the junction at North Pit is at 3.8 miles, but another sign about 0.4 mile ahead says the same thing. In the meantime, head slowly uphill on the crumbly a'a road; the walking is difficult but there are good views all around to take your mind off your feet. Directly across the saddle to the north is Mauna Kea, the highest point in Hawai'i at 13,796 feet. It is dormant now. To its left you can sometimes spot Kohala, the oldest volcano on the Big Island. To the left of Kohala and farther in the distance is much larger Haleakala, on the island of Maui. The peak to the farthest left is Hualalai, back on the Big Island, much lower and younger than Mauna Kea. It hasn't erupted since the early 1800s, but is still considered active.

▶ Thomas A. Jaggar, a geologist from the Massachusetts Institute of Technology, established and served as director of the Hawai'i Volcano Observatory in 1912. He and Lorrin Thurston (of Thurston Lava Tube fame), a local newspaper editor, were influential in the establishment of Hawai'i Volcanoes National Park.

At 0.4 mile meet the sign that says North Pit is *still* 3.8 miles away. It is mounted on a big ahu and marked with white paint on the ground. This is where you turn left (south) and leave the road, following the line of ahus marching up the slope. After about 1 mile cross a minimalist sort of road and continue following cairns straight ahead. There are occasional yellow paint splotches on the rocks to mark the route, but many have partly eroded away. At 1.7 miles reach two tall ahus side by side, marking a collapsed lava tube. Part of it has been bricked in with rocks to make a shelter, but there is toilet paper tucked into the some of the crannies. *Pack yours out!*

You have reached 12,000 feet by now, and except for the top of an antenna, this is the last you'll see of the observatory. Keep left (east) at the next TRAIL sign, then turn right (south) at another sign onto a road, walking alongside a ridge on the right that looks like somebody threw a plate of spaghetti at it. Not far beyond the road is blocked by a gate, so you turn right (west) onto the trail again. A riotously colored vent marks the beginning of an easy section of mostly packed golden olivine sand for which your feet will rejoice. At 3.5 miles cross the road again at another sign. After a bit of hard climbing the trail levels out and you walk along a rock-lined path that takes you past a beautiful little alcove where a pit toilet has been installed over a crack. The rock walls around the lua glow with shimmering reds, oranges, and purples, and the lava has solidified in wonderfully drippy textures. Just beyond the toilet, a very tall ahu marks the site of Jaggar's Cave and a three-way North Pit Junction at 13,000 feet. From the junction you can take the right fork toward the summit of Mauna Loa. The left fork heads toward the trail to Mauna Loa cabin.

Jaggar's Cave is not a cave at all, but a smooth flat area a few steps below ground level whose walls have been piled up more than head-high to form a shelter from the wind. There is no roof, so if you camp here and the weather is bad you will need a tent. Some maps show "waterholes" nearby, but don't count on finding them, or finding any water in them. Occasionally there are bits of ice in the cracks that you can chip free and melt; more often there is nothing at all. Return the way you came.

Trail across North Pit

Miles and Directions

0.0 Start (N19 32.17' / W155 34.32')

0.4 Second sign that posts the same mileages as the trailhead sign. Turn left, leaving the road.

1.3 Cross a road (N19 31.33' / W155 34.56')

1.7 Tall ahus mark a lava cave; last sight of the observatory at 12,000 feet

2.4 trail sign; keep left (east)

2.5 Turn right onto a road (south)

2.8 Turn right onto the trail, leaving the road (west)

3.5 Cross another road, staying on the trail

3.8 Jaggar's Cave, North Pit Junction (N19 29.36' / W155 34.38')

7.6 Return to the trailhead

Options: The routes to the summit and Mauna Loa Cabin offer more of the same kind of scenery, but the hiking gets harder. To bag the summit, head northwest around the rim of North Pit and follow the trail, 2.6 miles to the highest point marked by two tall ahus at 13,677 feet.

To continue on to Mauna Loa cabin where there is shelter and sometimes water, head south on the signed Mauna Loa Trail to another sign directing you toward the cabin, dropping right down into North Pit. Follow the trail 2.1 miles to the cabin on the rim of Moku'aweoweo crater.

12 Pololu Valley

This is the northernmost of the deep narrow valleys carved into Hawaii's windward Kohala coast, at one time home to a farming community of native Hawaiians but long since abandoned. It's mostly ranching country now, and the wider inland part of the valley is private property, blocked by a fence behind which cattle graze. Please keep out. Your reward for negotiating the steep, rocky, sometimes slippery trail is a pretty black sand beach shaded by ironwoods. It is popular with locals, some of whom camp among the trees though camping is officially illegal. The ocean currents are too dangerous for swimming. Pololu is a less-crowded alternative to Waipio Valley, which is not very far away to the south as the crow flies but is separated by a roadless area of the coast. To hike both, you have to drive all the way back to Waimea, across the Kohala peninsula, then up the opposite side.

Start: Pololu Valley Trailhead
Distance: 1.2 miles out and back
Elevation change: 440 feet
Difficulty: Moderate
Approximate hiking time: 1 hour
Trail surface: Rocky trail; slippery when wet
Seasons: Year-round
Land status: Department of Land and Natural Resources
Other trail users: Horses
Canine compatibility: Dogs permitted
Nearest town: Hawi
Fees and permits: None

Maps: *USGS Honokane*
Trail contact: Department of Land and Natural Resources, Division of Forestry and Wildlife; (808) 974-4217; www.hawaiitrails.org
Special considerations: Carry water. There is none at the trailhead and none at the bottom, nor are there any toilets. The walk back up the trail can be hot. You might encounter paniolos (cowboys) or hunters on horseback on the narrow trail. Livestock always has right of way, so stand quietly off to the side of the trail until they pass.

Finding the trailhead: From Hilo, drive HI 19 (the Hawai'i Belt Road) north then west for 54 miles, all the way to Waimea. Just past Waimea, turn right (west) onto HI 250 and continue until it ends at HI 270. Turn right (east) again on HI 270 and go all the way to its end at mile 28.

From Kailua-Kona, drive northeast on HI 190 (also the Hawai'i Belt Road) for 40 miles to Waimea. Turn left (west) on HI 250, then right (north) on HI 270. There is a small, usually crowded parking area at the trailhead.

Beach at Pololu Valley

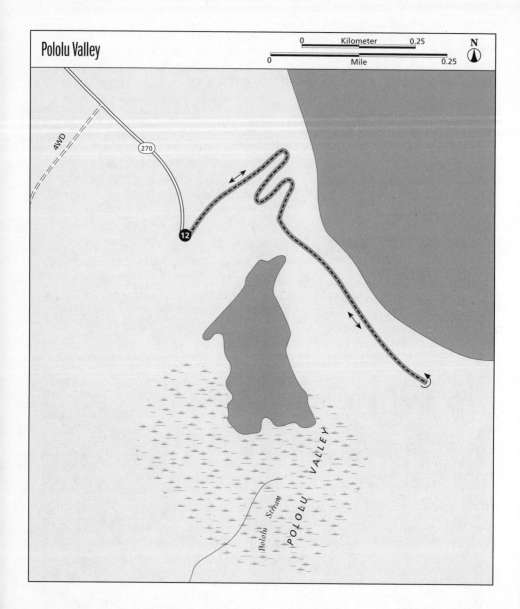

The Hike

There are so many warnings at the trailhead about falling rocks, dangerous ocean currents, and tidal waves, you might think you are descending into hell. The beach itself is quite benign and beautiful, but stay out of the water. Your main concerns are slipping if the trail is wet as you descend, and developing heat exhaustion as you climb back up.

Try to watch both your feet and the scenery as you drop down the rocky trail because the shoreline is spectacular where the Kohala Mountains drop into the sea.

The trail is lined with typical coastal vegetation, such as naupaka with its small white flowers that look like they have been torn in half. There is occasional shade from Brazilian pepper trees and ironwoods. Toward the bottom, take three long switchbacks, pass through a tunnel of hau, and emerge onto the gravel of the stream mouth. Just to the left (northeast) is the beach.

The Pololu Stream flows down out of the mountains to the sea and, except at rainy times and high tides, disappears underground at the beach, so you don't have to ford it. The ground is covered with nehe, little yellow native sunflowers. Back from the beach is an ironwood forest carpeted with "needles" and homemade swings attached to the branches—hard to resist. You can only wander upstream as far as the fence, beyond which is private property, and you can explore the far (south) end of the beach, but don't try to hike beyond the cliffs. The sea is much too dangerous. Retrace your steps back uphill to the parking lot.

Miles and Directions

0.0 Start (N20 12.14' / W155 44.02')

0.6 Pololu Beach (N20 12.13' / W155 43.54')

1.2 Return to the trailhead

13 Hawai'i Tropical Botanical Garden

At the Hawai'i Tropical Botanical Garden a wondrous array of beautiful growing things from all over the tropical world is packed onto a single hillside above a bay. This is one of the few hikes in this book that ventures into a commercial (though nonprofit) tourist attraction because it is simply a marvel, something you should not miss. You do not have to be a botanist or a gardener to be awestruck by the glorious and downright weird life-forms Mother Nature has dreamed up. In addition, there are screeching macaws, a waterfall, a lily pond, and a photogenic beach. There are also mosquitoes. Take repellent. The garden will provide an umbrella if it's raining.

Start: Botanical Garden visitor center
Distance: 1.5 miles
Elevation change: 400 feet
Difficulty: Easy
Approximate hiking time entry: 1 to 3 hours
Trail surface: Asphalt
Seasons: Year-round
Other trail users: Occasional golf carts ferrying
caretakers and disabled visitors
Canine compatibility: Dogs not permitted
Land status: Private
Fees and permits: Entrance fee
Maps: *USGS Papaikou*, but it isn't needed; a map of the garden is provided with admission
Trail contact: Hawai'i Tropical Botanical Garden; (808) 964-5233; www.hawaiigarden.com

Finding the trailhead: From the Hilo International Airport, turn right (north) onto HI 11, then left (west) at a signal onto HI 19 (Kamehameha Avenue). Drive north on HI 19 for 7 miles to the turnoff to Onomea Bay. A sign on the right says scenic route 4 miles long. Turn right onto the narrow road (Old Mamalahoa Highway or Scenic Road) and go about 2 miles to the botanic garden parking lot and visitor center on the left (west) side of the road. Buy your ticket at the visitor center/gift shop (where you'll also find restrooms and water) and cross the street. Give your ticket to the ukulele-strumming guy at the gate and enter the garden. Approximate **GPS:** N19 48.37' / W155 05.46'

The Hike

The garden path descends through a jungle of what seems to be hundreds of kinds of ginger in every color and size imaginable. Some have flowers as big as your head, some look like sponges, beehives, or torches. Overhead, red lobster claw heliconias dangle in 10-foot swags from banana-like trees.

You can travel in any direction through the maze of well-marked paths. You will find orchids in shapes and color combinations so peculiar you can hardly believe they are flowers, as well as ferns and palms, pineapples, and plumerias in bewildering variety. Don't miss the cannonball tree. (You have to look up!) Its huge, cannonball-size, perfectly round fruits do not dangle from its branches as they should, but are attached by the hundreds directly to its trunk. There is a miniature forest of Cook pines, an aviary of colorful macaws screaming "Aloha," and a lily pond with lotus flowers and giant carp.

You can have a rest and a snack at Turtle Point, the farthest point from the beginning, though Onomea Bay does not have a good swimming beach and the shore is rough and rocky. On your way back up to the entrance, be sure to take the short spur trail to the right to see Onomea Falls.

◀ *Trail through the garden*

14 Akaka Falls State Park

This is an easy stroll along a paved, winding path through a garden of showy tropical blossoms, bamboo groves, and along a pretty stream to an overlook of spectacular Akaka Falls, over 442 feet high. It's easy to understand why it's a standard stop for tour buses, but that's no reason to stay away. You can enjoy it in relative peace and solitude if you get there before 9:00 a.m.

Start: Akaka Falls Trailhead
Distance: 0.5-mile loop
Elevation change: 200 feet
Difficulty: Easy
Approximate hiking time: 45 minutes
Trail surface: Asphalt
Seasons: Year-round
Other trail users: None

Canine compatibility: Dogs not allowed
Land status: Hawai'i State Park
Nearest town: Honomu
Fees and permits: None
Maps: *USGS Akaka Falls,* but none needed
Trail contact: Department of Land and Natural Resources, Hawaii State Parks; (808) 974-6200; dlnr@hawaii.gov; www.hawaiistateparks.org

Finding the trailhead: From the Hilo International Airport, turn right (north) onto HI 11 and then turn left (west) on HI 19 (the Hawai'i Belt Road or Kamehameha Avenue). Drive north on HI 19, pass milepost 14, and watch for the sign for HI 220 and Akaka Falls. Turn left (mauka/toward the mountain) through the tiny town of Honomu, then turn right (west) at a sign directing you to Akaka Falls. Continue a little more than 3 miles to the end of road. There are bathrooms, picnic tables, and usually tour buses at the trailhead. **GPS:** N19 51.14' / W155 09.08'

The Hike

The walk begins at a gap in a low stone wall, where you begin to descend an asphalt stairway to a sign that recommends you walk the trail counterclockwise, beginning to the right. The first waterfall you see across the valley to the north is Kahuna Falls, an extra attraction on this hike. It's almost as high as Akaka Falls, but is tucked back into a notch in the cliff, and parts of it are obscured by vegetation, so you don't get as clear a view as you would like. Don't be discouraged, though. Keep going.

After a short uphill pull, then a shorter descent, you arrive at the star attraction, a clear, perfect view of extremely photogenic Akaka Falls, plummeting a straight, narrow 442 feet. You can see the entire fall from here, clear down to the dark pool at its base. There is a covered shelter nearby in case of rain.

Continue following the loop trail through plantings of colorful gingers of several kinds, a grove of massive bamboos, tall banyan trees dripping with aerial roots, epiphytic ferns and climbing vines, all beautiful but anticlimactic after you've seen the waterfall. Cross a tumbling stream on a little bridge and climb back up the short staircase to the parking lot. The little town of Honomu, once part of the sugarcane industry on the Big Island, is a great place to stop for ice cream or shaved ice after your hike.

15 Kalopa Native Forest Trail

Kalopa State Park is a hidden treasure. Its native forest is a tiny patch of the real Hawai'i that has not been trampled by cattle, plowed under for sugarcane, or bulldozed for development. The showy blossoms of ginger and plumeria that are usually associated with "natural" Hawai'i have actually been brought here from elsewhere as ornamentals. Even the coconuts, breadfruit, and bananas we think of as quintessentially Hawaiian were introduced by the original Polynesian settlers. You can pick up a pamphlet at the trailhead that tells about the loving care and hard work that have gone into maintaining this rare little piece of forest, and you can also borrow a trail guide to help you identify and appreciate the plants. Or you can simply stroll and soak up the beauty and solitude in a bit of Hawai'i not overrun by tourists. The park also hosts a campground, cabins, picnic area, and an arboretum with trees from all over the tropical world.

Start: Native forest nature trail trailhead
Distance: 0.7 mile
Elevation change: Negligible
Difficulty: Easy
Approximate hiking time: 1 hour
Trail surface: Maintained trail
Seasons: Year-round
Other trail users: None
Canine compatibility: Dogs not permitted

Land status: Hawai'i State Park
Nearest town: Honoka'a
Fees and permits: None
Maps: USGS Honoka'a; trail map provided at the trailhead
Trail contact: Department of Land and Natural Resources, Hawaii State Parks; (808) 974-6200; dlnr@hawaii.gov; www.hawaiistateparks.org

Finding the trailhead: From the Hilo International Airport turn right (north) onto HI 11 and then left (west) on HI 19 (the Hawai'i Belt Road or Kamehameha Avenue.) Drive north on HI 19 to milepost 39 and watch for a sign for Kalopa State Park on the right (east). Turn left (mauka/toward the mountain) and follow the signs uphill for 3 miles to the park entrance at the end of the road. Pass a spur road to the campground and park near the cabins. There is a big sign with a map at the trailhead.

Pick up a pamphlet about the park and native forest and leave a donation if you choose in a slot in a pipe. A minimal amount to cover copying of the nature trail map is all that is requested. What a deal! **GPS:** N20 02.18' / W155 26.24'

The Hike

The beginning of the trail doesn't seem obvious from the parking area, but follow the arrow that points you around the left edge of the grass of the arboretum, past a couple of brown storage buildings, and to another sign that says NATURE TRAIL 0.7 MILE LOOP. Pick up a trail guide from the box here (return it when you're finished). This is one of the few nature trails in Hawai'i whose signs are intact and whose guidebook corresponds to the stops on the trail.

▶ The state park cabins are very inexpensive accommodations in pricey Hawai'i. Each of them sleeps eight bunk-bed style, has a bathroom with a shower, and provides linens and blankets. At Kalopa there is a recreation hall with a fully equipped kitchen, a real bargain for families. Call (808) 794-2600 for information and reservations.

The nature trail begins at station 11, so don't go searching for 1 through 10. The guide is numbered counterclockwise, starting to the right. Watch for white splashes of paint on trees at about eye level to keep you on the trail. Whether you stop to read about each station or not, you'll love the quiet stroll through this forest. The whole route is shaded by shaggy ohia lehua trees, kolea trees whose new leaves sprout in a delicate pink color before turning dark green, and ie'ie (pronounced ee-yeh, ee-yeh) vines with bizarre sausage-shaped flowers. The forest floor hosts many kinds of ferns, including hapu'u, massive tree ferns much higher then your head. The final stop is at a strangler fig, a banyan tree whose seed was deposited by a bird on the branch of a native ohia. The fig developed aerial roots that grew downward to the soil, planted themselves, and developed new trunks and climbers until the original ohia was completely engulfed; it will eventually be killed for lack of sunlight.

If you have time, you can extend your stay with a stroll through the arboretum and a picnic at the covered picnic area where there is a barbecue and water.

Strangler fig

16 Waipio Valley

This isolated corner of the island is a favorite destination for tourists, who usually just peer over the cliff edge down onto the valley then go away. For hikers who are connoisseurs of fine beaches, waterfalls, and Hawaiian culture, and don't mind a short, stiff workout on a (mostly) paved road, the rewards are beyond anything sedentary tourists can imagine. The valley was home to a thriving community of native Hawaiians who grew taro and other traditional crops in the fertile soil until it was battered by a tsunami in 1946. Most of the inhabitants left, but those who still remain prefer the old ways, and value their isolation and privacy. They do not appreciate strangers wandering through their neighborhood gawking at them, but do not mind hikers sharing their access road, admiring their green fields from a distance, and enjoying their beach.

Start: Waipio Valley parking lot
Distance: 2.8 miles out and back
Elevation change: 900 feet
Difficulty: Moderate
Approximate hiking time: 2 hours
Trail surface: Asphalt road, dirt road
Seasons: Year-round, but don't try to cross the stream in winter or anytime the water is high
Other trail users: Four-wheel-drive vehicles
Canine compatibility: Dogs permitted
Land status: Private
Nearest town: Honoka'a
Fees and permits: None, unless you plan to continue on the Muliwai Trail to Waimanu Valley as a backpack trip. You can spend the night on the beach, but it's not recommended. You need a permit from the Division of Forestry and Wildlife (808-994-4221) to camp on the beach and to use the Muliwai Trail.
Maps: USGS *Kukuihaele*, but you don't really need a map
Trail contact: None
Special considerations: Do not try to drive an ordinary passenger car down the road from the overlook. Even if you have a four-wheel-drive vehicle, don't try it unless you know what you're doing. The residents of the valley don't mind if you visit the beach, but please do not wander through the "town."

Finding the trailhead: From the Hilo International Airport, turn right (north) onto HI 11, drive 1 block, then turn left (west) on HI 19 (the Hawai'i Belt Road or Kamehameha Avenue). Drive north about 40 miles to the marked turnoff to Honoka'a and Waipio Valley (HI 240), and follow it through the funky little town to its end at Waipio Valley Overlook.

The Hike

The steep paved road that serves as the trail into Waipio Valley begins right from the parking lot, but take a short detour to the overlook to see what you're in for. (There's a bathroom there, too.) The first part of the hike descends along a rushing stream, then crosses it at a switchback. Go down the very steep roadway for about 0.75 mile to a junction where you make a sharp right (east) turn. The other road goes straight

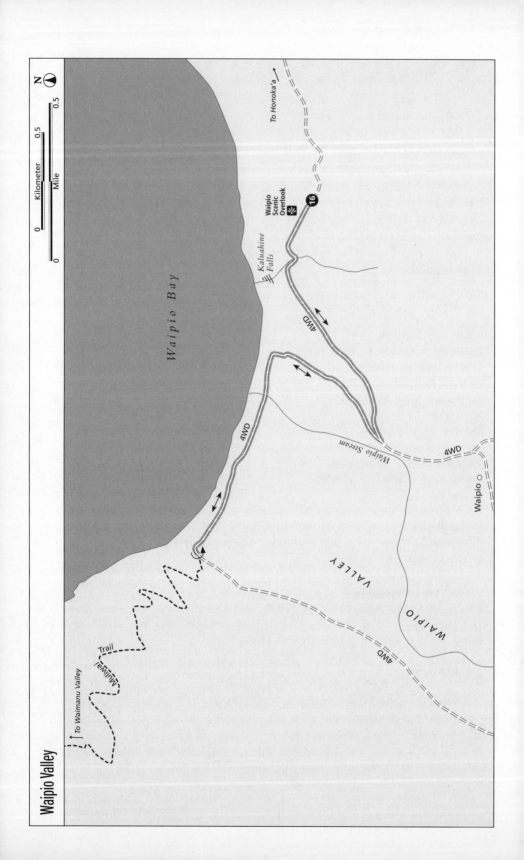

Waipio Valley

To Waimanu Valley

Muliwai Trail

Waipio Bay

4WD

4WD

Kaluahine Falls

Waipio Stream

4WD

WAIPIO VALLEY

Waipio

4WD

Waipio Scenic Overlook

16

To Honoka'a

N

Kilometer
0   0.5

Mile
0   0.5

ahead into the valley and onto private property. Your route flattens out and turns to packed earth and cobbles as it skirts taro fields and wetlands with sedges and papyrus, then emerges at the beach under ironwoods.

Walk out toward the shoreline, and, facing the ocean, look to your right (south). If you are lucky you will see beautiful Kaluahine Falls, dropping 620 feet to the sea. If you are unlucky, the water in the stream has been diverted for irrigation, and you will see a blank rock face. The beach is lovely anyway, perfect for a picnic, but too dangerous for swimming. There are dunes to explore on the far side of Waipio Stream, but make sure the water is low enough to cross safely before plunging in. It is subject to flash flooding. Camping is permitted on the beach with a permit from the Division of Forestry and Wildlife, but there are no facilities and it isn't highly recommended.

Miles and Directions

0.0 Start (N20 07.00' / W155 34.55')
1.4 Waipio Stream (N20 07.08' / W155 35.28')
2.8 Return to the trailhead

Option: The Muliwai Trail begins at the west end of the Waipio Valley beach, climbs very steeply up a cliff, drops into and out of twelve deep gulches, and descends into Waimanu Valley, 9 miles to the west. The trail is poorly maintained, slippery, and steep, and stream crossings in the gullies can be treacherous. If you crave an extremely vigorous and difficult backpack, try this one. A permit is required.

Waipio Valley and beach from the trail

17 Manuka Nature Trail

The Manuka Natural Area Reserve, on the southern slope of Mauna Loa, protects one of the least disturbed sections of original native forests on the island. It was last buried by lava more than 2,300 years ago, and has miraculously escaped development, so it has some very old trees by Hawaiian standards, many of which exist nowhere else on earth. While the nature trail itself starts at about 1,800 feet in elevation, the reserve as a whole extends all the way from sea level to 5,000 feet, so every habitat from lowland dry forest to wet rainforest is represented. It is also home to the 'elepaio, a tiny native bird with a cocked tail, and Hawaii's only native mammal, the hoary bat. There are remains of a native Hawaiian settlement, with many plants used by the original inhabitants on site as well. The nature trail takes you through the native forest along a path with numbered posts corresponding to a pamphlet sometimes available in a box at the trailhead.

Start: Manuka Nature Trail trailhead
Distance: 2-mile loop
Elevation change: 400 feet
Difficulty: Easy
Approximate hiking time: 2 hours
Trail surface: Rocky and uneven; don't try it in sandals
Seasons: Year-round
Other trail users: None
Canine compatibility: Dogs not permitted on the nature trail itself, though there is almost always at least one romping in the park
Nearest town: Captain Cook

Land status: Natural area reserve
Fees and permits: None
Maps: *USGS Pohue Bay*, but it's not necessary. It is nice to have the map that is sometimes available in a box near the trailhead. If you want to make sure you'll have one, visit the Department of Land and Natural Resources office in advance or ask for one by mail.
Trail contact: Department of Land and Natural Resources, Natural Area Reserve Systems; (808) 974-4221; dlnr@hawaii.gov; www.hawaii.gov/dlnr/dofaw

Finding the trailhead: From Hilo drive 81 miles south on HI 11 (just look for mile marker 81), then watch for the sign for the Manuka State Wayside area on the right (mauka/toward the mountain). There's a picnic area with a restroom and parking lot, but no water. From Kailua-Kona drive south on HI 11 about 40 miles to just before milepost 81 and turn left (mauka) into the Manuka State Wayside area. **GPS:** N19 06.35' / W155 49.33'

The Hike

Within the natural area reserve is a manicured park surrounding a parking area with a covered picnic area and toilets. It gets lots of use by people taking a break from driving and seems to be a favorite spot for dog exercising. The park itself has some unusual species from around the world, including a sausage tree from Africa with what appear to be great fat sausages dangling from every limb. The bunya-bunya tree from Australia, with its ten-pound "pine" cones, is worth investigating for its name alone. It's too bad that most of these curiosities are not labeled.

Not many people who stop here use the nature trail, but it is well maintained and has a trail guide that actually corresponds to the numbered stops. From the trailhead just beyond the parking area you walk gently uphill over blocky a'a lava and watch the vegetation change along with the footing. Several different lava flows have covered the hillside in the past, each leaving a different kind of surface.

▶ **Did you know that it is impossible to determine the age of tropical trees? Since there are no distinct seasons, no tree rings form, so you can't count them.**

Before you reach the first mile marker you'll pass a short spur to a pit crater to the right of the trail where the roof of a lava tube has collapsed. Among the more interesting plants to notice are the mamaki, the stingless Hawaiian nettle. Like most native Hawaiian species, these had no need to develop stinging hairs for protection, since there were not any (native) animals to eat them. Past the 1-mile marker are remnants of terraces constructed by the ancient Hawaiians, with several kinds of edible and otherwise useful plants growing among them. These include the kukui, or candlenut tree, whose oily nuts were used as lamps and whose seeds you will have seen strung together as necklaces in every shop in the islands. Even though the kukui is Hawaii's state tree, it is not a native, but was brought here by the original Polynesians.

Sausage tree with fruit and flower

As you near the end of the loop, the trail descends to emerge onto an unmarked grassy area that doesn't look anything like the place where you began and has no signs. To find your car head left (east) slightly uphill, across the grass at the edge of the forest for just a few yards and you will see the picnic shelter and parking lot slightly below you and to the right (south).

18 Pu'uhonua o Honaunau (Place of Refuge)

A stroll through this beautifully maintained and partly reconstructed site of pre-European Hawaiian life can't exactly be called a hike, but no visitor to the Big Island should miss it. Pu'uhonua o Honaunau National Historical Park is actually a part of the long, only partly developed Ala Kahakai National Historic Trail, which extends 175 miles along the western and southern coast of the island. (Much of this proposed trail runs through private property and is not open to the public.) This was not only the home of the ali'i, the chiefs of the region, but was a special place of sanctuary for anyone who had violated a kapu, or religious law, had been on the losing side of a battle, or otherwise feared for his life. It was a sacred place where no blood could be shed. It's also one of the best places to see endangered sea turtles up close.

Start: Visitor center
Distance: 0.5 mile
Elevation change: None
Difficulty: Easy
Approximate hiking time: 1 hour
Trail surface: Mostly asphalt, some sand
Seasons: Year-round
Other trail users: None
Canine compatibility: Dogs not permitted

Land status: National historical park
Nearest town: Captain Cook
Fees and permits: Park entrance fee, a Golden Age Pass, or another acceptable park permit
Schedule: 8:00 a.m.–5:30 p.m. daily
Maps: USGS Honaunau, but none needed
Trail contact: National Park Service; (808) 328-2326; www.nps.gov/puho

Finding the trailhead: From Kailua-Kona drive HI 11 (the Hawai'i Belt Road) south for about 22 miles to HI 160 (located between mileposts 103 and 104). Turn right (makai/toward the sea), and wind downhill to the park sign, then turn left (south) to the visitor center and parking lot, which are on the right.

From Hilo, drive south on HI 11 for 103 miles, passing Hawai'i Volcanoes National Park, around the south end of the island, and heading north to HI 160. Turn left (makai), and wind downhill to the park sign, then to the visitor center and parking lot. You can also get to the park from Hilo by driving north around the island, through Waimea, then south through Kailua-Kona (116 miles).

The Hike

Pick up a free map and guide to the site at the entrance and follow the numbered posts through the royal grounds, past an accurately reconstructed temple, work buildings, outrigger canoes, fishponds, plants used for food and tools of daily life, Hawaiian games, the Great Wall that marked safety for those who could reach it, and a heiau or temple guarded by reconstructions of wooden gods. This is all in a beautiful setting on the shore of a peaceful bay. If you can arrange to be there around July 1, during the cultural festival, you can participate in making tapa cloth, tasting traditional Hawaiian foods like poi, and even sail out into the bay on an outrigger canoe.

Option: Two other national historic sites, Kaloko-Honokohau and Pu'ukohola Heiau, lie many miles farther north along the Ala Kahakai route. If you are interested in the life and culture of real Hawaiians, both of these are worth a visit. Both also have walking trails.

Tikis at the Place of Refuge

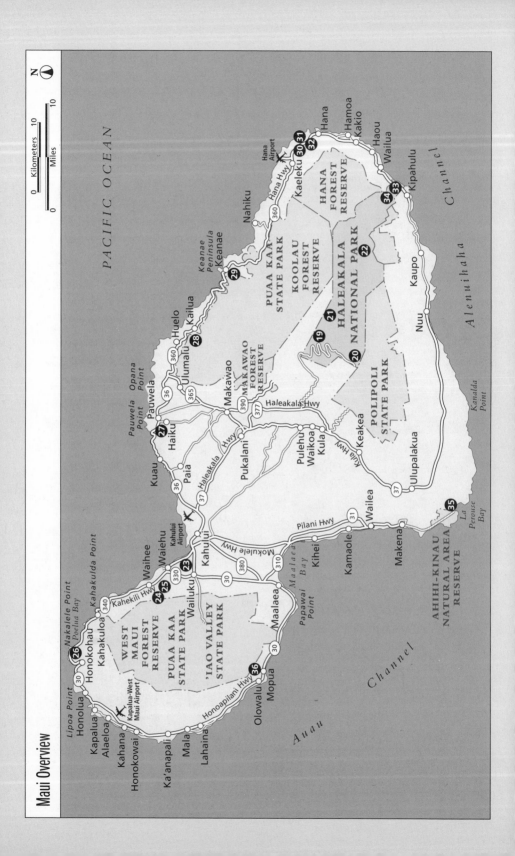

Maui Overview

Maui: The Valley Isle

aui is the second biggest and the second most frequently visited (next to O'ahu) of the Hawaiian Islands. It is known as the Valley Isle because it's made of two mountains joined by an isthmus. The two mountains are so different they might as well be separate islands, and at one time they were. Sediments poured down the side of the older mountain, and lava flowed down from the newer one, to form the land connection between them. At times of higher sea levels, when the climate was warmer between glacial periods, the isthmus was inundated and the two mountains became separate islands for a time. The deep sediment of the isthmus makes it a rich agricultural area that supports lots of sugarcane.

The older volcano that formed West Maui is extinct now. It is deeply grooved, weathered by wind and water, and clothed in dense vegetation. Pu'u Kukui on West Maui is second only to Mount Wai'ale'ale on Kaua'i in the amount of rainfall it receives (over 400 inches per year).

There are a number of river and ridgetop hikes on West Maui. You can get to most of them easily from Kahului, where the island's main population center and airport are, and you can find some of the island's cheapest accommodations in Wailuku, right next door. It is an interesting, slightly shabby old town, a little like Hilo on the Big Island, with a couple of hostels and inexpensive motels.

Most tourists gather in sunny Kihei, on the southern coast of the isthmus, in the rain shadow of the mountains. It's pretty heavily developed, but does have some superb coastline, especially southwest of town where there is good hiking. The other main attraction on West Maui is the historical whaling port of Lahaina, on the leeward side. It's fun to take a stroll down the main street, but it is an expensive place to stay. For a look at really old Hawai'i, take the short hike to the petroglyphs at Olowalu, south of Lahaina.

Haleakala, the younger of the two volcanoes that make up Maui, emerged from the sea not much more than a million years ago, and has erupted within historic times, so is still considered active. At 10,023 feet, it is twice as high as the highest of the West Maui mountains. Its northern coastline is surely one of the most beautiful in the world. The notorious Hana Highway winds its way past trailheads for several hikes to waterfalls, nature preserves, and botanical gardens. At the end is Hana, jumping-off point for hikes in the Kipahulu section of Haleakala National Park, home of the misnamed Seven Sacred Pools. The Hana Highway is such a long, slow drive that if you plan to hike from Kipahulu or explore any of the other trails nearby, you should stay somewhere near the eastern end of the island. Hana is charming, but tiny, expensive, and often wet. There is a free campground at Kipahulu, but the real bargain in accommodations is at Wai'anapanapa State Park, on the way to Hana. It has both camping and very inexpensive, fully equipped housekeeping cabins. For information, call (808) 984-8109. (They don't take online reservations.) Some of Maui's most exciting treks begin at Wai'anapanapa, and it's a good place to watch for sea turtles, dolphins, and whales.

The most extensive system of trails is in Haleakala National Park. Some begin in the Kipahulu District on the coast, but there is a whole network of trails inside Haleakala Crater itself. Do not miss the chance to spend some time in the crater, even if you can only manage a day hike. The scenery is wild and barren and indescribably beautiful, like nowhere else on earth. It is home to the endangered Hawaiian goose, the nene, and to the extremely rare silversword, with stalks of flowers up to 9 feet tall. There are two campgrounds and three cabins inside the crater, providing one of the few opportunities on Maui for a multiday hike or backpack. Permits are required. Reservations to stay in the cabins are in great demand and hard to come by: For information call (808) 572-4400 or visit www.nps.gov/hale. Haleakala is also notorious for catching visitors unaware. The air is thin at 10,000 feet, and it can get very cold, even if this is the tropics. It occasionally snows in winter.

There is no public transportation on Maui. If you are not a resident, you will need a rental car to get around. Never leave anything in your car at a trailhead!

The best map for finding your way around the island is "Map of Maui," published by the University of Hawai'i Press, available in bookstores and visitor centers, and sometimes at airports.

19 Hosmer Grove

Hosmer Grove may be the best place on Maui to see rare native Hawaiian birds with very little effort. You're likely to spot some interesting species even before you leave the parking lot. The hike is a cool, sometimes wet, ramble at almost 7,000 feet through a forest of both introduced and native Hawaiian trees, with a clearing partway through where an interpretive panel helps you identify the birds that are likely to show up.

Start: Hosmer Grove Nature Trail trailhead
Distance: 0.6-mile loop
Elevation change: About 100 feet
Difficulty: Easy, but with some ups and downs
Approximate hiking time: 30 to 45 minutes
Trail surface: Worn lava
Seasons: Year-round
Other trail users: None
Canine compatibility: Dogs not permitted

Land status: Haleakala National Park
Nearest town: Pukalani
Fees and permits: Park entrance fee
Maps: *USGS Kilohana,* but none needed. The trail is short and well marked, and there is a map display at the trailhead.
Trail contact: Haleakala National Park Headquarters; (808) 572-4400; www.nps.gov/hale

Finding the trailhead: From Kahului, drive southeast on HI 37 (the Haleakala Highway) for about 7 miles through the town of Pukalani. Just past town turn left (east) onto HI 377, staying on the Haleakala Highway. In another 6 miles you'll reach HI 378, also known as Haleakala Crater Road, where you turn left (east) to begin the slow, switchbacking ascent to the Hosmer Grove turnoff on the left (east) about 10 miles up. If you find yourself at park headquarters (on the right) you've gone too far. Follow the Hosmer Grove road to the campground. **GPS:** N20 46.04' / W156 14.04'

The Hike

Hosmer Grove has a free, first-come, first-served campground with water and toilets nearby. The trail begins at a sign at the low end of the campground where there are interpretive panels about the history of the place and the fate of many of Hawaii's native species.

The grove is planted with trees from all over the world, such as pines, spruces, cedars, and redwoods. It was a misguided attempt by forester Ralph Hosmer in 1910 to slow the rate of deforestation occurring at an alarming rate in Hawai'i, and perhaps to establish a timber industry at the same time. Now, of course, some of these alien trees themselves pose a threat to the local ecosystem. Still, the variety of vegetation does attract a variety of birds, and there are still plenty of ohia lehua trees and other natives left to appeal to i'iwis, apapanes, amakihis, and even Hawaiian owls.

Begin by crossing a little stream, then climb to an overlook where the park service has installed a panel to help you identify the birds. It's above an opening in the canopy to give you a better view. Be patient and spend at least ten to fifteen minutes at the overlook, and you're bound to see something beautiful and rare.

Beyond the overlook is a junction where you keep left, heading uphill. The path to the right cuts straight back down to the campground. Climb through native scrubland with fuzzy red ohia blossoms, short-leaved shrubs with pink and white berries called pukiawe, delicious plump ohelo berries, silvery hinahina geraniums, and the beautiful yellow-flowered pea called mamane. The trail tops out at a little bench where you can catch your breath and soak up the view before following the rest of the loop back down to the parking lot.

A wonderful little book that is easy to carry and shows all the birds you're likely to see in Hawai'i—and where to see them—is *Hawaii's Birds,* published by the Hawai'i Audubon Society in Honolulu.

Mamane blossom

Trails on Haleakala (Hikes 20 to 22)

Haleakala is known as the House of the Sun. According to legend, Hina, the mother of the demigod Maui, complained that the days were too short to allow her tapa cloth to dry. She would have to fold it up still damp and the designs would be smeared. Maui went to the mountain and lassoed a ray of the sun and would not let it go until it promised to move more slowly across the sky, at least for part of the year so that the days would be longer.

Haleakala Crater isn't really a crater in the strict sense, but a valley. When the volcano was younger and higher than it is now, eruptions ceased for a time, and wind and rain began to erode stream channels down its sides. The headwalls of the streams eventually coalesced to form a single long valley. Later, when volcanic activity resumed, lava poured down the stream channels, filling them. New spatter and cinder cones formed on the summit, so that today, the huge depression in the mountain looks like a crater. The volcano has been mostly quiet for centuries, though there have been minor eruptions as recently as the 1790s.

Haleakala is a hiker's paradise. There are three different trails into the crater, two of which can be done as day hikes. The third, the Kaupo Trail, involves a shuttle from one side of the island to the other, too complicated and time-consuming for most visitors, and rental cars are not permitted on the road to the trailhead. It's also extremely strenuous, but if you're looking for a challenge, you can get information about it at the visitor center.

Hiking inside Haleakala is an experience no physically fit visitor (or resident, for that matter) should miss. The sheer vastness and wildness of it, the silence, the unearthly shapes and colors, guarantee you an unforgettable peak experience (no pun intended).

The crater is so big that you can spend several days inside it. There are three cabins, two of which have adjoining campgrounds, connected by a network of trails. One hike between two of the cabins and campgrounds is described here, but there are so many options for multiday hikes that you will have to decide on your own itinerary. You will have to be flexible in your planning too. The cabins are in great demand, available only by lottery. You have a better chance getting campground space than cabin space, and camping permits are obtained on a first-come, first-served basis at the visitor center on the day you plan to begin your trip.

Cabins are available in a lottery system. They are relatively inexpensive and sleep one to twelve people. They have propane cooking stoves, woodburning stoves, outhouses, and water (that must be treated). You can enter the lottery no more than ninety days before your trip and can apply online at http://fhnp.org/wcr. You also can call (808) 572-4400 between 1:00 and 3:00 p.m., Monday through Friday for more information.

Even if you are planning only a day hike on Haleakala, you will be starting at an elevation near 10,000 feet, and even though you begin by going downhill, headache, nausea and vomiting, and shortness of breath are possible. It can sometimes be rainy and windy, too, and the weather changes quickly. Snow is possible, though unlikely, in winter. Make sure you have warm clothes and rain gear just in case. There is no shelter or water between trailheads and cabins. Carry lots of water and remember that you will be climbing on your way out, so will need more than you used on your way in.

If you are planning to backpack, you must carry a tent. It can rain at Holua Camp and probably will rain at Paliku Camp, at the edge of a cloud forest.

The trails described in this section are:

20 Sliding Sands Trail to Kapala'oa Cabin: 5.8 miles one way; 2,475-foot elevation loss.

21 Halemau'u Trail to Holua Cabin: 3.6 miles one way; 1,250-foot elevation loss.

22 Holua Cabin to Paliku Cabin: 6.3 miles one way; 550-foot elevation gain; 1,120-foot loss.

20 Sliding Sands Trail to Kapala'oa Cabin

Sliding Sands (Keonehe'ehe'e in Hawaiian) is the easiest trail into and out of Haleakala, with fabulous views all the way. You can make this a day hike to the cabin and back, or make it the first leg of a multiday adventure inside the crater, spending the first night at Kapala'oa Cabin. Camping is not allowed at Kapala'oa.

Start: Kapala'oa Trailhead near the visitor center
Distance: 11.6 miles out and back
Elevation change: 2,475 feet
Difficulty: Strenuous
Approximate hiking time: 5 to 7 hours
Trail surface: A little of everything: packed sand, loose cinders, a'a lava
Seasons: Year-round, but it does occasionally snow in winter
Other trail users: Horses
Canine compatibility: Dogs not permitted
Land status: Haleakala National Park
Nearest town: Pukalani

Fees and permits: Park entrance fee. No permit is needed for a day hike, but you will need a wilderness permit if you plan to spend the night in the crater.
Maps: USGS Kilohana and Nahiku; National Geographic Trails Illustrated Haleakala National Park map
Trail contact: Haleakala National Park Headquarters; (808) 572-4400; www.nps.gov/hale. Weather forecast: (808) 877-5111.
Special considerations: Remember that horses always have right of way, so please stop, step to the side, and stand quietly until they have passed.

Finding the trailhead: From Kahului, drive southeast on HI 37 (the Haleakala Highway) for about 7 miles through the town of Pukalani. Just past town turn left (east) onto HI 377, staying on the Haleakala Highway. In another 6 miles you'll reach HI 378 (Haleakala Crater Road, which is still called Haleakala Highway on the topo). Turn left (east) again to begin the slow, switchbacking ascent to park headquarters, where you can get weather information and pick up your permit if you need one. (Watch out for groups of bicyclists flying downhill around blind corners.) Continue on up the road to the visitor center and parking lot on the rim of the crater. You'll find water and toilets here, but no food and no gas.

The Hike

A sign at the visitor center points to the trailhead. Pass the hitching rail where the horses are unloaded in the parking lot, turn left for a few paces along the summit road, then swing left again toward the crater rim. A good interpretive panel shows you what the mountain looked like at its height, and reminds you that this volcano is only dormant, not extinct.

Now you plunge into a different world. The excellent, well-packed, well-graded trail, with broad switchbacks, allows you to appreciate the stupendous views without watching your feet. You can see usually the clouds crowding into the Kaupo Gap on the right and the Ko'olau Gap on the left. A little less than 2 miles down you see your first silversword, which grows only in the Haleakala Crater. At mile 2 meet the cutoff to Kalu'uoka'o'o, a beautiful, multicolored crater reached by a 1.2-mile round-trip detour.

For the next 0.5 mile the trail becomes slightly steeper and rockier. You go over a little rise, then descend on several more long switchbacks to the crater floor. At the junction with the Halemau'u Trail to Holua Cabin your trail goes straight ahead (east) to Kapala'oa. You begin to see a few beautiful yellow-flowered mamane shrubs, then pass through a patch of ferns. The cinder cones that looked like bumps from high ground are full-sized mountains now.

The last couple of miles are a bit tedious as the trail slogs through fairly deep soft cin-

▶ Be prepared for rapid and extreme weather changes on the mountain. Cold wind and rain can suddenly blow in through gaps in the crater wall, and there is very little shelter. Carry rain gear. On the other hand, tropical sun reflecting off black rock can be scorching, and there is no potable water in the crater. Water at the cabins must be purified. Carry lots of water and sunscreen. Guided horseback rides use this trail regularly.

ders. The ferns give way to grasses and you will meet a junction with another trail to Holua Cabin; go straight ahead (east) again. Continue a short distance through grassland to yet another junction heading north; again stay straight (east). Just beyond is Kapala'oa Cabin, with a water tank and lua (pit toilet) behind. Have a rest, spend the night, or return the way you came. Don't feed the nenes.

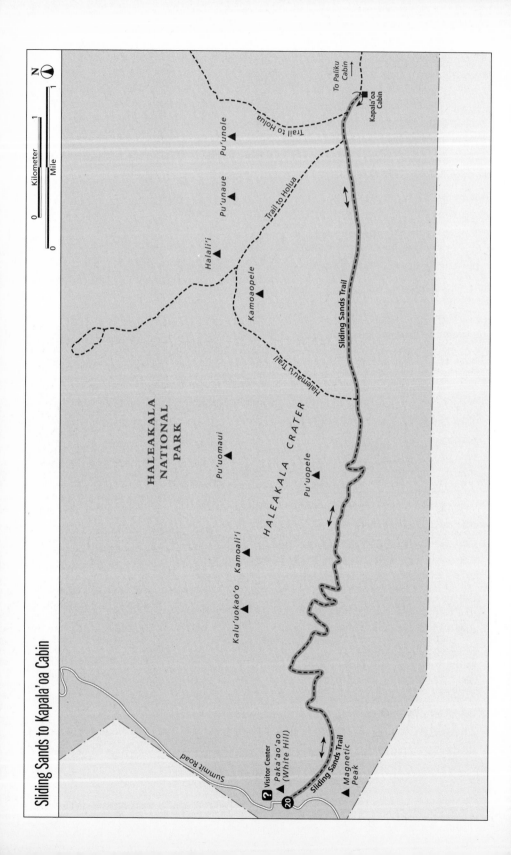

Sliding Sands to Kapala'oa Cabin

Miles and Directions

0.0 Trailhead (N20 42.47' / W156 15.04')

0.6 Turnoff to Kalu'uokao'o Crater; keep right (east) (N20 42.41' / W156 14.00')

4.0 Junction with Halemau'u Trail to Holua Cabin; go straight (east) (N20 42.24' / W156 12.46')

5.6 Second junction with trail to Holua Cabin; keep straight (east)

5.8 Kapala'oa Cabin (N20 42.24' / W156 11.03')

11.6 Return to the trailhead

Options: You can continue on to Paliku Cabin, another 3.6 miles to the east, losing almost 1,000 feet in elevation. This is an especially interesting section because of the change in environment. Kapala'oa lies in red, cindery desert, Paliku in cloud forest. Or you can hike northward from Kapala'oa to Holua Cabin, 3.5 miles away, visiting Pele's Paint Pot and the Bottomless Pit on the way.

Heading up the Sliding Sands Trail

21 Halemau'u Trail to Holua Cabin

This one of the two most popular routes into Haleakala Crater. You can make a rugged in-and-out day hike of it or, even better, spend the night at Holua Cabin or camp in the campground. You can also enter the crater at this trailhead and exit via the other main route, the Sliding Sands Trail (or vice versa), either in a day or as an overnight backpack. You will need a car shuttle for this second option.

Start: Halemau'u Trailhead
Distance: 7.2 miles out and back
Elevation change: 1,250 feet
Difficulty: Moderate as a backpack; strenuous as a day hike
Approximate hiking time: 5 to 7 hours
Trail surface: Clear, well-graded trail partly on smooth pahoehoe, partly on rougher a'a
Seasons: Year-round, but it does occasionally snow in winter
Other trail users: Bicyclists, occasional horse tours

Canine compatibility: Dogs not permitted
Land status: Haleakala National Park
Nearest town: Pukalani
Fees and permits: Park entrance fee. No permit is needed for a day hike, but you will need a wilderness permit if you plan to spend the night in the crater. Contact the park service for more information on cabins and camping.
Maps: *USGS Kilohana; National Geographic Trails Illustrated map of Haleakala National Park*
Trail contact: Haleakala National Park Headquarters; (808) 572-4400; www.nps.gov/hale

Finding the trailhead: From Kahului, drive southeast on HI 37 (the Haleakala Highway) for about 7 miles through the town of Pukalani. Just past town turn left (east) onto HI 377, staying on the Haleakala Highway. In another 6 miles you'll reach HI 378 (Haleakala Crater Road, which is still called Haleakala Highway on the topo). Turn left (east) again to begin the slow, switchbacking ascent to park headquarters, where you can get weather information and pick up a permit if you need one. (Watch out for groups of bicyclists flying downhill around blind corners.) Three miles farther up the road, just past a sharp bend, you'll see the Halemau'u Trailhead on the left (east). There is plenty of parking and pit toilets, but no water.

The Hike

The Halemau'u Trailhead is a favorite hangout for nene (Hawaiian geese) who relish the mist-fed grass that grows there, but they also practice looking pitifully hungry so tourists will toss them a few crumbs of more interesting treats. Please do not give in. They are just coming back from the brink of extinction and do not need junk food.

The trail begins on a gentle descent through typical Hawaiian subalpine scrubland consisting of yellow-flowered mamane bushes, white-flowered, silvery leaved hinahina geraniums, and pukiawe shrubs studded with tasteless (in flavor, not appearance) pink and white berries. The trail trends generally eastward toward Ko'olau Gap, where clouds swirl and tumble and pile up from below, and, if conditions are right, drift into the crater a wisp at a time.

The fence you might notice now and then runs around the entire perimeter of Haleakala to keep out goats who would otherwise chew the native vegetation to stubble. In about 0.5 mile a trail climbing up from Hosmer Grove Campground joins this one, and shortly thereafter the trail makes a dogleg turn to the south and steepens. The braided, twisting pahoehoe flow that poured through the gap and down the mountainside looks as though it might have solidified only yesterday, except for the tinge of green vegetation staining its surface.

▶ Be prepared for rapid and extreme weather changes on the mountain. Cold wind and rain can suddenly blow in through gaps in the crater wall, and there is very little shelter. Carry rain gear. On the other hand tropical sun reflecting off black rock can be scorching, and there is no potable water until you reach the cabin. Carry plenty of water and sunscreen.

Holua Cabin

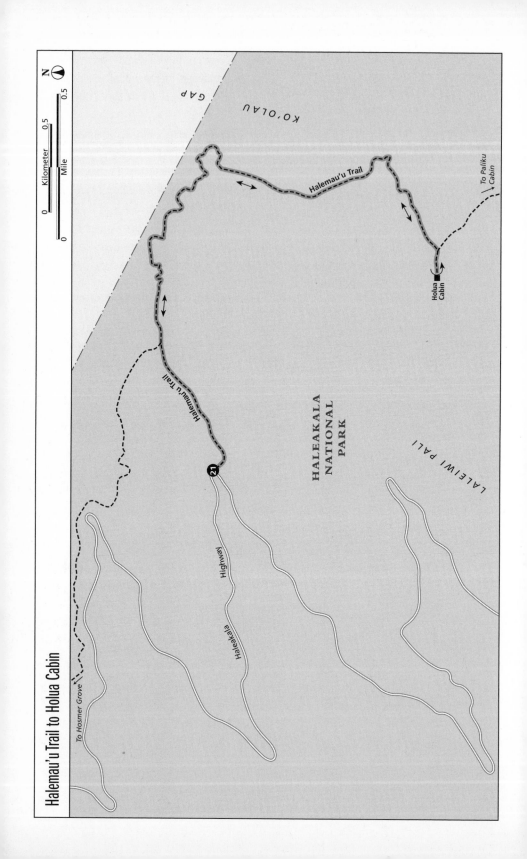

Halemau'u Trail to Holua Cabin

N

Kilometer
0   0.5

0   0.5
Mile

KO'OLAU GAP

Halemau'u Trail

To Paliku
Cabin

Holua
Cabin

Halemau'u Trail

21

Highway

Haleakala

HALEAKALA
NATIONAL
PARK

LALEIWI PALI

To Hosmer Grove

At 1.2 miles round a corner and find yourself on the inside of the crater for the first time, where you can see the beginning of the no-nonsense switchbacks that will drop you onto its floor. From here you can look northeast to another break in the crater wall where clouds creep—or sweep—in. This is the Kaupo Gap, at the top of which is Paliku Cabin. These openings in the crater wall keep the western end of the crater green while the eastern portion is barren, but beautiful, cinder desert. The pathway that might be visible climbing the farthest red slope is the Sliding Sands Trail.

At 2 miles you'll get your first glimpse of your goal, Holua Cabin, tucked beneath a big lumpy ridge that runs perpendicular to the part of the crater wall known as Leleiwi Pali. When you reach the crater floor, pass through a gate near a hitching rail and strike out across flat grassland on smooth, even trail. Enjoy it while you can. Soon you'll be climbing a rough and rocky ridge clothed in dense masses of the silvery lichen called Hawai'i snow. When the trail reaches the ridgetop it turns right (southwest) and continues on to Holua Cabin. You may find a welcoming committee of hopeful nenes awaiting you. There is a water spigot at the cabin, but the water must be purified.

If you are backpacking follow the signs to the campground, which is just over a rise and out of sight of the cabin. From the campground on spring nights listen for the sad calls of the very rare dark-rumped petrels who nest in the cliffs above you. The sound they make gives them their Hawaiian name of ua'u.

Return the way you came.

Miles and Directions

0.0 Start at the Halemau'u Trailhead heading east/downhill (N20 45.11' / W156 13.45')

0.5 Trail from Hosmer Grove joins Halemau'u Trail (N20 45.21' / W156 17.21')

1.9 First sighting of Holua Cabin to the east

2.7 Reach the crater floor and pass through a gate

3.6 Reach Holua Cabin (N20 44.29' / W156 13.06')

7.2 Return to the trailhead

Option: You can hike all the way across the crater to its western end if you continue southeast along the Halemau'u Trail to the Sliding Sands Trail. Turn westward on the Sliding Sands Trail and climb to the Sliding Sands Trailhead at the visitor center. It is a very long, hard day hike, but a delightful backpack. You will need a car shuttle, but it's easy to get a ride from one trailhead to the other. In fact, there is a pullout along the park road across from the Halemau'u Trailhead parking entrance for picking up and dropping off hikers.

22 Holua Cabin to Paliku Cabin

This leg of the journey through Haleakala Crater is probably the most varied and exciting of all. It includes vivid splashes of color at Pele's Paint Pot, a visit to the Bottomless Pit, and a stroll through a garden of silverswords, the stars of Hawaii's plant world, to mention only a few of the highlights. Holua and Paliku are the only spots where camping is permitted in Haleakala Crater.

Start: Holua Cabin
Distance: 6.3 miles point to point
Elevation change: 550 feet gain, 1,120 feet loss
Difficulty: Moderate. The distance between cabins is short, but footing is sometimes rough and irregular.
Approximate hiking time: 3 to 5 hours
Trail surface: Lava in all its forms: soft cindery sand, smooth ropy pahoehoe, and rough, blocky a'a
Seasons: Year-round, but it does occasionally snow in winter

Other trail users: Occasional horse tours
Canine compatibility: Dogs not permitted
Land status: Haleakala National Park
Nearest town: Pukalani
Fees and permits: Park entrance fee. You will need a wilderness permit if you plan to spend the night in the crater. Contact the park service for more information on cabins and camping.
Maps: *USGS Kilohana; National Geographic Trails Illustrated Map of Haleakala National Park*
Trail contact: Haleakala National Park Headquarters; (808) 572-4400; www.nps.gov/hale

Finding the trailhead: From Kahului, drive southeast on HI 37 (the Haleakala Highway) for about 7 miles through the town of Pukalani. Just past town turn left (east) onto HI 377, staying on the Haleakala Highway. In another 6 miles you'll reach HI 378 (Haleakala Crater Road, which is still called Haleakala Highway on the topo). Turn left (east) again to begin the slow, switchbacking ascent to park headquarters, where you can get weather information and pick up a permit if you need one. (Watch out for groups of bicyclists flying downhill around blind corners.) Continue on up the road to the visitor center and parking lot on the rim of the crater. You'll find water and toilets here, but no food and no gas.

The Hike

From the sign in front of Holua Cabin, head southeast on the Halemau'u Trail over a low rise for about 1 mile to the beginning of the Silversword Loop on your left (northeast). Don't miss it! It's only 0.1 mile out of your way, and you're not likely to see these bizarre gigantic daisies anywhere else in the world.

The Silversword Loop Trail reconnects with the main Halemau'u Trail and crosses a fairly young flow (3,000 years old) that is utterly devoid of life. It's a sea of boiling lava with crashing waves and bits of flying froth frozen in time. To add to the illusion, the deep sandy trail underfoot feels like walking on a beach. Off to your right (south)

Pu'uomaui (Maui's Hill), the highest cinder cone in Haleakala, rises 640 feet above you. Beyond it you can trace the route of the Sliding Sands Trail all the way to the western crater rim.

As you proceed, you will meet several junctions with trails that cut off to the right (south) toward Kapala'oa and the Sliding Sands Trail, but your route sticks to the Halemau'u Trail, keeping left (east) every time. Climb a little "pass" where wildly beautiful streaks of volcanic minerals stripe the sides of Pele's Paint Pot. Not far beyond you'll find another colorful spatter cone surrounding the Bottomless Pit, which is, in fact, only 65 feet deep. Beyond, the trail climbs to its highest point at 7,500 feet.

▶ **Paliku Cabin sits in the Kaupo Gap, where howling winds and driving rain can roar through with unbelievable force. Be sure to have good rain gear with you and, if you plan to camp at Paliku, stake your tent down very securely. Remember that unless it is raining, there is no water or shelter between Holua and Paliku.**

On your long and mostly gradual descent, watch for rows of monstrous jagged teeth sticking up out of the mountainside. They are remnants of younger, more resistant lava intrusions called dikes, left standing after the older, softer lava that encased them eroded away. As you pass Maunahina, the lighter colored mountain to the north, you can see rock walls, obviously of human origin, running up its sides. These were built by ranchers to hold cattle before Haleakala became a national park. If the sky is clear you might glimpse Mauna Loa (the smooth rounded peak) and Mauna Kea (the bumpier one) on the Big Island of Hawai'i off to the southeast.

The way becomes easier as the footing turns to pahoehoe and the narrow trail passes through tall grass and ohelo and pukiawe scrub, with occasional clumps of mamane glowing bright yellow in spring. Turn left (east) at the final junction, where the Kaupo Trail splits off to the right (south) and drops 6,100 feet in 8 miles south to the tiny hamlet of Kaupo on the coast. Climb a slight rise and in minutes you'll find Paliku Cabin tucked back in a notch surrounded by mature ohia and mamane trees, and a huge berry patch.

A sign in front points the way to the campground, just out of sight to the left. Campers and cabin users share the water spigot and pit toilet near the cabin. Just beyond the cabin is a park service building not open to the public, as well as a horse pasture. From the cabin you can explore the narrow path that winds up the cliff behind the building for a look down onto the forest canopy, where you might see native Hawaiian birds foraging in the ohia trees.

You can return the way you came to Holua Cabin. If you plan to hike on to Kapala'oa Cabin, turn back to the junction in front of Paliku Cabin and hike 3.6 miles southwest (right). If you're a real glutton for punishment and have a ride waiting for you at the bottom, you can hike all the way down to the beach on the Kaupo Trail.

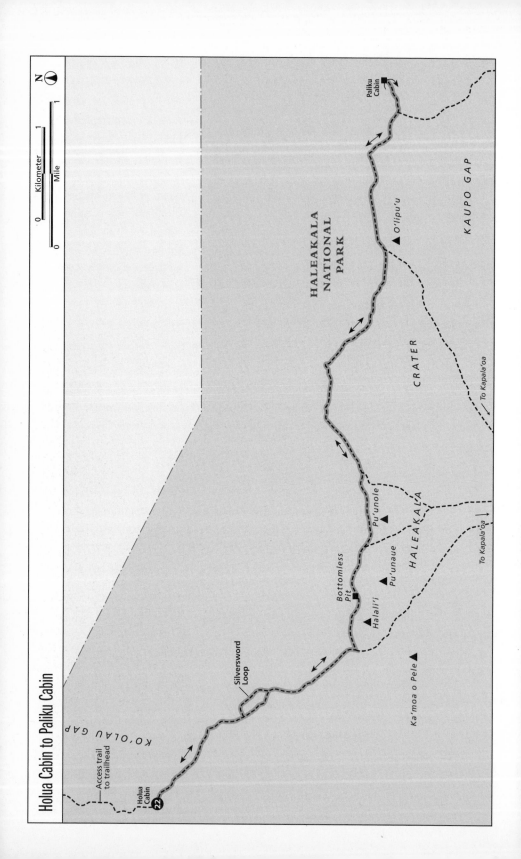

Holua Cabin to Paliku Cabin

N

0   Kilometer   1
0   Mile   1

HALEAKALA NATIONAL PARK

KO'OLAU GAP

Access trail to trailhead

Holua Cabin
22

Silversword Loop

Bottomless Pit

Halali'i ▲

Ka'moa o Pele ▲

Pu'unaue ▲

Pu'unole ▲

HALEAKALA

To Kapala'oa

To Kapala'oa

CRATER

O'lipu'u ▲

KAUPO GAP

Paliku Cabin ■

Miles and Directions

0.0 Start at Holua Cabin (N20 44.29' / W156 13.06')

0.9 Turn left onto the Silversword Loop.

1.3 Silversword Loop rejoins the Halemau'u Trail; keep left.

1.9 Keep left (east) at a junction with a trail heading southeast toward Kapala'oa Cabin (N20 43.02' / W156 11.57')

2.3 Keep left (east) at the next junction beside the Bottomless Pit. Just beyond, reach the highest point of your hike at 7,500 feet.

2.7 Keep left (east) again at another junction to Kapala'oa. (N20 43.05' / W156 09.35')

3.4 Yet another junction to Kapala'oa and Sliding Sands; keep left (east) as usual.

4.9 Yep, another one. Keep left (east).

6.1 Meet the final junction with the Kaupo Trail heading south down to the coast. Paliku Cabin is minutes away, up the hill to the right (east). (N20 43.06' / W156 08.29')

6.3 Arrive at Paliku Cabin

Photographing a silversword

In Addition

The Haleakala Silversword

Haleakala Crater is the only place in the entire world where the silversword plant grows. Its scientific name is a mouthful: *Argyroxiphium sandwicense macrocephalum*. Its Hawaiian name, ahinahina, means gray-gray, or very gray. Its silvery color is due to a coat of fine hairs that cover the plant, reflecting back the intense sunlight that would overheat it and gathering moisture as well.

Silversword is perfectly adapted to this alpine desert landscape, able to tolerate extremes of heat, cold, wind, and drought. Its leaves are both narrow and succulent, and form a rosette low to the ground for protection. It bides its time in this condition for anywhere from seven to thirty years, storing up energy for the day when it can thrust up a flowering stalk as tall as 9 feet, covered with big purple daisylike flowers. Then it dies.

The plant is of special interest to botanists since it is related to a group of smallish, sticky members of the daisy or sunflower family called tarweeds, which come from California. Most of Hawaii's flora originated in Southeast Asia, but about 20 percent came from the other direction, in North America. When the newcomers arrived, they found so many open environmental niches on these remote and geologically young islands they rapidly evolved new forms. Relatives of the silversword live on Hawai'i and Kaua'i as well, though they are extremely rare everywhere. They almost disappeared from Haleakala not long ago, eaten by goats and uprooted by humans, but their population is increasing since they are protected in Haleakala National Park.

23 'Iao Needle

This hike takes you into the misty green forest at the western end of the island to one of Maui's most famous landmarks. 'Iao Needle is a lava spire thrusting up out of the dense, damp foliage lining the walls of a gorge sacred to native Hawaiians. It is one of the sites where King Kamehameha won a victory on his way to uniting the Hawaiian Islands. This hike is best in the morning, before clouds and rain fill the valley.

Start: 'Iao Valley Trailhead
Distance: 1 mile out and back, with several interconnecting loops
Elevation change: 100 feet
Difficulty: Easy
Approximate hiking time: 1 hour
Trail surface: Asphalt
Seasons: Year-round
Other trail users: None
Canine compatibility: Dogs permitted on leash
Land status: 'Iao Valley State Monument

Nearest town: Wailuku
Fees and permits: None
Schedule: 7:00 a.m.–7:00 p.m. daily
Maps: USGS *Wailuku*, but none needed
Trail contact: Hawai'i State Parks; (808) 984-8109; www.hawaiistateparks.org
Special considerations: Stay on the path. You will see little use trails that head off into the forest here and there, but these all lead onto private property where visitors are not welcome.

Finding the trailhead: From Kahului, drive HI 32 west through Wailuku, where the road becomes West Main Street. In the center of town, among government buildings, you will pass the junction with HI 330 on the right (north), then HI 30 on the left (south). HI 32 becomes HI 320 at a sign pointing straight ahead to 'Iao Needle. About 1 mile along HI 320 you will reach a Y junction; follow the right fork for 4 miles, all the way to the end of the road at the monument in the parking lot. **GPS:** N20 52.51' / W156 32.43'

The Hike

Be sure to stop at the interpretive panels at the trailhead that explain the geologic and (sometimes bloody) human history of this sacred valley. The path begins at a showy red-orange flowered royal poinciana tree. You can choose any of a series of circular routes. The lowest one, the Lu'au Trail, is planted with species of plants brought to Hawai'i by the early Polynesians, including a terraced taro patch.

▶ Watch for flash floods here. Don't go wading along the stream when it's raining hard.

Above this is a trail to the Middle Lookout, the closest you can get to the needle itself. You'll have to crane your neck to spot the top of the landmark at 2,250 feet, almost 1,300 feet above you. The Kinihapai Stream tumbles down far, far below. You can leave the lookout and follow a third trail around the ridge separating Kinihapai and 'Iao Streams, and descend to skirt 'Iao Stream back to where the three paths meet. The two streams themselves meet below the parking lot.

Option: Right next door to the entrance to 'Iao Needle is Kepaniwai Park and Heritage Gardens. Take few minutes to stroll among the flowers, ceremonial structures, and statuary celebrating the various cultures that have been stirred into the melting pot that has become present day Hawai'i. There is a picnic area nearby.

24 Waihe'e Ridge Trail

This is a good steady workout, conveniently close to Kahului. There is a surprising variety of scenery for such a short hike, and the views out over the coast are wonderful if the weather is clear, as it is more likely to be early in the morning. Hunting is permitted here on weekends and holidays, so wear bright clothing, but you don't need to be unduly nervous. Leave nothing in your car at the trailhead.

Start: Waihe'e Ridge Trailhead
Distance: 4.2 miles out and back
Elevation change: 1,500 feet
Difficulty: Moderate
Approximate hiking time: 2 to 3 hours
Trail surface: Mostly lava trail, sometimes wet and slippery
Seasons: Year-round
Other trail users: None
Canine compatibility: Dogs permitted on leash

Land status: Hawai'i Department of Land and Natural Resources
Nearest town: Wailuku
Fees and permits: None
Maps: *USGS Wailuku,* but the trail is not shown on the topo
Trail contact: Department of Land and Natural Resources; (808) 984-8100; www.hawaiitrails.org

Finding the trailhead: From Kahului drive HI 340 north for about 8 miles (it starts as Kahului Beach Road, then becomes Waiehu Beach Road then Kahekili Highway) to Maluhia Road. Turn left, and drive less than 1 mile to where a small brown sign on the left says WAIHE'E RIDGE TRAIL.

The Hike

From the parking area at the clearly marked trailhead, go around a gate and start climbing up an old road. It's dirt for the first few feet, then becomes cement. At 0.2 miles a yellow arrow on a rock directs you to the left (south), leaving the road. Walk alongside a wire fence through open pastureland where weedy, but pretty, bright blue Jamaica vervain blooms in spring.

Soon you enter welcoming shady forest, climbing beneath eucalyptus, guava, kukui, and some spiky Cook pines. As you climb the views open up more, the vegetation becomes scrubbier, and you're among uluhe ferns and ohia with the song of wind through leaves in your ears. From a little knob at 0.5 mile glorious views open down the canyon over a patchwork of farm plots and treetops in more shades of green than you ever imagined existed.

Waihe'e Ridge Trail, Waihe'e Valley (Swinging Bridges)

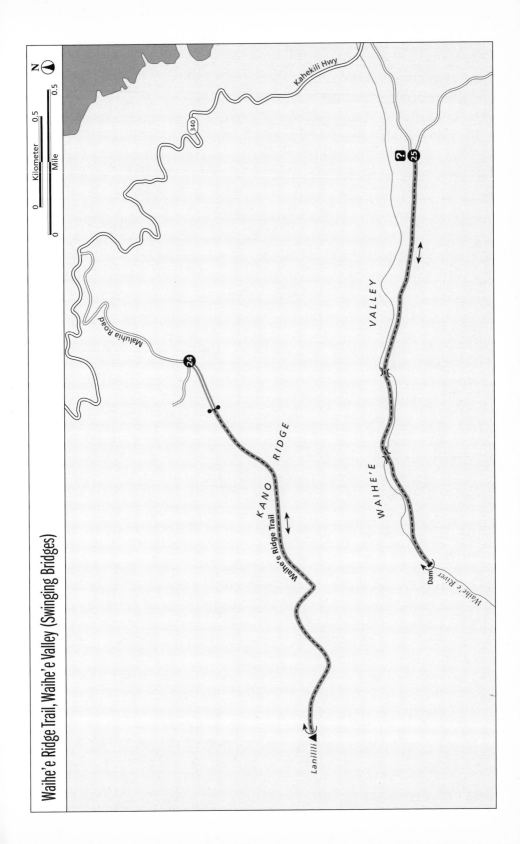

Cross a saddle where you can look out over the isthmus, with Wailuku and Kahului and cloud-shrouded Haleakala to the east. Around the next curve you can hear the roar of the Waihe'e River rushing through the Waihe'e Valley far below. Watch for waterfalls tumbling down the distant cliffs. A short steep set of switchbacks, with a few recycled plastic stairs in the steeper parts, takes you past mile 1.5 and to another high point. Then you drop down through a sometimes boggy saddle and climb again, passing muddy little seeps and a brown pool.

By mile 2 you are in a tropical high-scrub plant community, where beautiful fountains of purplish grasses, along with sedges, club mosses, and lichens, tell you there is plenty of moisture here . . . if it isn't already raining. You reach the summit of Lanilili peak (2,563 feet) at 2.1 miles, where there is a picnic table for resting and enjoying the sweeping view. If it's clear enough, you can see some distance up the northwest coast, way back into the West Maui mountains, and all across the isthmus.

Retrace your steps to the trailhead . . . very carefully! The views will draw your attention away from your feet, and the trail is very slippery when it's wet—it's almost always wet toward the top.

Miles and Distance

- **0.0** Start (N20 57.11' / W156 31.54')
- **0.2** Leave the road and turn left onto trail
- **2.1** Lanilili summit (N20 93.48' / W156 54.77')
- **4.2** Return to the trailhead

25 Waihe'e Valley (Swinging Bridges)

The trail's informal name comes from the two suspension bridges across the stream. The route is on private property belonging to the company that owns the irrigation ditch that in earlier days supplied water to sugarcane fields. You used to have to contact the company in Wailuku to get a permit to enter (a rule that was often ignored), but now entrance is controlled at a kiosk where you can buy sodas and snacks and sample macadamia nuts. This has been a very popular hike for many years. The swinging bridges are fun to cross and there is a perfect little pool to swim in at the end. It's on the rainy side of the island, so the earlier in the day you go the better, but expect to get wet anyway.

Start: In the parking area just beyond the entrance kiosk

Distance: 3.8 miles out and back

Elevation change: 100 feet

Difficulty: Easy

Approximate hiking time: 1.5 to 2.5 hours

Trail surface: Part road, part good trail, sometimes rocky

Seasons: Year-round, except during heavy or steady rain

Other trail users: Cyclists

Canine compatibility: Leashed dogs permitted

Land status: Private; owned by Wailuku Agribusiness

Nearest town: Wailuku

Fees and permits: Entrance fee, used for maintenance

Schedule: 9:00 a.m.–5:00 p.m.

Maps: USGS Wailuku, but the trail is not shown on the topo

Trail contact: Wailuku Agribusiness; (808) 244-9570

Finding the trailhead: From Wailuku drive north on HI 340 about 5 miles, through the little town of Waihe'e. About 1 mile beyond the town turn left (west) on Waihe'e Valley Road. Follow it about 0.5 mile to a T intersection. A sign directs you to the right; the road ends at a gate and the entrance kiosk.

The Hike

Park in a wide spot just beyond the kiosk and hike up the road to a Y junction with chains across both forks. Step over the chain on the left (south) fork, indicated by a sign. Soon you will begin to hear the water flowing through the ditch on the left. Shortly thereafter you'll reach a second fork and turn left (south) again, stepping over or around another gate. The road levels out for awhile and you stroll alongside sugarcane and laua'e (maile-scented ferns) to the first swinging bridge. It looks pretty rickety, but it's firm.

At times there is very little water in the stream beneath the bridge because most has been diverted for irrigation, though it can run fast and deep if it's raining upstream. You will notice irrigation ditches, some of them running through tunnels blasted through the lava, along with the machinery that opens and closes them.

▶ The valley is subject to flash flooding. Don't go in if rain is forecasted.

About 50 yards after the road turns into trail, you come to the next swinging bridge, on which you cross back over the stream. Now that you're above the place where the water gets diverted, there is more water in the stream. Walk through a bamboo forest and cross the stream two times more. If the water is low enough you can cross on dry rocks. The wet ones are *very* slippery. There's a nice pool along this stretch, but the best is yet to come.

Continue up a narrow rocky path/streambed beneath wild ginger that sometimes grows higher than your head. As you draw nearer to the streamside you'll notice the stream is full and roaring now because you have passed another diversion ditch. It's feeling much more like wilderness. A short rise then a short drop in the trail takes you to the dam, where a "waterfall" pours into a perfect diving pool at the end of the trail.

Upstream, clouds permitting, you can see where the valley widens a bit to reveal phenomenally steep cliffs at the head with a narrow, long, vertical string of silvery waterfalls.

Return the same way.

Miles and Directions

0.0 Entrance kiosk (N20 14.16' / W156 52.65')

0.1 First Y junction; take the left (south) fork

0.2 Second Y junction; go left (south) again

1.9 Swimming hole at the dam (N20 93.48' / W156 54.77')

3.8 Return to the trailhead

26 Nakalele Blowhole

Blowholes are created when the sea undercuts a lava cliff. If there is a crack or other opening in the overhanging rock shelf, when the surf crashes into the shore the water is forced up through the hole like a geyser. The height of the fountain varies with the tides and the size of the surf. It's fun to go when the tide is coming in and watch the water shoot higher and higher. There are blowholes on all the major islands—maybe some on the minor ones too—but the setting for this one is arguably the most scenic of all, and it isn't surrounded by souvenir stands. On a weekday you'll only share the scene with a few goats, but summer weekends are busier.

Start: Parking area on HI 30 near milepost 38

Distance: 0.6 mile out and back

Elevation change: 100 feet

Difficulty: Easy

Approximate hiking time: 1 hour

Trail surface: Lava rock; sometimes slippery, sometimes jagged

Seasons: Year-round

Other trail users: None

Canine compatibility: Dogs permitted

Land status: Private

Nearest town: Ka'anapali or Wailuku

Fees and permits: None

Maps: *USGS Napili*, but none needed

Trail contact: None

Special considerations: Watch your step and, especially, watch your children. There really isn't a defined trail, the rocks can be slippery and sharp, and the surf can be dangerous. Do not stand too close to the blowhole!

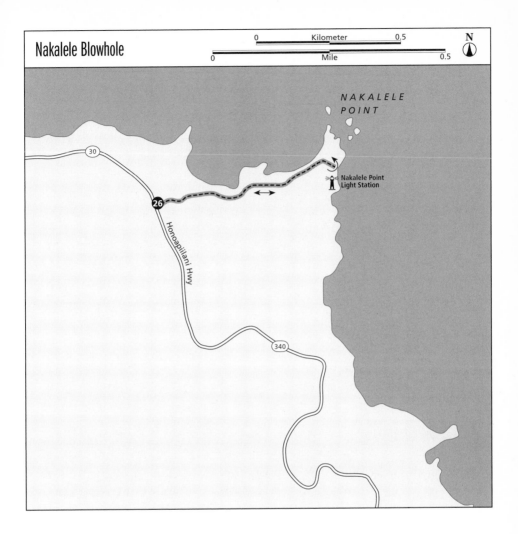

Nakalele Blowhole

NAKALELE POINT

Honoapiilani Hwy

Nakalele Point
Light Station

Finding the trailhead: From Lahaina or Ka'anapali, drive HI 30 north and east to milepost 38 and watch for a parking area on the makai (ocean) side. From Wailuku, drive HI 340 west and north, including a section of winding one-lane road, to where the route becomes HI 30. Pull out near milepost 38 in the parking area on the right. There are no facilities of any kind here. Leave nothing in your car.

The Hike

There are several informal routes from the highway to the blowhole. The easiest way to reach it is to start down the orange-gated road over windswept, goat-mowed ground, wandering downhill and to the right (east) toward the Nakalele Point Light Station. Along the way you'll see hundreds—maybe thousands—of cairns of stacked lava rocks. Making cairns is a tourist tradition, not a native Hawaiian one.

As you near the light station (there is no house, just a light), you'll see a small area enclosed with a wire fence. Below that you can see the top of a ladder sticking up from the cliff edge. (You don't have to use it; it's just a reference point.) Below are some of the world's most beautiful tide pools, wonderful places to explore very carefully at low tide. To continue to the blowhole, pass to the right (north) of the light to a gully where white paint splashed on the rocks marks the easiest path down to the blowhole.

The fabulous, eerie sculptures and patterns in the eroded lava make this worth a trip even if there were no blowhole at the end. Be careful, though. The lava is very sharp and a slip could cause a nasty gash. Stop now and then to enjoy the stunning views west across Honokohau Bay to the jutting fin-shaped rock called Kahakuloa Head. You will be able to hear the intermittent roar and whoosh of the blowhole as you cross a low flat area before you see the blowhole itself, shooting a fountain of water out of the middle of a flat terrace downhill and to the right. When you can tear yourself away, just head back uphill toward the highway, keeping slightly to the right (west).

Miles and Directions

0.0 Start (N21 01.42' / W156 35.40')
0.3 Blowhole (N21 01.47' / W156 35.20')
0.6 Return to the trailhead

27 Twin Falls

Don't expect solitude on this very popular hike because the swimming is great and the falls are beautiful. It isn't exactly unspoiled wilderness, and it isn't even marked on the road, but everybody knows where it is. There's even a little fruit and drink stand at the entrance, and a jar for donations to help with upkeep. The trail has been closed at times because the path does go right past people's homes. It's open now, but please stay on the trail, away from private property, and don't trash the neighborhood.

Start: Unmarked Twin Falls trailhead
Distance: 1.2 miles out and back
Elevation change: Minimal
Difficulty: Easy
Approximate hiking time: 30 to 40 minutes
Trail surface: Gravel road; worn lava trail; streambed
Other trail users: None
Canine compatibility: Open to friendly dogs, even off leash

Land status: Private
Nearest town: Pa'ia
Fees and permits: None
Maps: *USGS Pa'ia,* but none needed
Trail contact: None
Special considerations: This stream can be very dangerous in heavy rain. The narrow valley is subject to flash floods that could sweep you away in an instant. Stay away in bad weather.

Finding the trailhead: From Kahului, drive east on HI 36 toward Hana for about 6 miles to the funky old ex-sugar mill/art colony/hippie haven town of Pa'ia. In another 6 miles HI 36 becomes HI 360 (the Hana Highway). Just past mile marker 2, and just before you cross a bridge over Ho'olawa Stream, look for a small parking area on the shoulder and lots of activity on the right (mauka/mountain) side of the road. There is no sign.

The Hike

Go through the gate, where a little farm stand provides fresh fruit and a pot for donations to help maintain the area. Begin walking down the gravel road, noting that there are lots of minor roads and side trails that lead to little pools along Ho'olawa Stream, and many others that are driveways to private residences. The road is lined with wonderful vegetation, including huge elephant ears called ape (pronounced ah-pay) in Hawaiian and appropriately named *Monstera deliciosa* leaves with Swiss cheese-like holes in them.

At 0.5 mile a Y intersection is marked by a painted rock whose colors are faded and chipped. Both forks of the trail take you to waterfalls. If you want to keep your feet dry, follow the right fork. You cross an irrigation ditch in a tangled hau forest, then walk along the retaining wall that separates the ditch from the stream itself. You'll have to step over a concrete block with a pipe on it that looks like the end of the ditch wall, but the wall actually keeps going. Where the wall ends at a big old banyan tree, continue straight ahead a few more yards, picking your way over roots and rocks,

Octopus tree

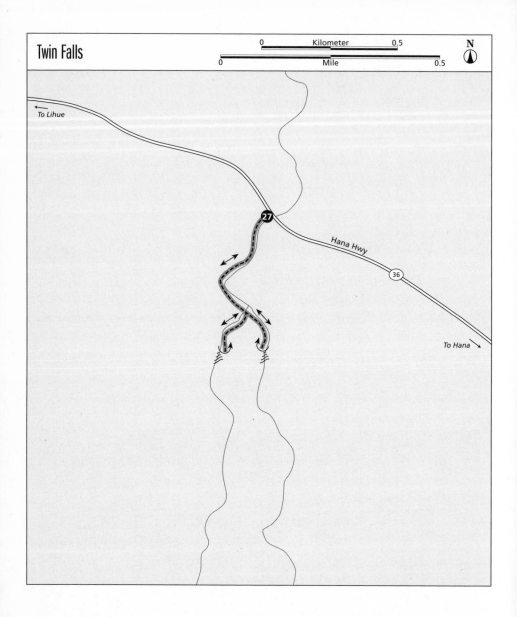

Kilometer 0.5

Mile 0.5

N

To Lihue

27

Hana Hwy

36

To Hana

to a fall pouring over a ferny lava cliff into a deep pool. Kids love to make the 25-foot leap from the top of the fall into the swimming hole.

To see the other waterfall, return to the painted rock and follow the left fork until you reach another stream with a ditch running parallel to it. You'll have to wade from here: You can walk along the top of the wall separating stream from ditch for perhaps 50 yards, or just wade up the middle of the stream. The rocks underfoot are round and smooth and slippery, but it's not much more than knee deep. Keep your camera or anything else that can't get wet wrapped in plastic in case you slip.

The second fall is higher than the first one, perhaps 50 feet, and the water flows over a deep fern grotto. It's deep enough for swimming. Retrace your steps to the painted rock, and from there back to your car.

Miles and Directions

0.0 Start at the gate (N20 54.42' / W156 14.33')

0.5 Painted rock junction. There are waterfalls both ways; take your pick.

0.6 Highest waterfall on the left fork (N10 54.17' / W156 14.62')

1.2 Return to the trailhead

28 Waikamoi Ridge Nature Trail

This is a good place to stretch your legs on the long road to Hana. It involves a steep climb but is very short, traveling through magnificent old forest with views of Waikamoi Stream and the ocean. There are no facilities of any kind here. Take mosquito repellent.

Start: Waikamoi Ridge Nature Trailhead
Distance: 1 mile out and back
Elevation change: 240 feet
Difficulty: Easy
Approximate hiking time: 45 minutes to 1 hour
Trail surface: Gravel path; worn lava with some slick tree roots
Seasons: Year-round
Other trail users: None

Canine compatibility: Leashed dogs permitted
Land status: Hawai'i Division of Forestry and Wildlife
Nearest town: Wailua
Fees and permits: None
Maps: USGS Ke'anae; map at trailhead, but not needed
Trail contact: Division of Forestry and Wildlife; (808) 984-8100; www.hawaiitrails.org

Finding the trailhead: From Kahului follow HI 36, the Hana Highway, eastward. After about 10 miles HI 36 becomes HI 360, and the numbers on the mileposts start over again. Continue to milepost 9.5 and a parking area on the mauka (toward the mountain) side of the road. There's a sign and other cars will be present. **GPS:** N20 52.28' / W156 11.08'

The Hike

The sheer size of the trees along this trail will leave you gasping. This is a nature trail and many of the big trees are labeled. You might be surprised to discover that most of them are kinds of eucalyptus, but eucalyptus bigger than you ever imagined. The vines climbing up into their branches, sometimes completely covering the trunks, should also seem familiar, but are so large you might not recognize them as ordinary houseplants. Among them are philodendron and pothos, whose leaves are the size of

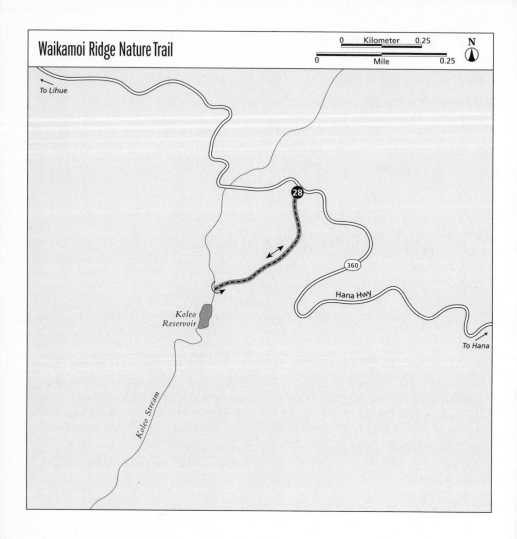

umbrellas. Among the deep greens are startling red bunches of heliconias. You can see how they earned their common name of lobster claws.

You climb on a terraced gravel path, past a sign warning QUIET. TREES AT WORK, to a covered picnic area with a barbecue overlooking the sea. The gravel path ends at 0.3 mile, and the path continues upward to the right on sometimes slippery rocks and tree roots. You enter a forest of bamboo, ti, and hala, picking your way carefully over slippery roots. Just after a road joins the trail from the right (north), you arrive at a grassy flat with another covered picnic table. This one overlooks a valley that is a sea of waving bamboo, below which is the real ocean. This is the end of the trail. Return the way you came.

29 Ke'anae Arboretum

This easy stroll follows a stream through a garden of trees and flowers from all over the tropical world. The trail meanders gently up a series of broad terraces originally built by native Hawaiians for growing taro. The lower portion is planted with exotic trees, while the upper end is devoted to plants introduced and used by the Polynesians. It's a perfect opportunity to take a break from concentrating on the winding Hana Highway to stretch your legs and even splash in the stream.

Start: Ke'anae Arboretum entrance
Distance: 1 mile out and back
Elevation change: Negligible
Difficulty: Easy
Approximate hiking time: 1 hour or less
Trail surface: Asphalt road narrowing to smooth trail
Seasons: Year-round
Other trail users: None
Canine compatibility: Dogs not permitted

Land status: Hawai'i Department of Land and Natural Resources
Nearest town: Hana
Fees and permits: None
Maps: USGS Ke'anae, but a map is not required
Trail contact: Department of Land and Natural Resources; (808) 873-3509; www.hawaiitrails.org

Finding the trailhead: From Kahului drive HI 360 southeast to a sharp bend around mile marker 17. The arboretum is on your right (mauka/toward the mountain), where there is some parking, but there is more space across the road on the makai (toward the sea) side. There are no facilities of any kind at the trailhead, but there are toilets back (northward) up the road at the Kaumahina State Wayside rest area. You will have to bring your own picnic, as well as your mosquito repellent.

The Hike

Go past the gate and down the broad asphalt path lined with the ubiquitous red and white impatiens that thrive in damp places all over Hawai'i. The noisy stream that was invisible at first appears from behind a dense patch of ginger, and you follow it the rest of the way. As the ground levels out a wide lawn begins, dotted with clumps of palms and other tropical trees with identifying labels. Even if botany leaves you cold, there are wondrous things to see here: teak trees with impossibly enormous leaves and dozens of kinds of eucalyptus, including the painted gum with beautiful multicolored pink, green, yellow, and purple stripes running down its trunk. Some of the forest giants have huge sculptural prop roots or buttresses flowing out along the ground in wavy patterns like the train of a bridal gown. There are also showy patches of red torch gingers, and heliconias called lobster claws.

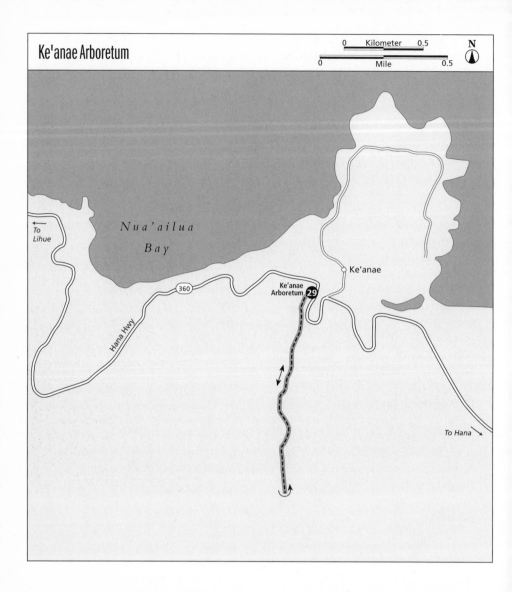

At 0.3 mile the asphalt ends and you come to a collection of plants brought here and used by the native Hawaiians: papaya, coconuts, breadfruit, noni, wild yams, ti, taro, and paper mulberry used to make tapa cloth. Follow the stream back the way you came when you have had enough.

Miles and Directions

0.0 Ke'anae Arboretum entrance (N20 51.30' / W156 08.57')

0.5 Maintained trail ends

1.0 Return to the trailhead

Options: For a taste of true Hawaiian rain forest travel, you can continue on past the taro patch into the canyon beyond for another mile or so, following a "path" marked by occasional plastic ribbons, scrambling steeply upward through mud, bugs, and dense, wet vegetation to a forest clearing. Return the same way.

Torch ginger

30 Sea Caves and Black Sand Beach

This is a short tour of several natural wonders created when flowing molten lava poured into the sea. The coastline is classic Hawai'i, picture postcard pretty with swaying palms and turquoise water. It is also the setting of a romantic . . . and tragic . . . Hawaiian myth.

Start: Black Sand Beach Trailhead at Wai'anapanapa State Park
Distance: 0.4-mile modified loop
Elevation change: 40 feet
Difficulty: Easy
Approximate hiking time: 30 to 40 minutes
Trail surface: Lava, asphalt, and sand
Seasons: Year-round
Other trail users: None
Canine compatibility: Dogs not permitted

Land status: Wai'anapanapa State Park
Nearest town: Hana
Fees and permits: None
Schedule: The parking lot gate is open Mon–Fri, 7:00 a.m.–6:00 p.m.; weekends and holidays, 8:00 a.m.–6:00 p.m.
Maps: USGS Hana, but none needed
Trail contact: Hawai'i Department of Land and Natural Resources; (808) 873-3509, (808) 248-4844; www.hawaiitrails.org

Finding the trailhead: From either Kahului (heading east) or Hana (heading north), drive to mile marker 32 on HI 360 (Hana Highway), where a sign points makai (toward the sea) or northeast to Wai'anapanapa State Park. Drive about 0.5 mile down the narrow park road to a T intersection. Turn left (north) toward the campground and park at road's end. There are toilets and water at the campground. **GPS:** N20 47.14' / W156.00.07'

The Hike

A sign in the parking lot directs you to the left where an interpretive panel tells one of several versions of the story of a Hawaiian princess who was killed in a sea cave by her jealous husband. Now and then the water at the base of the cave turns red with her blood, according to the myth—or with a bloom of aquatic life, according to biologists. Descend on lava stairs just a few yards to find the first cave on the right (west). The caves are the remains of a lava tube whose roof has collapsed in places. The walls above are hung with ferns and other deep green tropical foliage, and the cave itself is properly dark and drippy and mysterious. When you emerge from the other end, the path is bright with cheerful begonias and impatiens. The intricate pattern of branches arching overhead are from a native Hawaiian shrub called hau, often planted as natural fencing. You can see why: "Hau will I ever get to the other side?" Its flowers are bright yellow with purple centers, fading to deep orange with dark centers when they fall.

A few steps up bring you to a short spur to the left that leads north to a gorgeous view of the bay. Skirt the edge of the second cave, then ascend a few more steep stairs to close the loop. There is another spectacular viewpoint behind a railing at the top.

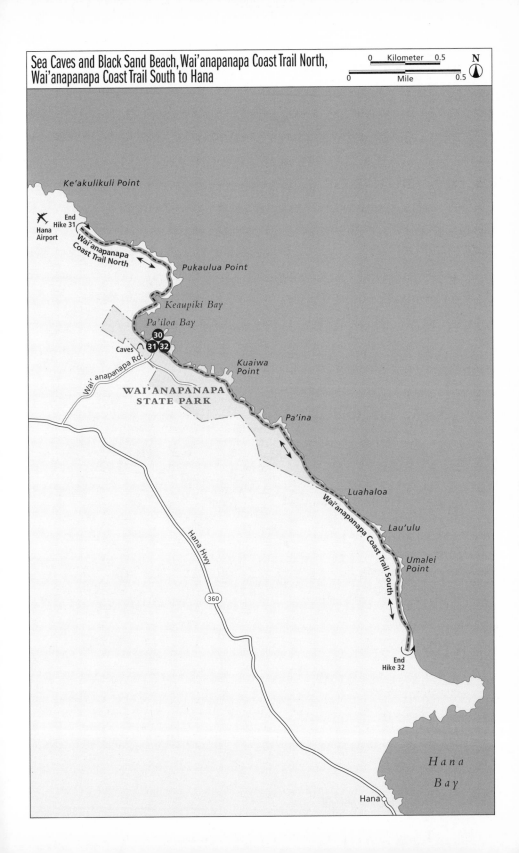

0   Kilometer   0.5

0   Mile   0.5

N

Ke'akulikuli Point

Hana Airport

End Hike 31

Wai'anapanapa Coast Trail North

Pukaulua Point

Keaupiki Bay

Pa'iloa Bay

30

31 32

Caves

Wai'anapanapa Rd.

WAI'ANAPANAPA
STATE PARK

Kuaiwa Point

Pa'ina

Luahaloa

Lau'ulu

Umalei Point

Wai'anapanapa Coast Trail South

Hana Hwy

360

End Hike 32

Hana Bay

Hana

Back at the fork at the trail's beginning, where you first turned left to the cave, you now turn right (north) and descend another steep path curving left down toward the black sand beach. There is a veritable forest of warning signs here, all of which you should take very seriously, most having to do with swimming in the little cove ahead. Accidents due to tricky currents and unexpected waves have been all too frequent. The beach at the bottom is small and usually crowded, unless you're there early or late in the day. The black sand is coarse and sharp and hard on bare feet.

Once you're down on the beach, follow the rock face around to the right for just a few feet and you will find a tunnel in the cliff that goes about 25 yards clear through to the ocean. Be careful! The water can rush in with great force, smash you against the wall, or suck you out to sea. Return the way you came.

Lava formation in the bay at Wai'anapanapa State Park

31 Wai'anapanapa Coast Trail North

Crashing surf, several blowholes, ancient burial sites, and breathtaking scenery are the rewards of this walk along a wild and lonely coast. It follows a historic Hawaiian route known as the Kings Trail, dating back to the 1550s. The park calls it the Ke Ala Loa O Maui/Piilani Trail. The way is marked by ahus (cairns) since the trail is rough and rocky and indistinct in places. The hike ends at the edge of the little Hana airport.

See map on page 119.
Start: Black Sand Beach trailhead
Distance: 2.2 miles out and back
Elevation change: Negligible
Difficulty: Moderate due to difficult footing over uneven lava
Approximate hiking time: 1 to 2 hours
Trail surface: Rough, blocky a'a lava with sharp edges
Seasons: Year-round
Other trail users: None
Canine compatibility: Not recommended for dogs. The route is over very rough lava with knife-sharp ridges and points, pocked with deep holes the size of small dogs. Dogs are not permitted on the first few dozen yards along the beach in the state park anyway.
Land status: Wai'anapanapa State Park
Nearest town: Hana
Fees and permits: None
Schedule: Parking lot gate open Mon–Fri, 7:00 a.m.–6:00 p.m.; weekends and holidays, 8:00 a.m.–6:00 p.m.
Maps: USGS Hana
Trail contact: Hawai'i Department of Land and Natural Resources; (808) 984-8100; www.hawaiitrails.org, www.hawaiistateparks.org

Finding the trailhead: From either Kahului (heading east) or Hana (heading north), drive to mile marker 32 on HI 360 (Hana Highway), where a sign points makai (toward the sea) to Wai'anapanapa State Park. The park is only about 3.5 miles north of Hana. Drive about 0.5 mile down the narrow park road to a T intersection. Turn left (north) toward the campground and park in the lot at road's end. There are toilets and water at the campground next door. Do not leave valuables in your car.

The Hike

Follow the trailhead sign to the right, makai, toward the Black Sand Beach, pausing to admire the spectacular coastline at an overlook: turquoise sea, white foam, and black lava against a background of intense green mountains. Descend steeply on a path that curves left (north) down toward the beach. When you reach the little cove, you might take a few minutes to explore a 25-yard tunnel through the lava cliff that runs out to the sea. Stay away from the opening. The surf can rush in with considerable force.

Turn north (left, if you're facing the ocean) and follow along the cliff edge (you might get your feet wet at high tide). Climb over a lava hump, descend to the shore again, then climb immediately to a shelf above the reach of the waves, but not the spray. The rocks are carpeted with beach naupaka, with succulent leaves and white flowers that look as though they are missing half their petals. Spirals of hala leaves supported by prop roots, along with swaying palm trees, make this shoreline postcard pretty, but watch your feet. The trail is rough. Resist the temptation to slide down the cliff to sample any of the little pocket beaches below. The lava cliffs are loose and crumbly and will not hold your weight.

Hala or pandanus forest

At about 0.5 mile you pass a lonely gravesite that overlooks a cove with dramatic sea stacks just a few yards offshore. From here on you'll have to watch for ahus (rock cairns) to find the easiest path through the boulders.

Beyond the gravesite a blowhole shoots water up like a geyser through an opening at the top of a sea cave. It only blows intermittently, best when the sea is rough and the tide is high, but you can tell where it is even if it's not blowing at the moment by the chunks of white coral that have been spewed up onto the black lava. A little beyond this, keep watch for another blowhole that doesn't shoot such a high fountain of water, but does echo with a loud thump and hiss as the surf smashes against the narrow slot.

After passing yet another, bigger, blowhole, you'll catch sight of the Hawai'i state flag flying ahead (unless it's raining). It marks the edge of the Hana airport, your turnaround point. If you continue on you'll find yourself right at the end of the runway, and will be in for a big surprise if somebody is just taking off. If the weather is bad enough to obscure the runway, a bright orange trail marker indicates the end of the trail.

Miles and Directions

0.0 Start at the Black Sand Beach Trailhead (N20 47.14' / W156 00.07')

0.3 Second beach

0.6 First blowhole

1.1 Hana Airport boundary (N20 47.44' / W156 00.28')

Options: You can return the way you came, or you can follow a faint trail mauka (toward the mountain) to a paved road alongside the airport until you reach the highway. You can return to the trailhead by following the highway.

32 Wai'anapanapa Coast Trail South to Hana

Like the walk northward along the coast, this one follows a shoreline of incomparable beauty, with dozens of blowholes and sea arches, fascinating lava formations, archeological sites, and possible sightings of sea turtles and dolphins. The catch is that, beyond the first mile, the route is very rough, indistinct, and dangerous if you aren't very, very careful. You can't get lost, but there are cracks and holes and collapsed caves, as well as big chunks of lava with very sharp edges to negotiate. The Ke Ala Loa O Maui/Piilani Trail will take you almost all the way to Hana Bay, but you will need a car shuttle or a ride back to the trailhead. A one-way hike on this trail is enough!

See map on page 119.
Start: Black Sand Beach Trailhead at Wai'anapanapa State Park
Distance: 2 miles out and back, or 4 miles one way if you go to trail's end near Hana
Elevation change: Negligible
Difficulty: Moderate
Approximate hiking time: 1 hour to half day
Trail surface: Fairly smooth lava at first, rougher a'a as you progress; indistinct
Seasons: Year-round
Other trail users: None
Canine compatibility: Dogs not permitted in state park

Land status: Wai'anapanapa State Park and Hawai'i Department of Land and Natural Resources
Nearest town: Hana
Fees and permits: None
Schedule: Parking lot gate open Mon-Fri, 7:00 a.m.–6:00 p.m.; weekends and holidays, 8:00 a.m.–6:00 p.m.
Maps: USGS Hana
Trail contact: Department of Land and Natural Resources; (808) 873-3509; www.hawaiitrails.org, www.hawaiistateparks.org

Finding the trailhead: From either Kahului (heading east) or Hana (heading north), drive to mile marker 32 on HI 360 (Hana Highway), only about 3.5 miles north of Hana. A sign points makai (toward the sea) to Wai'anapanapa State Park. Drive about 0.5 mile down the narrow park road to a T intersection. Turn left (north) toward the campground and park in the lot at road's end. There are toilets and water at the campground. Do not leave valuables in your car.

The Hike

From the parking lot take the short concrete sidewalk straight toward the ocean and sea arch overlook. Turn right (north) onto an asphalt trail, passing the picnic area, then the old cemetery with the campground behind. At the CAUTION WATCH YOUR STEP sign leave the asphalt path, which winds back up to the caretaker's house, and go left down the dirt path toward the ocean. There's a picture of hikers marking the trail. Pass another section of the cemetery. Skirt the cliff edge through hala and naupaka, passing below the cabins. There are tempting but dangerous tide pools below.

The ground shakes and thunders when the surf is up. Almost at once you reach a wide spot in the trail where hissing and rumbling tells you there is a blowhole near. When the tide is in, you are likely to get wet with its spray.

From here on, you will pass one blowhole after another, one sea arch after another. At 0.6 mile cross over a lava tube on a lava bridge, where the sea rushes in beneath you with every wave. Beyond, a few stair steps hacked out of the lava take you down to a pebbly cove. When you climb out you come to the remains of a heiau or Hawaiian temple. Beyond that you pass through a sort of portal to an overlook with a bench. At the end of the first mile, a road heads off to the right (west) in a grassy spot that goes back up toward the highway and the Hana School. This is the place to turn around if you don't have much time or don't want to walk the whole route.

If you decide to continue, the trail climbs higher over the ocean, so for a while you're not so close to the shore, the a'a is much rougher to walk on, and the route is harder to find. The lava is twisted into grotesque forms, and there are deep holes and caves to watch out for. Watch for a section of cliff that seems to be carved into regular stone columns. These are formed when lava cools at such a uniform rate that it cracks in natural hexagons. Devils Tower in Wyoming and the Devils Postpile in California are examples of the same phenomenon. Don't forget to watch for dolphins and sea turtles offshore. The route drops into a gully, then goes along a cobblestone beach, where a sign marks the end of the trail at mile 4. You can cut up to the highway from here if you have a ride back to Wai'anapanapa, or continue on another 0.5 mile to Hana Bay for a swim.

Miles and Directions

- **0.0** Start (N20 47.15' / W156 00.07')
- **1.0** Optional turnaround point (N20 46.40' / W155 59.30')
- **4.0** Trail's end near Hana (N20 46.03' / W155 59.05')

One of several blowholes on the coast

33 'Ohe'o Gulch and the Seven Pools

The Seven "Sacred" Pools are the most popular attraction at this end of Maui. There are more than seven of them, depending on where you begin your count, and there is nothing sacred about any of them—the name was an invention of the tourist industry. Still, the setting is beautiful, with Pipiwai Stream flowing down 'Ohe'o Gulch, dropping over one waterfall after another, into one lovely pool after another, on its way to the sea. The last several of these pools, just before the stream flows into the ocean, are perfect for swimming.

Start: Kipahulu Visitor Center
Distance: 0.5-mile loop
Elevation change: 80 feet
Difficulty: Easy
Approximate hiking time: 30 to 40 minutes, not counting time out for swimming
Trail surface: Mostly asphalt
Seasons: Year-round, except just after a big rainstorm
Other trail users: None
Canine compatibility: Dogs not permitted
Land status: Haleakala National Park
Nearest town: Hana

Fees and permits: Park entrance fee. No permit is needed.
Maps: USGS Hana, but a map isn't really needed
Trail contact: Kipahulu Visitor Center; (808) 248-7375; www.nps.gov/hale
Special considerations: Pipiwai Stream flows down a narrow gorge that makes it subject to flash flooding. Check with the visitor center to make sure conditions are safe, and heed all park service warning signs. Do not swim in the ocean in this area. The shore is rugged and rocky and the currents deadly.

Finding the trailhead: From Hana, drive 10 miles south and west on HI 31, past the boundary of Haleakala National Park, and across the bridge over 'Ohe'o Gulch. Turn left (makai/toward the sea) into the Kipahulu Visitor Center parking lot. (*Note:* HI 360 [the Hana Highway] coming from Kahului, ends at Hana. It becomes HI 31 as it continues south.) **GPS:** N20 39.43' / W156 02.28'

The Hike

From the parking lot, walk straight toward the ocean and the visitor center, then turn left toward a big trail sign. Just beyond is a model traditional Hawaiian house with information panels telling about how it was constructed. There is a Y trail junction here. Follow the right fork (marked trail) and walk beneath an overarching canopy of kukui nut trees and a big banyan tree with hundreds of aerial roots reaching down to the ground to form new trunks.

You emerge, blinking, into sunshine where the path curves gently to the left, passing an ancient burial site. You can cut off the main trail here and walk a few yards toward the cliff above the sea for a look at the wild coastline, then return to the path and follow the asphalt steps down to the pools.

One of the lower pools

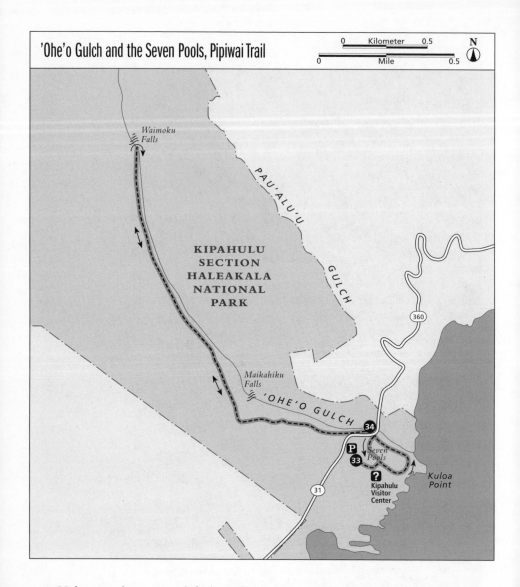

'Ohe'o Gulch and the Seven Pools, Pipiwai Trail

0   Kilometer   0.5

0   Mile   0.5

N

Waimoku Falls

PAU'ALU'U

KIPAHULU SECTION HALEAKALA NATIONAL PARK

GULCH

Maikahiku Falls

'OHE'O GULCH

34

P

Seven Pools

33

?

Kipahulu Visitor Center

31

360

Kuloa Point

Unless you have arrived fairly early in the morning, at least before 9:00 a.m., you'll find yourself part of a crowd. This is, understandably, a very popular place. The asphalt trail continues uphill, passing spur trails down to the pools. There are interpretive panels along the way explaining the origin of the pools. Continue upward along the stream almost to the highway, where a sign directs you to the left, back toward the visitor center, to complete the loop.

34 Pipiwai Trail

This is the best day hike on Maui. It takes you up alongside 'Ohe'o Stream, first through a guava orchard, then through a magical, musical bamboo forest, and on to an enchanting pool at the base of Waimoku Falls. Try to go early in the morning so you can savor the place in solitude.

See map on page 128.
Start: Kipahulu Visitor Center Parking lot entrance on HI 31
Distance: 3.6 miles out and back
Elevation change: 800 feet
Difficulty: Moderate
Approximate hiking time: 2 to 3 hours
Trail surface: Worn lava, often muddy, with large tree roots and two rock-hopping stream crossings
Seasons: Year-round, though not after a heavy rain
Other trail users: None
Canine compatibility: Dogs not permitted
Land status: Haleakala National Park
Nearest town: Hana

Fees and permits: No permit required. Kipahulu is the coastal extension of Haleakala National Park. Park entrance fee may be paid at the visitor center.
Maps: *USGS Hana*
Trail contact: Kipahulu Visitor Center; (808) 248-7375; www.nps.gov/hale
Special considerations: Pipiwai Stream flows down a narrow gorge that makes it subject to flash floods when there is heavy rain in the mountains. Check with the visitor center to make sure conditions are safe before you set out. Also heed the signs advising hikers against jumping into the stream from the rocks above. There have been many, many injuries here.

Finding the trailhead: From Hana drive 10 miles south, then west, on HI 31, past the boundary of Haleakala National Park and across the bridge over 'Ohe'o Stream. Turn left (makai/toward the sea) into the Kipahulu Visitor Center parking lot. (*Note:* HI 360 [the Hana Highway] coming from Kahului, ends at Hana. It becomes HI 31 as it continues south.) There is an official trailhead with a large sign to the right (north) of the parking lot, or you can cross the street from the parking lot, turn right, and follow the trail that parallels the road for a few yards to where it turns left (mauka/toward the mountain).

The Hike

From the parking lot, cross HI 31, turn right (northeast) and follow the verge for about 50 yards to where an obvious trail cuts off to the left (west). The trail follows the edge of the cliff above Pipiwai Stream, among mountain apple and guava trees, both of which produce delicious fruit in spring and summer. Picking your way over tangles of roots, climb past several openings in the dense vegetation leading to trail spurs where you can watch cascades tumble into pools below. In about 0.5 mile you reach a lava-walled overlook of Makahiku Falls, 184 feet high. It can be spectacular or just a trickle, depending on recent weather. Do not try to climb down the cliff to get to the falls.

Boardwalk toward Waimoku Falls

FREE TROPICAL EDIBLES

Guavas are lemon-sized and lemon-colored fruits with smoother skins. The insides are pink, juicy, seedy, and delicious. You can eat the whole thing, but most people just slurp out the middle and discard the husk. They grow on large shrubs to small trees. They are invasive weeds, so eat all you want.

Mountain apples grow on larger trees than guavas. Their red-skinned fruits look like slightly elongated, slightly pear-shaped apples. Their flesh is crisp and white, much like an apple. The trees have showy pinkish-red powder puff flowers in spring.

Pass through a gate, closing it behind you, and begin to climb more steeply, passing a huge old mango tree, and beyond that a truly awesome banyan tree with hundreds of aerial roots growing down toward the earth to become new trunks. You emerge into sunshine amid more guava trees, where you can glimpse the mountains ahead above a waving sea of bamboo. Reenter the forest, and at about the 1.0-mile point cross a bridge over the stream, then promptly cross back on a second bridge.

The trail enters one of the most magical hiking experiences ever, through a very tall, very dense bamboo forest where the *klok-klok* sound of the stems knocking together in the wind makes weird and beautiful music, and the rest of the world disappears. The illusion is slightly disturbed by the recycled plastic faux wood boardwalk that keeps you off the muddy path and prevents erosion from countless tourist feet.

When you finally emerge from the bamboo forest, round a corner, climb some big steps, rock hop a little stream, and enter a different kind of forest altogether. The canopy is made up of flamboyant African tulip trees with gigantic red flowers and huge bird's-nest ferns clinging to their branches. These alternate with silvery kukui trees, whose nut shells pave the forest floor like cobblestones.

Cross another stream on sometimes slippery rocks, and in a few yards you'll find yourself at the edge of a pool beneath Waimoku Falls. It flows over the cliff 400 feet above in beautiful filmy patterns, with hundreds of tiny rivulets trickling from cracks in the rocks, nourishing rock gardens of delicate ferns. You're in a kind of lava amphitheater, surrounded by falling water and hanging gardens. This is a perfect spot to sit and have lunch or a snack, and you can splash in the pool and shower under the falls. Do be aware, though, that rocks sometimes get washed over the cliff into the pool, so swim and shower at your own risk. Return the way you came.

Miles and Directions

0.0 Start at visitor center parking lot (N20 39.50' / W156 02.37')

1.8 Waimoku Falls (N10 40.44' / W156 03.24')

3.6 Return to parking lot the way you came.

35 La Perouse Bay (Hoapili Trail)

The Hoapili Trail is named for a one-time chief and governor of the island of Maui. La Perouse was a French explorer who landed here in 1786, then left without claiming the island for France! A trail known as the King's Highway circled the whole island in pre-contact times, but this section, among others, was buried by an eruption in the 1700s. Governor Hoapili built the "new" road between 1826 and 1831 to serve a village that has now been abandoned. There are dozens of archeological sites along the way. Please do not disturb them.

Start: End of the road at La Perouse Bay
Distance: 4 miles out and back
Elevation change: 40 feet
Difficulty: Moderate
Approximate hiking time: 2 to 3 hours
Trail surface: a'a lava
Seasons: Year-round, but very hot in summer
Other trail users: Horses and bicycles allowed, but certainly not recommended
Canine compatibility: Leashed dogs permitted, but also not recommended
Land status: Hawai'i Department of Land and Natural Resources

Nearest town: Makena
Fees and permits: None
Maps: USGS Makena
Trail contact: Department of Land and Natural Resources; (808) 873-3509; www.hawaiitrails.org
Special considerations: The trail is easy to follow, but the footing is very rough. You will want hiking boots—don't even think about doing this in sandals. Even running shoes will be shredded. It can also get very hot, so take lots of water and sunscreen. Don't leave anything in your car.

Finding the trailhead: From Kahului follow the signs for Kihei until you reach HI 311. The road becomes narrower and narrower as it goes through Makena, narrower and rougher still through the Ahihi-Kina'u Natural Area Reserve. Continue to the road's end at an unpaved parking lot, a total distance of about 25 slow miles.

The Hike

The hike begins at La Perouse Bay, one of the prettiest on the island with views of Kaho'olawe and Molokini Islands, and ends at Kanaio Beach, though you can go several very difficult miles farther if you wish. From the dirt parking area, head toward a closed four-wheel-drive road (just mauka) and follow it mostly along the shore, past foundations and other remains of an old fishing village in a grove of kiawe trees. At 0.5 mile look for a stone structure on your right and a fence on your left. Turn left (northeast) through an opening in the fence and you're officially hiking the King's Highway. At 0.7 mile a sign confirms this, though it exaggerates the distance to Kanaio Beach.

On the Hoapili Trail the a'a has been broken up into small pieces to make walking possible, but the rocks still shift and roll under your feet. The tortured lava on either side of the road gives you an idea of what went into building this trail, and maybe you'll be a little less irritated with the footing.

For a time the highway runs inland, out of sight of the ocean, but about 0.5 mile from the hike's end you top a little rise, the sea reappears, and so does the breeze. The

The King's Highway

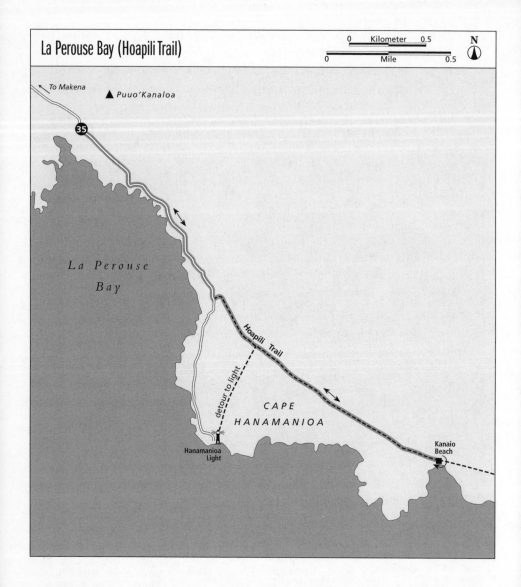

0   Kilometer   0.5

0   Mile   0.5

N

To Makena

▲ Puuo'Kanaloa

35

*La Perouse
Bay*

Hoapili Trail

detour to light

*CAPE
HANAMANIOA*

Hanamanioa
Light

Kanaio
Beach

last 0.25 mile reveals a welcome patch of green toward the ocean, but hang on a little longer until the path descends into a beautiful little inlet at Kanaio Beach. It's lined with naupaka and kiawe, and has smooth sand and refreshing tide pools.

You can hike another 3 miles before you run into private land, but you've seen the best by this point and are probably ready to find better footing. Return as you came.

Miles and Directions

0.0 Start at road's end at La Perouse Bay (N20 36.04' / W156 25.14')

0.7 Meet the official Hoapili Trail; go through the gate on the left (N20 35.29' / W156 24.43')

2.0 Kanaio Beach (N20 34.50' / W156 23.45')

4.0 Return to trailhead

Option: At about 1 mile you can make a 0.5-mile detour to the right (southwest) for a look at the lighthouse on Cape Hanamanioa. In fact, you can continue along the shoreline all the way if you choose, but it is a longer and harder hike.

36 Olowalu Petroglyphs

These are some of the most accessible petroglyphs on Maui (not counting those on hotel grounds, some of which are reproductions). They are incised geometric designs and stylized human figures whose meanings are unknown. They are in fairly good condition, though there has been some vandalism. The hike to see them is short and mostly level, but can be hot so it's best done early or on an overcast day.

Start: Gate behind Olowalu Store
Distance: 1.2 miles out and back
Elevation change: 40 feet
Difficulty: Easy
Approximate hiking time: 40 minutes to 1 hour
Trail surface: Dirt road

Seasons: Year-round; hot in summer
Other trail users: Bicycles, occasional cars
Canine compatibility: Dogs permitted
Land status: Private
Nearest town: Kahului
Fees and permits: None
Maps: USGS Olowalu

Finding the trailhead: From the Kahului Airport take HI 380 (the Kuihelani Highway) south to HI 30 (the Honoapi'ilani Highway). Turn left and continue south about 12 miles to the Olowalu Store and Chez Paul Restaurant. You won't miss it; there isn't much else there. Pull around in back of the store and park by a water tank at a road that runs mauka (toward the mountain), perpendicular to the highway. You'll see an open gate and a sign that says OLOWALU PETROGLYPHS. Please stay on the road and do not block the gate as this is private land.

The Hike

To reach the petroglyphs just follow the dirt road mauka, through weedy wasteland and canefields. You will see a paved road swing off to your right (east), but stay on the main (dirt) one, ignoring any side trips.

A small volcanic cone to the right, at the mouth of the valley, marks the spot. Cross over an irrigation ditch and look for some iron railings on the hillside on your right, behind a tin shack. These lead up to what used to be a viewing platform. Scramble up the slope over chunks of broken concrete to a level spot and look to the

Olowalu petroglyphs

left (up the canyon) to see the petroglyphs. The designs are similar to those found all over the Hawaiian Islands, so they surely have some religious significance, but their meaning has been lost. They are not in the best condition, but very much worth seeing. While you're in the area, Olowalu has good snorkeling.

Olowalu Petroglyphs

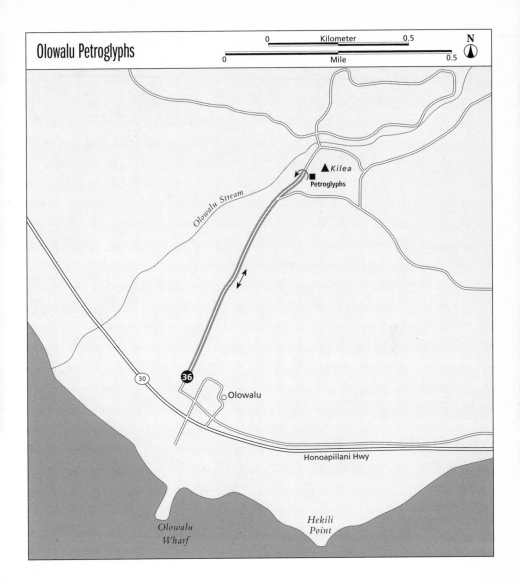

Miles and Directions

0.0   Start (N20 48.44' / W156 37.21')

0.6   Petroglyphs (N20 49.07' / W156 37.07')

1.2   Return to starting point.

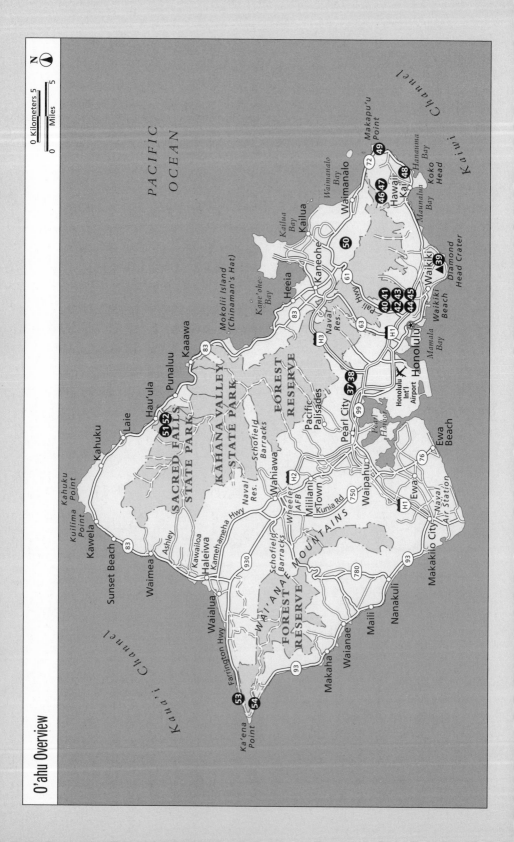

O'ahu Overview

O'ahu:
The Capital Isle

O'ahu is the place most people think of when they think of Hawai'i, and Honolulu and Waikiki Beach are what they think of when they think of O'ahu. Honolulu is the state capital, as well as the population, business, and visitor center of the entire state. It's a busy city with terrible rush hour traffic, jammed with tourist hotels, glitzy shops, and crowded beaches. What isn't devoted to commerce or tourism on the rest of the island seems to be devoted to the military. Still, O'ahu has a surprising number of very fine hiking trails scattered all over the island. Most of these are maintained by Na Ala Hele, part of the state's Division of Forestry and Wildlife.

O'ahu is the third largest and, not coincidentally, the third youngest of the main Hawaiian Islands. It was formed by two volcanoes, the first of which erupted three to four million years ago. All that is left of this one is the Wai'anae Range, the smaller of the two volcanoes, though its summit, Mount Ka'ala, is O'ahu's highest point at 4,025 feet.

The younger volcano, whose remains make up the Ko'olau Range, erupted a million years later, but experienced a more recent spurt of activity 30,000 years ago when it built the cones of Diamond Head, Koko Head, and the Punchbowl. Sediment eroded from the two mountains has washed down into the center of the island to form a plateau between them.

As on all the Hawaiian Islands, the mountains and the trade winds determine all weather activity on O'ahu. The long Ko'olau Range, which runs from northeast to southwest, blocks the trade winds, whose moisture carves deep green canyons on the windward side and keeps the central plateau and the leeward coast relatively dry. Hiking the canyons and ridgetops of the windward coast is often wet, but the views through the clouds down to the shoreline are spectacular, and the forests have an incredible variety of tropical vegetation. The southeastern peninsula, culminating in Makapu'u Point, is sunny and dry enough to harbor a botanical garden devoted to desert species. The best and most extensive trail system is not far from Honolulu in the foothills of the Ko'olau Mountains, where you can put together a hike of any length and difficulty you desire. It can get busy on weekends, but never really crowded. The most remote and relatively unspoiled hiking can be found at the western end of O'ahu. Ka'ena Point, in particular, is one of the few places where you can still see the real Hawai'i, including native wildlife.

None of the hikes described here are overnight backpacks, though some backpacking possibilities exist on the island. Most of these are too close to trailheads to be worth the trouble of carrying a pack, and many are used mainly by hunters and are not especially scenic. Others are on military property and require tedious paperwork. All overnight hikes require a permit from the Department of Land and Natural Resources (DNLR) office in Honolulu. Call (808) 973-9778 for more information; online reservations are not accepted.

The DLNR, through the Na Ala Hele Hawai'i Trail and Access System, also has maps of all the trails they administer. They are copies of USGS topos, not always perfectly up-to-date, but more so than the topos themselves. Call (808) 973-9782 for information and maps, or better, visit www.hawaiitrails.org. Get a good, detailed street map, such as the AAA map, for getting around on O'ahu. The map published by the University of Hawai'i Press is useful, too, but does not have the detail you need for navigating your way out of Honolulu.

Unlike the other islands, O'ahu does have public transportation in the form of TheBus, which is very useful for getting around Honolulu and Waikiki but does not go to most trailheads. If you don't live on the island, you'll need to rent a car. It's too bad, because Honolulu has one of the most illogical, confusing, maddening road and freeway systems ever! You can get a schedule for TheBus at www.thebus.org or by calling (808) 848-5555, or you can pick one up at any number of locations in the city. Keep in mind that the problem of trailhead vandalism is especially bad on O'ahu simply because there is a big city nearby, and lots of tourists.

There are a surprising number of inexpensive hotels and hostels all over O'ahu, even in Waikiki. There are many campgrounds, too, all of which require a permit. Information about camping and permits for Honolulu city and county parks is available at (808) 523-4525 or www.co.honolulu.hi.us/parks. For camping in state parks call (808) 587-0300; online reservations are not accepted.

37 Waimano Loop

There are so many kinds of wild fruits and berries on this trail, you won't make much forward progress in spring and summer if you try to sample them all. This loop is a short sample (and the best part) of the much longer Waimano Trail, which struggles steeply up toward the rainy Ko'olau Mountains. You can hike the loop in either direction, but it is described counterclockwise here, beginning on the upper trail and returning on the lower. There are overlooks along the upper section of the loop that offer views out over the myriad lacy textures and colors of the treetops in the Waimano Valley. When you drop into the valley itself, you can experience the forest more intimately below the canopy on an easy pathway along a stream.

Start: Waimano Trailhead
Distance: 2-mile loop
Elevation change: 200 feet
Difficulty: Easy unless the trail is very wet
Approximate hiking time: 1 to 2 hours
Trail surface: Worn lava; good, with a few short, steep, sometimes slick sections
Seasons: Year-round, but can be wet and slippery in winter
Other trail users: Hunters, mountain bikes

Canine compatibility: Leashed dogs permitted
Land status: Hawai'i Department of Land and Natural Resources Waimano Gulch State Park Reserve
Nearest town: Pearl City
Fees and permits: None
Maps: USGS Waipahu
Trail contact: Department of Land and Natural Resources; (808) 973-9782; www.hawaiitrails.org

Finding the trailhead: From Honolulu, take HI 1 (the Lunalilo Freeway) west to exit 10 at Pearl City. Turn right (west) onto Moanalua Road. Go just over 1 mile to Waimano Home Road and turn right (north). Follow Waimano Home Road for 1 mile to the end of the road, and park in a wide spot on either side. There is a guard station at the trailhead that is manned twenty-four hours a day, seven days a week. The guard is not, of course, responsible for your car, but it would take a very bold or stupid thief to break in there. The security guard will also know if hunters are around.

The Hike

Begin walking along the road, keeping to the left of the chain-link fence. In just a few paces the upper and lower trails split. Keep right on the upper trail, which soon veers away from the road a little. You are surrounded by Surinam cherry, strawberry guava, Java plum, and mountain apple, all edible in season. Scramble up an eroded bare dirt gully to an overlook of Waimano Valley for a gorgeous view over the forest with the mountains as backdrop.

Descend a little, and at about a 0.5 mile pass a tunnel, part of an old irrigation system. Turn left at a junction that drops downhill steeply on switchbacks to the lower section of the trail. The route is easy to follow, marked with plastic strips, but some-

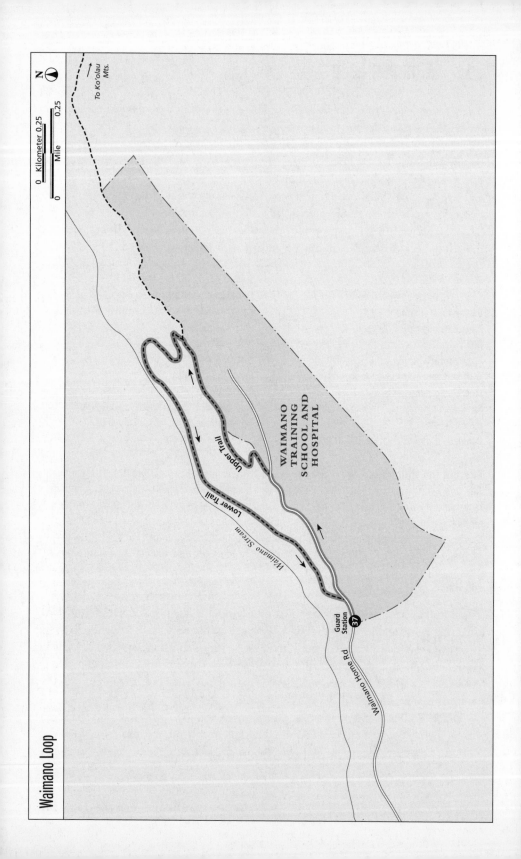

Waimano Loop

N

0   Kilometer 0.25

0   Mile   0.25

To Ko'olau
Mts.

Upper Trail

Lower Trail

Waimano Stream

WAIMANO
TRAINING
SCHOOL AND
HOSPITAL

Guard
Station

37

Waimano Home Rd

what overgrown. Watch your head for low branches. Veer left and go through a hau tunnel, beyond which you meet Waimano Stream. Stroll along the stream through a forest of dwarf bamboo, ferns, fishtail palms, and kukui trees. When the path leaves the stream you head gradually uphill on an old road, back to the first junction and the trailhead.

Miles and Directions

0.0 Start (N21 24.55' / W157 57.23')

0.6 Junction with the connector to the lower trail; turn left/downhill (N21 23.23' / W157 56.23')

2.0 Return to the trailhead

Option: If you crave real adventure and a strenuous workout, you can continue along the trail above Waimano Stream for another 6 miles all the way to the very base of the Ko'olau escarpment, but the farther you go, the more the trail deteriorates. It's not well maintained and is steep, muddy, overgrown, and sometimes washed out.

View from the Waimano Trail

38 'Aiea Loop

This relatively level loop just above Honolulu is high enough into the foothills of the Ko'olau Mountains to feel wild and is a great favorite with both locals and visitors. In fact, it can be crowded on weekends. The route offers some interesting views and a variety of tropical trees and flowers. Like most of the trails on the (geologically) older islands, this one can be muddy and slippery when wet. The trailhead has water, toilets, picnic facilities, and a heiau to visit as an added bonus. You can hike this trail in either direction, but most people prefer to start at the upper end and wind up at the lower, so that is how it is described here. Either way, you have to walk back up to your car at the end.

Start: Upper 'Aiea Loop Trailhead
Distance: 4.7-mile loop
Elevation change: 900 feet
Difficulty: Moderate
Approximate hiking time: 2.5 to 3.5 hours
Trail surface: Good lava; you must negotiate some downed trees and tree roots
Seasons: Year-round, though wet and muddy in winter
Other trail users: Mountain bikes, rarely horses

Canine compatibility: Dogs permitted
Land status: Keaiwa Heiau State Recreation Area
Nearest town: 'Aiea
Fees and permits: None
Schedule: Open 7:00 a.m.–7:45 p.m. in summer; 7:00 a.m.–6:45 p.m. in winter
Maps: USGS Kaneohe, Waipahu
Trail contact: Department of Land and Natural Resources, Hawai'i State Parks; (808) 587-0166; www.hawaiistateparks.org

Finding the trailhead: Take HI 1 (the Lunalilo Freeway) west to HI 201. The exit is from the left lane. Almost at once, go left (northwest) again onto HI 78. Follow this to the Stadium/'Aiea exit. Turn right (north) toward 'Aiea. Follow Moanalua Road for 2 blocks to 'Aiea Heights Drive. Turn right (northeast) and wind up and up through suburbs to the Keaiwa Heiau State Recreation Area. Continue on up as the road becomes one way, and park at the highest point in the road. There is plenty of parking, restrooms, water, a picnic area, and a small brown and gold trail sign.

The Hike

The trail begins in a grove of swamp mahogany and travels through a forest of all the usual weedy suspects, including strawberry guava, Cook pine, and ironwood, to an open area of red dirt crisscrossed with tangled tree roots. Enjoy the view out toward Honolulu from the clearing, then swing left (north) and follow the nearly flat path, ignoring side trails that shoot off here and there. Along with weeds like lantana and the notorious Koster's curse you will find orchids and clumps of bamboo. In the steeper, shadier valleys, however, you can still find real Hawaiian natives like koa, and lots of different kinds of ferns.

'Aiea Loop

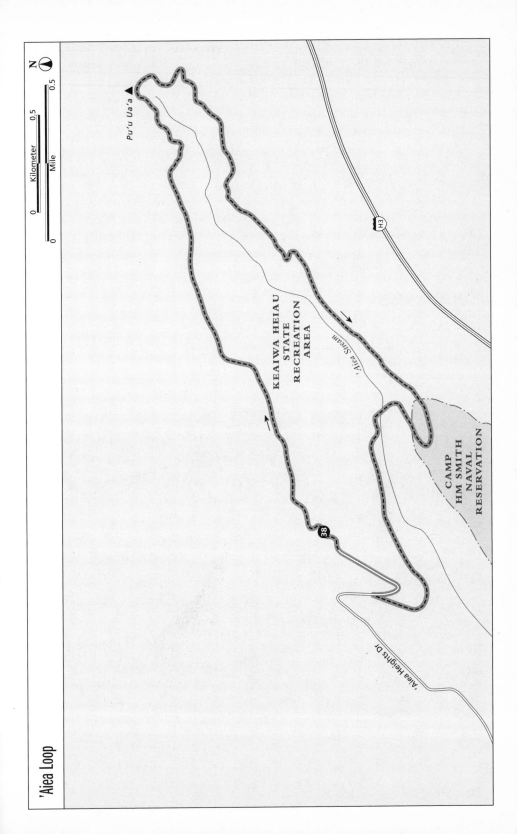

N

Kilometer
0   0.5

Mile
0   0.5

Pu'u Ua'a ▲

KEAIWA HEIAU
STATE
RECREATION
AREA

'Aiea Stream

38

H3

'Aiea Heights Dr

CAMP
HM SMITH
NAVAL
RESERVATION

At about mile 0.6 there is a bench where you can sit and enjoy a slice of the coast. In another 0.5 mile you reach the high point of the hike on Pu'u'ua'u at more than 1,600 feet, and just beyond it another bench at which you can sit and enjoy a view of . . . the freeway! The next opening in the trees gives you a look out over a bit of the Salt Pond and Pearl Harbor. There are several fallen trees at intervals on this section of the trail (the farthest from either trailhead) that you must clamber over or scrunch under.

About three-quarters of the way along you begin to descend through ti, ginger, and octopus trees whose pink arms stick up like a broken umbrella's (or a surprised octopus) when in bloom. Cross the 'Aiea streambed and start back uphill again. As you level out, the trail surface changes to what looks like cobblestone paving; these are actually shells of kukui nuts, whose branches are now overhead. Reach another open red-dirt spot with a view, swing around a corner, and find yourself at a grassy campground. Climb up the slope beside the restroom to the road, turn right (northeast) and follow it back up to your car.

Miles and Directions

0.0 Start (N21 23.47' / W157 54.20')

1.6 Pu'u Ua'a; high point on trail (N21 24.20' / W157 52.59')

4.7 Arrive back at the trailhead

Slippery, tangled tree roots on the trail

39 Diamond Head

The name is Le'ahi to Hawaiians. This is the most famous landmark in all Hawai'i, the classic hike everybody must do when they come to O'ahu. Wilderness it is not. From opening to closing a steady stream of hikers of all ages, sizes, and states of physical fitness (or lack thereof) puffs up and down the steps. For many locals, it's a popular conditioning run. (Yes, run!) The view from the top is superb in all directions, as you would expect.

Start: In Diamond Head State Monument, where the sidewalk begins at the end of the parking lot
Distance: 1.6 miles out and back
Elevation change: 560 feet
Difficulty: Easy, depending on your condition and the weather
Approximate hiking time: 45 minutes to 1.5 hours
Trail surface: Partly paved, some dirt, some concrete stairs, and a fairly steep metal spiral staircase
Seasons: Year-round

Other trail users: None
Canine compatibility: Dogs not permitted
Land status: Diamond Head State Monument
Nearest town: Honolulu
Fees and permits: Park entrance fee
Schedule: 6:00 a.m.–6:00 p.m. daily
Maps: *USGS Honolulu*, but the only one you need is the excellent map on the brochure you receive as you enter the park.
Trail contact: Department of Land and Natural Resources, Hawai'i State Parks; (808) 587-0300; www.hawaiistateparks.org

Finding the trailhead: You can see Diamond Head from almost anyplace in Honolulu or Waikiki unless you are in a canyon of high-rise buildings. The trick is to head toward the mountain, sticking as close to the coast as you can, and pick up Monsarrat Avenue near the Honolulu Zoo and the east side of Kapiolani Community College. It's a one-way road heading eastward and turns into Diamond Head Road, which circles the crater. Watch for the well-marked entrance on your right. If you reach Eighteenth Street, you've gone too far. Drive up the park road, through a tunnel and emerge at the entrance kiosk and parking lot. **GPS:** N21 15.49' / W157 48.23'
  Note: This hike may be as easy to reach by TheBus as it is by car if you're already staying in Honolulu or Waikiki.

The Hike

The hike is well described in the brochure you receive at the kiosk as you enter. The maps are detailed, easy to follow, and the accompanying information is interesting and entertaining. In a nutshell, however, you begin along a flat concrete walkway that gradually begins to gain elevation. The concrete ends and a trail with handrails begins zigzagging more steeply uphill.

▶ Diamond Head got its English name when calcite crystals sparkling in the sun looked like diamonds to sailors approaching from the sea. Its Hawaiian name, Le'ahi, means something like tuna-head. Go figure.

▶ This hike is short but steep, and it can be hot. Start as early in the morning or as late in the afternoon as possible, allowing enough time to get back down before closing. If you are a regular hiker, it's a very easy walk. If you are a sedentary tourist, it's very strenuous. Take water and sunscreen, and wear good shoes with nonslip soles.

Shortly after passing a lookout you climb a stairway of seventy-four steps, then go through a dimly, though adequately, lit tunnel, climb a second staircase, and enter the bottom of the original Fire Control Station. Inside, climb a circular metal staircase to reach the top, and squeeze out through a low doorway into the open air. A last set of metal steps takes you to the wonderful 360-degree view spot over Waikiki, Koko Head, and back toward the misty Ko'olau Mountains. Go back down the way you came up.

Option: If you take TheBus, or prefer to enter the park on foot, you can walk up from the bottom of the hill and avoid the parking fee. It will add 1 mile to your climb. (Take care: There are few legal places to park your car around Diamond Head Road.) You will have to walk through the tunnel very carefully. The sidewalk isn't that wide, and drivers sometimes don't notice pedestrians in the dim light.

View of Honolulu from Diamond Head

40 Manoa Falls

This is one of the prettiest and most popular hikes on O'ahu. Hardcore wilderness buffs might find it a bit tame compared to some of the other muddy scrambles that pass for trails on O'ahu, but this well-engineered and more-or-less maintained trail does make the going easier and prevents erosion. This is a perfect family hike along a stream to a waterfall and pool.

Start: Parking lot at the Manoa Falls Trailhead
Distance: 1.6 miles out and back
Elevation change: 750 feet
Difficulty: Easy
Approximate hiking time: 1 to 2 hours
Trail surface: Mostly crushed rock trail, some worn lava, and slippery roots
Seasons: Year-round
Other trail users: None
Canine compatibility: Leashed dogs permitted

Land status: Hawai'i Department of Land and Natural Resources
Nearest town: Honolulu
Fees and permits: None for the hike; small parking fee
Maps: *USGS Honolulu*
Trail contact: Department of Land and Natural Resources (DLNR); (808) 973-9782; www.hawaiitrails.org

Finding the trailhead: From the east end of Honolulu drive HI 1 (the Lunalilo Freeway) to exit 23 for Punahou Street and go mauka (toward the mountain). Punahou Street soon turns into Manoa Road. Drive Manoa Road almost all the way to the end, about 3 miles, to a parking lot on the right.

From the west side of Honolulu, drive the Lunalilo Freeway to exit 24 for Wilder Avenue, and drive past three signals to Punahou Street. Turn right on Punahou Street and proceed as above. You can park for free on the street, but there has been such a high rate of theft from cars at the trailhead that it's worth paying the fee for supervised parking in the lot.

The Hike

From the parking lot, walk a few hundred yards farther up the road to a chain-link fence. Just to your left is the entrance to Lyon Arboretum. Go through the gate and find yourself on the clearly marked Manoa Falls Trail.

You'll be following Waihi Stream all the way to the falls. In the stream gully to your right are several monstrous strangler figs dripping with aerial roots, vines, and creepers, many of which you will recognize as ordinary houseplants like philodendrons and pothos run amok. You'll feel as though you've entered a Tarzan movie.

Cross a tributary creek on a bridge and proceed amid wild ginger, bamboo, huge tree ferns, and tangled thickets of hau. You can occasionally see, and usually hear, Waihi Stream tumbling over rocks on your right. The trail gradually becomes steeper and rockier, but in the worst places the DLNR has installed metal stair steps to help you up (and especially down) the hill.

Reach an opening near the base of Manoa Falls where there is a junction with the 'Aihualama Trail on the left. The falls flow gracefully down a 60-foot, absolutely vertical cliff into a little pool. People do take dips into the pool, but a huge sign cautions you against going beyond a fence to get closer. A major rockfall in 2002, while harming nobody, created a state of panic about lawsuits among local agencies. Swim at your own risk.

After you have enjoyed the falls, retrace your steps to the trailhead.

Miles and Directions

0.0 Start (N21 19.56' / W157 48.02')

0.8 Junction with the 'Aihualama Trail. A view of the falls is a few steps straight ahead. (N21 20.35' / W157 47.55')

1.6 Return to the trailhead

Aerial roots of banyon tree entrance gate

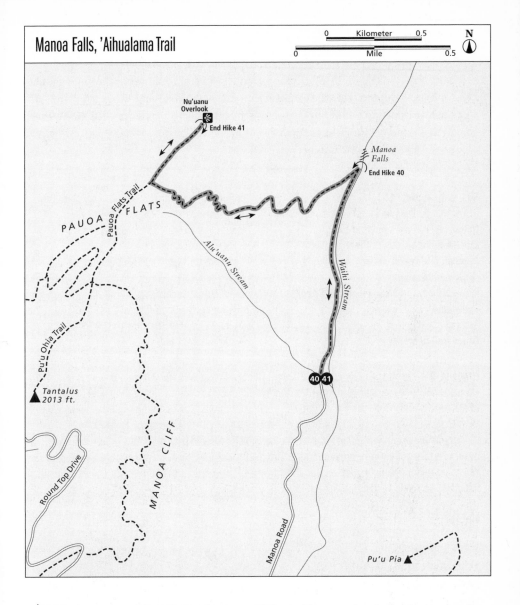

Nu'uanu
Overlook

End Hike 41

Manoa
Falls

End Hike 40

Pauoa Flats Trail

PAUOA FLATS

'Alu'uanu Stream

Waihi Stream

Pu'u Ohia Trail

40 41

Tantalus
2013 ft.

MANOA CLIFF

Round Top Drive

Manoa Road

Pu'u Pia

▶ Hau (pronounced "how"), also known as Hibiscus tileaceus, is a large shrub or small tree found all over the South Pacific. Often planted as natural fencing, its branches are long and spread horizontally, putting down roots whenever they touch the soil so that they form a tangled mass of interlocking limbs. The flowers are bright yellow with purple centers, fading to deep orange with darker centers when they fall, as they do after only one day. Early Hawaiians used the bark to make rope and the corky inner wood to make floats for fishing nets. Hau was considered so valuable that a commoner had to have permission from the chief to cut any for personal use.

41 'Aihualama Trail

If Manoa Falls isn't enough of a hike for you, you can continue farther along the edge of Manoa Valley to the Nu'uanu Overlook for fabulous views as far as Diamond Head in one direction and Kailua in the other. This trail also connects with the Pauoa Flats Trail, linking to more of the wonderful Honolulu Mauka Trail System and any number of hike and trail combinations.

See map on page 151.
Start: Manoa Falls Trailhead
Distance: 4.2 miles out and back
Elevation change: 1,200 feet
Approximate hiking time: 2 to 3 hours
Difficulty: Moderate
Trail surface: The usual rocks, mud puddles, and slippery tree roots
Seasons: Year-round
Other trail users: None
Canine compatibility: Leashed dogs permitted
Land status: Hawai'i Department of Land and Natural Resources
Nearest town: Honolulu
Fees and permits: None for the hike; small parking fee
Maps: *USGS Honolulu*
Trail contact: Department of Land and Natural Resources (DLNR; (808) 973-9782; www.hawaiitrails.org

Finding the trailhead: From the east end of Honolulu drive HI 1 (the Lunalilo Freeway) to exit 23 for Punahou Street and go mauka (toward the mountain). Punahou Street turns into Manoa Road. Drive Manoa Road almost all the way to the end, about 3 miles, to the trailhead parking lot on the right.

From the west end of Honolulu, drive the Lunalilo Freeway to exit 24 for Wilder Avenue and drive past three signals to Punahou Street. Turn right (north) on Punahou and proceed as above. You can park for free on the street, but considering the high rate of theft from cars at the trailhead, supervised parking is worth paying for.

The Hike

From the parking lot, walk a few hundred yards farther up the road to a chain-link fence. Just to your left (west) is the entrance to Lyon Arboretum. Go through the gate to the clearly marked Manoa Falls Trail. You will follow Waihi Stream all the way to the water-fall. In the stream gully to

Pu'u Ohia bamboo forest

your right are several monstrous strangler figs, dripping with aerial roots, vines, and creepers. You'll feel as though you've entered a Tarzan movie.

Cross a tributary creek on a bridge and proceed amid wild ginger, bamboo, huge tree ferns, and tangled thickets of hau. The trail gradually becomes steeper and rockier, but in the worst places the DLNR has installed metal stair steps to help you up (and especially down) the hill. At about 0.8 mile you'll reach an opening near the base of Manoa Falls, flowing gracefully down a 60-foot, absolutely vertical cliff into a little pool. People do take dips in the pool, but a big sign cautions you against going that close to the cliff. A major rockfall in 2002, though it harmed nobody, created a state of panic about lawsuits among local agencies. Swim at your own risk.

The signed 'Aihualama Trail cuts off to the left (west) as you face the waterfall. The first few yards involve a steep climb over boulders, but the path soon levels off in a bamboo forest. There are marvelous—or horrendous—strangler figs on your left, their clasping aerial roots slowly enveloping and killing their host trees. The trail winds in and out of gullies around a ridge above the Manoa Valley, rising and falling (mostly rising) for another mile. Most of the trail is decent, but when it's bad (lots of slippery rocks and mud puddles) it's slow going. Metal steps have been set into the path in the trickiest stretches, but these can be slick too.

In another 0.5 mile you leave the bamboo grove and begin climbing two series of switchbacks. The trailside vegetation makai (toward the sea) becomes sparse in some places, allowing green, misty views down Manoa Valley, and in one spot, just past two concrete posts, you can see all the way to Diamond Head.

Toward the end of the switchbacks you'll enter a deeper, denser bamboo grove, the stems making a wonderful klok-klok sound when the wind picks up. At 1.9 miles you reach a junction with the Pauoa Flats Trail in a clearing where the floor is a maze of tangled roots. Turn right (northeast) here. The left fork connects with other trails of the Honolulu Mauka Trail System. About 0.2 mile beyond you reach Nu'uanu Overlook, the end of the trail, and, bracing yourself against the stiff wind, gaze down the Nu'uanu Valley all the way to Kailua.

You can continue along the Pauoa Flats Trail extend your exploration, or return the way you came.

Miles and Directions

0.0 Manoa Falls trailhead (N21 19.56' / W157 48.02')

0.8 Manoa Falls and 'Aihualama Trail junction; with your back to the falls, turn right (west) (N21 20.35' / W157 47.55')

1.9 Pauoa Flats Trail junction; keep right (northeast) (N21 20.32' / W157 48.33')

2.1 Nu'uanu Overlook (N21 20.41' / W157 48.24')

4.2 Return to the trailhead

42 Pu'u Pia

This short hike takes you through a forest of gaudy tropical flowers and singing birds to the top of a local landmark for a great view of the Ko'olau pali (cliff), Honolulu, and the sea. It's an easy, steady climb on a good trail.

Start: Pu'u Pia Trailhead
Distance: 1.6 miles out and back
Elevation change: 500 feet
Difficulty: Easy
Approximate hiking time: 45 minutes to 1 hour
Trail surface: Good packed dirt, some tree roots, some grass
Seasons: Year-round
Other trail users: None

Canine compatibility: Dogs permitted
Land status: Hawai'i Department of Land and Natural Resources
Nearest town: Honolulu
Fees and permits: None
Maps: USGS Honolulu
Trail contact: Department of Land and Natural Resources; (808) 973-9782; www.hawaiitrails.org

Finding the trailhead: From downtown Honolulu eastbound drive HI 1 (the Lunalilo Freeway) to exit 23 for Punahou Street and go mauka (toward the mountain). Punahou Street turns into Manoa Road. Where Manoa Road splits at a Y intersection, take the right fork (East Manoa Road), and continue to its end at Alani Drive. Turn left (north) on Alani Drive, continue to Woodlawn Drive, and park on the street at this intersection. Please do not block local residents' driveways. There are no facilities at the trailhead.

The Hike

Beyond a trail sign on Alani Drive, the street turns into Alani Lane and becomes very narrow. The pavement ends after you have passed a few houses and a graffiti-covered wall. Step over the low cable that blocks vehicle access and find yourself in deep forest at once, beneath tall dark trees dripping with vines and creepers, most of them escaped houseplants.

The trail splits after only about 0.1 mile, at a sheltered picnic table. The right fork is the Kolowalu Trail. Keep left on the Pu'u Pia Trail. The trail is lined with spectacular gingers and heliconias in varied colors, and white-rumped shamas warble (they really do warble) in the trees. Ascend easily on a path that seems entirely surfaced with interwoven tree roots. Swing to the left (southwest) and cross a grassy ridge in more open country, where native plants like ohia lehua and uluhe ferns take over, to the top of Pu'u Pia (2,236 feet). Take a seat on the little bench to enjoy the view: It is spectacular, looking out over the Manoa Valley down to sparkling Honolulu and the sea beyond. Behind you the Ko'olau Mountains rise in a massive green wall. It's a big reward for minimal effort.

Pu'u Pia, Manoa Cliff Trail, Makiki Valley Loop

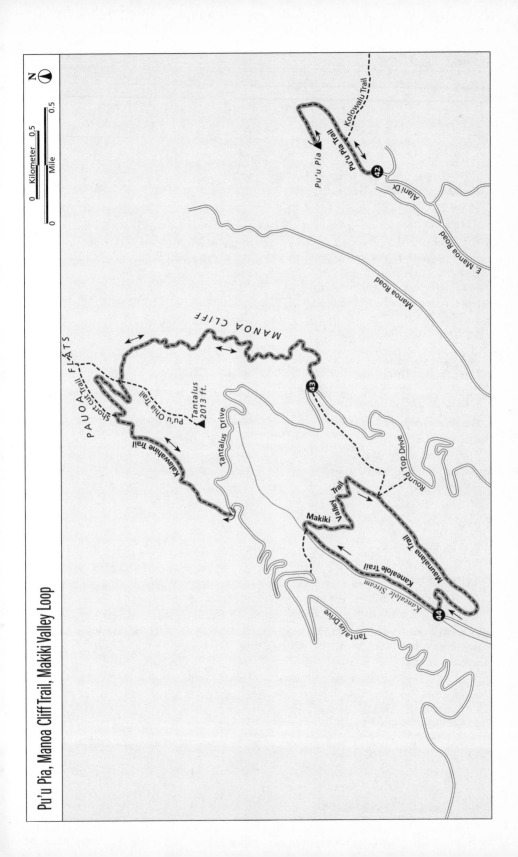

Miles and Directions

0.0 Start (N21 19.17' / W157 47.54')

0.8 Pu'u Pia (N21 19.31' / W157 47.47')

1.6 Return to the trailhead

43 Manoa Cliff Trail

This hike along a section of the crest of the Ko'olau Mountains gives you views (weather permitting, of course) over much of the island, both up the windward coast and out over Honolulu. There are lots of beautiful and interesting plants and flowers, and a rare native Hawaiian snail. Along the way you have an opportunity to make an easy climb of Mount Tantalus (Pu'u Ohia) at 2,013 feet. It's the high point on the rim of a volcanic crater.

See map on page 155.
Start: Manoa Cliff Trailhead
Distance: 2.5-mile shuttle (trail signs and DLNR maps erroneously say 3.4 miles)
Elevation change: 600 feet
Difficulty: Easy
Approximate hiking time: 1 to 2 hours
Trail surface: Part gravel, part worn lava, some rocks and roots
Seasons: Year-round, but expect more mud from December through March

Other trail users: None
Canine compatibility: Leashed dogs permitted
Land status: Hawai'i Department of Land and Natural Resources
Nearest town: Honolulu
Fees and permits: None
Maps: USGS Honolulu
Trail contact: Department of Land and Natural Resources; (808) 973-9782; www.hawaiitrails.org

Finding the trailhead: From eastbound HI 1 (the Lunalilo Freeway) in Honolulu, take exit 23 for Punahou Street. Go right (mauka/toward the mountain) on Punahou Street for 3 blocks to Wilder Avenue. Turn left (west) on Wilder and drive 3 blocks to Makiki Street, then turn right (mauka again). Stay on Makiki Street for a little over a 0.5 mile to Round Top Drive, and follow this about 3.5 miles to the trailhead. There's a parking area on the left (makai/toward the sea), along with a trailhead for the Moleka Trail. The Manoa Cliff Trail is just across the street. The trailheads are not conspicuous, though they are marked. Watch for street numbers 4059, 4059A, and 4063 on a rock wall nearby.

From HI 1 westbound, take exit 24B for Wilder Avenue, and follow Wilder left (northwest) to Makiki Street. Turn right (mauka) on Makiki Street and proceed as above.

To find the shuttle trailhead, from eastbound HI 1 (the Lunalilo Freeway) in Honolulu, take exit 23 for Punahou Street. Go right (mauka) on Punahou Street for 3 blocks to Wilder Avenue. Turn left (west) on Wilder and drive 3 blocks to Makiki Street, then turn right (mauka again.) Keep right on

Makiki Street and turn right again on Tantalus Drive. Just past mile marker 4.5, look for a big turn-out on the right (makai) side. It is marked by posts painted with red and white rings and a couple of trash cans. The trailhead is just across the street. It isn't terribly conspicuous, but there is a sign if you look for it. Do not leave anything in your car.

From HI 1 westbound, take exit 24B for Wilder Avenue, and follow Wilder left (northwest) to Makiki Street. Turn right (mauka) on Makiki Street and proceed as above.

The Hike

Begin on a good gravel trail, climbing gently through an especially beautiful forest that soon becomes a strawberry guava thicket. Turn a corner to find a sign announcing you've come 0.4 miles. You are now officially on the Manoa Cliff and will continue to contour along it for most of the way, with little change in elevation. Pass through a bamboo grove singing its wonderful klok-klok song in the wind—and there is usually plenty of wind here. In case you hadn't already noticed, there's a sign announcing that you are, indeed, in a bamboo grove.

There are plenty of native Hawaiians here—ohia lehua, koa, ie'ie, and white hibiscus—as well as the usual suspects brought by the original Hawaiians and Europeans: ti, eucalyptus, ginger, and the infamous Koster's curse. In the damper places the cliffs drip with nearly a dozen different species of ferns.

Watch for a railing at an opening in the forest for a great view down Manoa Valley. The wind picks up as you approach a gap in the mountains. Just beyond the highest point on the trail, at 1,860 feet, you meet a junction with the Pu'u Ohia (Mount

Honolulu from Pu'u Ohia (Mount Tantalus)

Tantalus) Trail cutting off to the left (south). You can make an easy 1.8-mile round-trip detour, gaining only about 200 feet, to climb the peak. Otherwise the trail keeps right (west).

In another 0.1 mile you'll arrive at another junction, where the Pauoa Flats Trail goes right (north). This time keep left (south). At this point you've rounded a corner and can look down the other side of the ridge to Honolulu and a good distance up the coast. After two long switchbacks, arrive at yet another junction, this time with the Kalawahine Trail, and turn left (south) onto it. The right fork is a "shortcut" to Pauoa Flats. This shortcut is not shown on the USGS topo.

More and more introduced species appear along the trail: guavas, coffee, even bananas. Amid all these foreign species you come upon a sign declaring that you are entering the habitat of the rare native Hawaiian land snail. Very shortly thereafter, another sign indicates that you are leaving snail habitat. Stop to examine the leaves of the plants along that section of trail and sure enough, you'll find hundreds of very tiny black snails. Why they like this one little patch of hillside is a mystery, but it's about all the habitat they have left. Do not disturb them.

Within ten to fifteen minutes of leaving the snails you'll reach the end of the trail at the Kalawahine Trailhead on Tantalus Drive. Pick up your shuttle back to the trailhead from here.

Miles and Directions

0.0 Start (N21 19.51' / W157 48.46')

1.3 High point

1.4 Pu'u Ohia junction; keep right (west) (N21 20.17' / W157 48.43')

1.5 Pauoa Flats shortcut junction; keep left (south)

1.8 Kalawahine Trail junction; keep right (south) (N21 20.17' / W157 48.52')

2.5 End at Tantalus Drive (N21 19.57' / W157 48.54')

44 Makiki Valley Loop

This patch of hills and valleys above Honolulu was almost completely denuded by agricultural uses before it was reclaimed. Now a crazy mix of trees from all over the world makes a fascinating and beautiful setting for a hike. Along the trail you'll find interpretive panels about the history, archaeology, and ecology of the area, as well as an area of plants used by the original Polynesians.

See map on page 155.
Start: Arboretum Trailhead at the parking lot
Distance: 2.7-mile loop
Elevation change: 1,100 feet
Difficulty: Moderate
Approximate hiking time: 1.5 to 2.5 hours
Trail surface: Some gravel, worn lava with slippery rocks and tree roots
Seasons: Year-round
Other trail users: None
Canine compatibility: Dogs permitted on leash; discouraged on weekends and holidays when hunting allowed. Hunting dogs excepted.

Land status: Hawai'i Department of Land and Natural Resources (DLNR), Division of Forestry and Wildlife (DOFAW)
Nearest town: Honolulu
Fees and permits: None
Schedule: Gates are open sunrise to sunset
Maps: *USGS Honolulu* and the DLNR map, which may be available at the Division of Forestry and Wildlife Office at the trailhead
Trail contact: Department of Land and Natural Resources; (808) 973-9782; www.hawaiitrails.org

Finding the trailhead: From the Honolulu area eastbound, take HI 1 (the Lunalilo Freeway) to exit 23 for Punahou Street. Head right (mauka/toward the mountain) for 3 blocks to Wilder Avenue. Turn left (west) on Wilder Avenue and drive 3 blocks to Makiki Street. Turn right (north) on Makiki Street. At the Y intersection take the left fork onto Makiki Heights Drive. In about 0.25 mile, at the top of a hairpin turn to the left, go straight ahead (north) toward a group of mailboxes. Follow the driveway-like narrow road through a gate and park in the lot on the left.

From westbound HI 1 exit at Wilder Avenue (exit 24B) and follow it to Makiki Street. Turn right (north) and proceed as above.

The Hike

The deforestation of this area started with the original Hawaiians, who introduced new plants and animals, cleared and terraced land for farming, and cut down forests. The Europeans followed, clearing more land, planting coffee, and grazing livestock, until the damaged soil could no longer hold moisture or stay in place. Landslides and flooding destroyed sugarcane fields and anything else that grew below. Even in the days of the monarchy, the danger was recognized and efforts at reforestation were begun.

Hawaii's first territorial forester, Ralph Hosmer, planted all kinds of native and introduced plants to control erosion. He hoped to begin a sustainable timber industry in Hawai'i. Some of the introductions were successful, others failed, still others became noxious weeds, out of control to this day. Today, an interesting hodgepodge of species surrounds the loop.

You might be able to pick up a free booklet at the nature center that includes a map of the trail and descriptions of some of the things you'll see on your walk. The markers along the trail, which at one time corresponded with descriptions on the map, have not been maintained, and the brochure describes the route in a counter-clockwise direction, opposite the way it's described in this guide, but the booklet is full of interesting and useful information.

The trail begins at a sign in the parking lot, climbs some stairs, turns left, makes one switchback to the right, then parallels the narrow road for about 0.1 mile through the arboretum. A gravel trail takes you out to this road above the nature center and below the DOFAW office. Do not walk up the road. Cross the street and walk to a big map located across the Kanealole Stream from the cinderblock toilets. Your trail, the Kanealole Trail, goes left; you will be returning on the Maunalaha Trail.

Set out on a gravel path beneath a luxuriant tapestry of vegetation, a riot of trees, shrubs, ferns, and vines, under a canopy of big African tulip trees. Cross a little stream on a bridge to an interpretive panel about the history and archeology of these valleys. Many plants are labeled with their names, their uses, and how they were brought to Hawai'i.

After re-crossing the stream, there's another panel about Hawaiian freshwater aquatic life. The path has been relatively flat so far, but now you begin to climb steeply up alongside the stream. Don't hurry. There is a lot to enjoy, including an almost solid curtain of vines and creepers hanging from the extended branch of a huge tree to form a little high-ceilinged room, a kid's delight. Even in winter, when not much is in bloom, you can peer through the openings in the dense greenery at brilliant splashes of orange wiliwili blossoms that seem to burst out of the bare branches on the tree before the leaves appear.

Listen for the clear melodious song of the shama thrush, an introduced bird that is easy to identify with a black head, chestnut front, and two bright white feathers along the sides of its tail. When it flies, you can see a white patch on its rump.

At 0.8 mile reach a junction where you turn right (southeast) on the Makiki Valley Trail. The left fork cuts west toward Tantalus Drive. Now your route both roller-coasters and zigzags into and out of several small gullies. The "pine needles" underfoot are not from pines at all but from ironwood, or Casuarina, trees introduced from Australia. Here and there, through forest openings, are views down the valley to Honolulu. An informative panel about the 2003 Makiki Valley Fire explains why fires are especially dangerous in Hawai'i. Another sign warns about the plant pest micronia, another threat to the island ecosystem.

After crossing another stream on a sturdy new bridge you come to a three-way junction. The left (southeast) fork is the continuation of the Makiki Valley Trail, which goes to Round Top Drive. Keep right (southwest) on the Maunalaha Trail and begin a steep and slippery descent down a narrow ridge through koa forest until, in three switchbacks, you drop into the valley bottom and cut back to the trailhead sign. From here, retrace your steps to your car.

Miles and Directions

0.0 Start (N21 19.02' / W157 49.39')

0.8 Turn right (southeast) on the Makiki Valley Trail (N21 19.34' / W157 49.18')

1.5 Again keep right (southwest), on the Maunalaha Trail, leaving the Makiki Valley Trail (N21 19.17' / W157 49.11')

2.7 Return to the trailhead

Makiki Valley Loop Trail

45 Judd-Jackass Ginger Pool

This may be the most popular short-hike destination on O'ahu, a place for socializing and swimming as much as communing with nature. Nu'uanu Stream flows along the southwest side of the elongated loop and widens into a pretty ginger-lined pool fed by a 10-foot cascade. The short loop trail is named for Lawrence Judd, who was a governor of Hawai'i in territorial days, and tradition has it that somebody grazed a donkey in the grass near the pool at one time. It is often crowded, especially on weekends, and parking is sometimes a problem. The best time for a hike is early in the morning on a weekday. You can walk directly to the pool, or hike the loop the long way 'round, rewarding yourself with a swim toward the end.

Start: Judd Trailhead
Distance: 1-mile loop
Elevation change: 200 feet
Difficulty: Easy
Approximate hiking time: 40 minutes to 1 hour
Trail surface: Lava
Seasons: Year-round; muddy in winter
Other trail users: Mountain bikes

Canine compatibility: Leashed dogs permitted
Land status: Hawai'i Department of Land and Natural Resources
Nearest town: Honolulu
Fees and permits: None
Maps: USGS Honolulu
Trail contact: Department of Land and Natural Resources; (808) 973-9782; www.hawaiitrails.org

Finding the trailhead: From Honolulu take the HI 1 (the Lunalilo Freeway) west for a little more than 1 mile to HI 61 (the Pali Highway) northbound. Turn off the Pali Highway at the Nu'uanu Pali Drive exit, turn right (east) and go for about 1 mile through suburbs to the parking area and trailhead on the right (south). The trailhead is not terribly conspicuous, but it's just past the bridge over the stream, and there are bound to be cars there—possibly so many you'll have to find a spot farther along the road. Theft from parked cars is all too common here. Leave nothing in yours.

The Hike

Drop down to the stream from the parking lot, passing beneath big banyan trees, and cross Nu'uanu Stream on slippery rocks. Signs on the other side point both ways. Go left (clockwise) and follow the wide trail up through bamboo forest and swamp mahogany

Jackass Ginger Pool

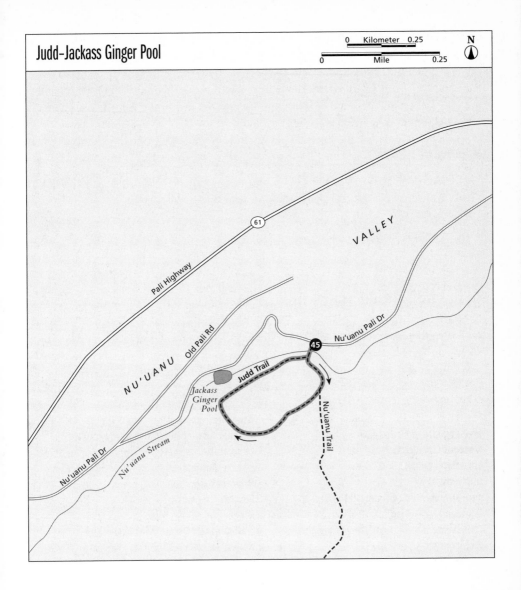

(a kind of eucalyptus), then through a grove of Cook pines. Signs at intervals keep you on the trail so you don't end up in somebody's backyard.

You will climb at first, then drop down to a junction with the Nu'uanu Trail on the left (southeast) at 0.4 mile. The Nu'uanu Trail connects with the Honolulu Mauka Trail System, where you can choose from any number of hiking trails if you want to extend your trip. Continue on the Judd Trail.

You'll begin to hear Nu'uanu Stream below at about 0.75 mile. Watch for an iron post on the left (downhill side) to guide you to the pool. The spur down to it is steep and slippery. The water is a bit murky, but nobody seems to mind. There is a rope to swing over the cascade, and plenty of rocks for sitting. Do not dive in, though; the pool isn't very deep. Swat a few mosquitoes, sniff the clumps of ginger surrounding the pool, then hike back up the spur to the main trail. This gradually descends to the bank of the stream again, where there are a few more little pools. When you reach the intersection at the stream crossing, you have closed the loop. Cross the stream and hike back uphill to the parking area.

Miles and Directions

0.0 Start (N21 20.49' / W157 49.17')

0.4 Junction with Nu'uanu Trail; keep right on the Judd Trail

0.7 Jackass Pool

1.0 Complete the loop

46 Kuli'ou'ou Valley Trail

A shady stroll takes you through a lush green valley toward the heart of the Ko'olau Mountains. Take your time beside a little stream to savor the ferns, flowers, and birdsong. You'll begin at the trailhead for the much more strenuous Kuli'ou'ou Ridge hike.

Start: Kuli'ou'ou Valley and Kuli'ou'ou Ridge Trailhead

Distance: 2 miles out and back

Elevation change: 350 feet

Difficulty: Easy

Approximate hiking time: 40 minutes to 1.5 hours

Trail surface: Well-maintained lava with a few slippery rocks

Seasons: Year-round

Other trail users: Mountain bikes and hunters

Canine compatibility: Dogs permitted

Land status: Hawai'i Department of Land and Natural Resources

Nearest town: Honolulu

Fees and permits: None

Maps: USGS Koko Head

Trail contact: Department of Land and Natural Resources; (808) 973-9782; www.hawaiitrails.org

Finding the trailhead: From Honolulu take HI 1 (the Lunalilo Freeway) eastbound until the freeway ends and the route becomes HI 72 (the Kalaniana'ole Highway). Continue on HI 72 for 4 miles after the freeway ends, then turn left (mauka/toward the mountain) on Kuli'ou'ou Road. The street might not be well marked, but there is a signal. About 1 mile up, in a suburb, turn left (north) at a fork where signs say both roads dead-end. Follow Kuli'ou'ou Road for a few blocks to Kala'au Place, turn right (east) and go to the end of the street. Park at the curb. **GPS:** N21 18.12' / W157 42.27'

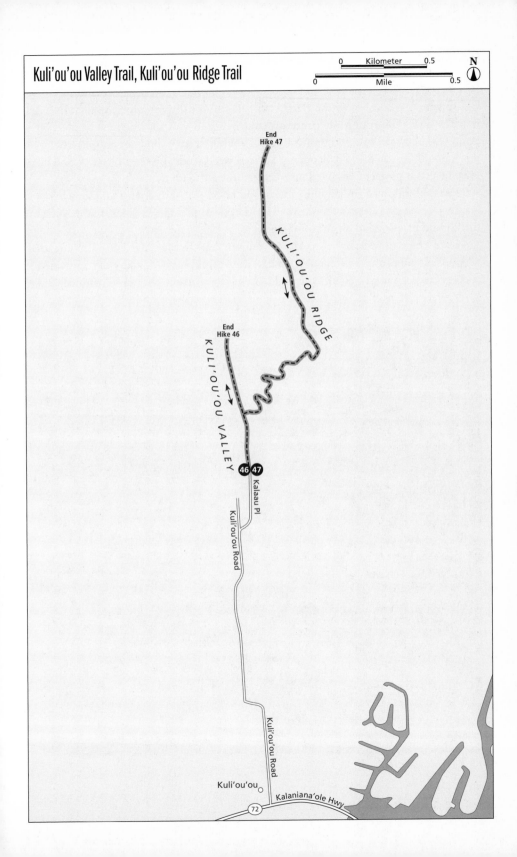

The Hike

Pass the stone barrier marked Kuli'ou'ou Reservoir, sign in on the sheet in the mailbox to your left, and follow the clearly marked trail northward into the valley. In 0.2 mile the trail splits. Your route continues straight ahead (north), while the Kuli'ou'ou Ridge Trail cuts off to the right (northeast). There is a set of built-in boot brushes at this junction so you can scrape off any noxious weed seeds you might have picked up elsewhere and protect Hawaii's native vegetation in this area.

The trail follows a (usually) dry streambed lined with dense ferns and strawberry guava trees. You're almost certain to hear the clear, melodious song of the shama thrush, and have a good chance of seeing one.

After 1 mile of walking on good trail, you can cross to the other side of the stream (a couple of tall cairns mark the way), but beyond this point the trail is not maintained and becomes a muddy, brushy scramble. If you want to see the top of the Ko'olau Range, take the Kuli'ou'ou Ridge Trail. Return the way you came.

Kuli'ou'ou Valley Trail

47 Kuli'ou'ou Ridge Trail

This is a beautiful, though often wet hike to the top of the Ko'olau Mountains. If the sun is out, you will be grateful for the fact that it is shady almost all the way to the top. There are spectacular views out over Koko Head, Koko Crater, and the ocean.

See map on page 165.
Start: Kuli'ou'ou Ridge and Kuli'ou'ou Valley Trailheads
Distance: 5 miles out and back
Elevation change: 1,750 feet
Difficulty: Moderate
Approximate hiking time: 2 hours
Trail surface: Fairly smooth lava with some eroded sections
Seasons: Year-round, but wet and slippery in winter
Other trail users: Mountain bikes and hunters
Canine compatibility: Dogs permitted

Land status: Hawai'i Department of Land and Natural Resources
Nearest town: Honolulu
Fees and permits: None required
Maps: *USGS Koko Head*
Trail contact: Department of Land and Natural Resources; (808) 973-9782; www.hawaiitrails.org
Special considerations: This trail can be very slippery and steep toward the top. Since hunting is allowed here on weekends and holidays wear bright clothing and stay on the trail.

Finding the trailhead: From Honolulu take HI 1 (the Lunalilo Freeway) eastbound to where the freeway ends and the route becomes HI 72 (the Kalaniana'ole Highway). Continue on HI 72 for 4 miles after the freeway ends, then turn left (mauka/toward the mountain) on Kuli'ou'ou Road. The street might not be well marked but there is a signal. About 1 mile up, in a suburb, turn left (north) at a fork where signs say both roads dead-end. Follow Kuli'ou'ou Road a few blocks to Kala'au Place, turn right (east) and go to the end of the street. Park at the curb.

The Hike

Pass the stone barrier marked Kuli'ou'ou Reservoir, sign in on the sheet in the mailbox to your left, and follow the clearly marked trail northward into the valley. In 0.2 miles the trail splits. Take the right fork, which heads uphill (northeast) toward the ridge (the Kuli'ou'ou Valley Trail continues straight ahead or north) At the split is a pair of boot brushes for you to clean your boots before and after your hike. Hawai'i has a terrible problem with introduced weeds, many arriving on hikers' shoes.

The trail climbs up well-graded switchbacks, first among strawberry guava and Brazilian pepper, then in ironwood forest (that's the tree that looks like a pine, but isn't). Watch your step. The shallow roots are slippery, even when dry, and are hard to avoid. Beyond the ironwoods is a grove of Cook pines (another tree that looks like a pine, but isn't). Above a short section of famous bare Hawaiian red dirt, reach a covered shelter with picnic tables (1.9 miles).

After a rest, slip and slide over ironwood roots to a huge old banyan tree, where the trail passes right through a gap in its aerial roots. Just beyond is a little bench and another boot brush. This one is here because you are now entering a more open zone of Hawaiian native plants. Soon the trail becomes steeper . . . and steeper . . . and steeper. Metal bars have been emplaced to keep the earth from being washed down the hill—and give you some flat spots. Haul yourself up on giant steps to reach one disappointing false summit after another. At last you reach a bare patch that is the summit, where a sign announces that this is the end of the Kuli'ou'ou Ridge Trail, just in case it's so socked in that you can't see there's nothing below you.

It is often windy here and if you can't see anything but mist, just wait a few minutes. The clouds will probably blow away, revealing an eye-popping view down the green ridgeline, out over Koko Crater and Koko Head to the sea. You'll probably want to stop frequently on the way down to admire the view or take pictures, but watch your step back down to the trailhead.

Miles and Directions

0.0 Start (N21 18.12' / W157 42.27')

0.2 Kuli'ou'ou Ridge and Kuli'ou'ou Valley Trails split. Turn right (northeast) (N21 18.22' / W157 43.28')

1.9 Picnic shelter

2.5 Summit (N21 19.13' / W157 43.23')

Koko Head and Koko Crater from Kuli'ou'ou Ridge

48 Koko Crater Botanical Garden

This is one of the City and County of Honolulu's five botanical gardens, ~~~~ ~~gu~~-ably the most interesting. It's the only one that offers a real "hike," with a beginning and end. The setting is inside Koko Crater, the largest cone made of volcanic ash on O'ahu. Each of Honolulu's gardens has its specialty, and this one features plants of dry lands and deserts all over the world. It's not a trim, well-manicured grassy lawn, but a more-or-less wild spot where the plants at least appear to have been left alone to be themselves.

Start: Entrance to the botanical garden
Distance: 2-mile loop
Elevation change: None
Difficulty: Easy
Approximate hiking time: 1 to 2 hours
Trail surface: Dirt road
Seasons: Year-round
Other trail users: None
Canine compatibility: Dogs not permitted

Land status: Honolulu Botanical Gardens
Nearest town: Honolulu
Fees and permits: None
Schedule: Open 9:00 a.m.–4:00 p.m. daily; closed Christmas and New Year's Day.
Maps: *USGS Koko Head,* but none needed
Trail contact: Honolulu Botanical Gardens; (808) 522-7060; www.co.honolulu.hi.us/parks/hbg

Finding the trailhead: From Honolulu take HI 1 (the Lunalilo Freeway) east. Once you're out of Honolulu the freeway ends and turns into HI 72 (the Kalaniana'ole Highway). Continue on HI 72 for about 8 miles. You'll pass over a saddle between Koko Crater and Koko Head, and the Hanauma Bay turnoff on the right (south). Turn left (mauka/toward the mountain) onto Kealahou Street. It's not well marked but there is a traffic light. In less than 1 mile there is a sign that says KOKO CRATER BOTANICAL GARDEN. What you'll actually see is a golf course. Turn left (north) anyway and go a few hundred yards to where the road ends at a smaller sign that announces the botanic garden and Koko Crater Stables. Turn right into the driveway and park near the gate. **GPS:** N21 18.53' / W157 41.41'

The Hike

Yes, you did come to Hawai'i to see things Hawaiian (if you don't already live here), but you are not likely to see such a crazy mix of botanical oddities together anyplace else in the world. Walk past the gate, and be sure to pick up a free guide to the gardens before setting off down the road amid a fragrant cloud wafting from a forest of plumeria trees of every color imaginable. These are the flowers you're most likely to see in a lei. There are also bougainvillea in masses of color.

The garden houses an American section with giant saguaros, fat barrel cacti, and big "old man" cacti with gray beards. The African section has real baobabs from Madagascar, with fat jug-like trunks and leaves and branches much too small to fit them.

here are sausage trees, dripping with enormous seedpods that look like sausages on steroids. These also have gaudy red-purple flowers in spring.

It's such an exceptional place that as you return to the start of the loop, you'll be startled to see housing developments spreading up the hillside like cancerous growths just outside the crater rim.

Exotic tree at Koko Center

49 Ka Iwi (Makapu'u Point)

This popular hike in the Ka Iwi State Scenic Shoreline offers some of the best sea views on O'ahu, a photogenic lighthouse, and a special bonus from December through April; migrating humpback whales—lots of them, just off shore. It's the easternmost point of O'ahu, affording views southwest back to Koko Crater and Koko Head, and northwest along Waimanalo Bay, over several islands protected as sanctuaries for sea birds. The dramatic spires of the Ko'olau Mountains poke up out of the clouds behind. The walk is sunny and shadeless, but open to the sea breeze. Take water and sunscreen. Take binoculars too, if you have them.

Start: Makapu'u Point parking area
Distance: 2.5 miles out and back
Elevation change: 500 feet
Approximate hiking time: 1 to 2 hours
Difficulty: Easy
Trail surface: Paved road
Seasons: Year-round
Other trail users: None
Canine compatibility: Dogs permitted

Land status: Ka Iwi State Scenic Shoreline
Nearest town: Honolulu
Fees and permits: None
Schedule: Open during daylight hours daily
Map: *USGS Koko Head,* but none needed
Trail contact: Hawai'i Department of Land and Natural Resources, Division of State Parks; (808) 587-0300; www.hawaiistateparks.org

Finding the trailhead: From Honolulu take HI 1 (Lunalilo Freeway) east. Once you're out of Honolulu the freeway ends and becomes HI 72 (the Kalaniana'ole Highway). Continue on HI 72 for about 10 miles. You'll pass over a saddle between Koko Crater and Koko Head, and the Hawai'i Kai Golf Course. Less than 1 mile past the golf course, after the road makes a sharp curve and begins to climb, watch for a turnoff to the right (east) marked Ka Iwi. Turn here and head down through a valley, then back up to the parking area. You'll likely see other cars and people moving up the hillside. There is a second turnoff beyond this one that just goes to an overlook. If you reach this second turn, or get to Sea Life Park, you've gone too far.

The Hike

Start the gentle climb up a hill covered with koa haole, kiawe (mesquite), and prickly pear cactus, enjoying ever-improving views back toward the rocky coastline toward Koko Head. If you are here between December and April and notice an excited group of people staring out to sea, you can bet you'll see humpback whales blowing, breaching, and doing whale things. A little more than 0.5 mile up the route there is an official whale-watching spot with some public binoculars and an interpretive panel with information about the whales.

At a turn in the road and a break in the cliff (on the left side), get a glimpse of the mistier windward shore and Waimanalo Beach. After the road curves back to the south side of the point again, watch for the stubby little lighthouse clinging close to the cliff below you.

Toward the top of the point you'll find concrete piles and foundations of structures left from World War II, along with a plaque honoring navy pilots who died here in 1942. Ascend between iron railings to a fabulous northward view over the ocean, which changes color as it passes over coral reefs, over Manana (Hawaiian for "rabbit,"

Makapu'u lighthouse

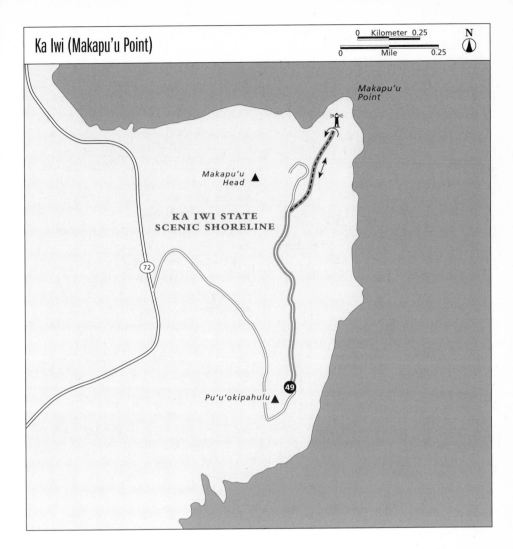

Makapu'u
Point

Makapu'u
Head ▲

**KA IWI STATE
SCENIC SHORELINE**

72

Pu'u'okipahulu ▲

49

not Spanish for "tomorrow") Island, and the smaller Kaohikaipu Island. A few steps higher and the whole glorious 360-degree panorama is yours, from Diamond Head to the Ko'olau Range and, in clear weather, all the way to Moloka'i. From the viewpoint you look almost straight down upon the little lighthouse, bright white and red against the drab hillside and the blue sea.

From the overlook, return as you came to the parking lot.

Miles and Directions

0.0 Start (N21 18.04' / W157 39.05')

1.2 Makapu'u overlook (N21 18.32' / W157 39.04', approximate)

2.5 Return to the trailhead

50 Maunawili Falls

This is a very popular hike to a pretty little waterfall and pool. You will enjoy it more if you get there early in the day to avoid the crowds. The surrounding area was once farmed by the early Hawaiians, later planted with sugar, coffee, rubber, and grazed by cattle, but is now lush and green again, and blooming with flowers. It is shady most of the way, usually damp and sometimes muddy, with three slippery stream crossings.

Start: Maunawili Falls Trailhead
Distance: 2.8 miles out and back
Elevation change: 420 feet
Difficulty: Easy, though the trail can be slippery
Approximate hiking time: 2–3 hours
Trail surface: Worn lava, tree roots, slippery rocks, mud
Seasons: Year-round
Other trail users: None
Canine compatibility: Leashed dogs permitted
Land status: Hawai'i Department of Land and Natural Resources

Nearest town: Kailua
Fees and permits: None
Maps: *USGS Koko Head* and *Honolulu,* but the trail is too new to show on the topo
Trail contact: Department of Land and Natural Resources; (808) 973-9782; www.hawaiitrails.org
Special considerations: This hike is rated easy because it is short and there is not too much elevation gain. However, in winter it can be slippery and the stream, which you must cross several times, can be dangerous at high water.

Finding the trailhead: From Honolulu drive HI 1 (the Lunalilo Freeway) to HI 61 (the Pali Highway). Head north on HI 61, through the tunnels, past an intersection with HI 83 (the Kamehameha Highway), and past the first Auola Road intersection. At the second Auola Road intersection, turn right (south) at a signal, then almost immediately turn left (south) on Maunawili Road. The road gradually narrows to one lane and reaches an intersection with Kelewina Street. There is no official trailhead parking, but you can park on Kelewina. Please do not block homeowners' driveways. The trail begins on a private road with a trail sign.

The Hike

Follow the shady private paved road alongside Olomana Stream, audible but not visible, to where the road is very clearly marked closed. Turn right (north) onto the Maunawili Falls Trail, which is fairly flat and wide at first, passing beneath tall straight trees draped with huge houseplants. There are several different kinds of colorful gingers, showy heliconias (lobster claws), and bird-of-paradise, as well as occasional coffee plants left over from agricultural days.

Descend to Maunawili Stream and cross to the right side for the first time . . . carefully. The rocks are slimy. Once across, keep left along the stream bank. Cross the

Maunawili Falls and Pool ▶

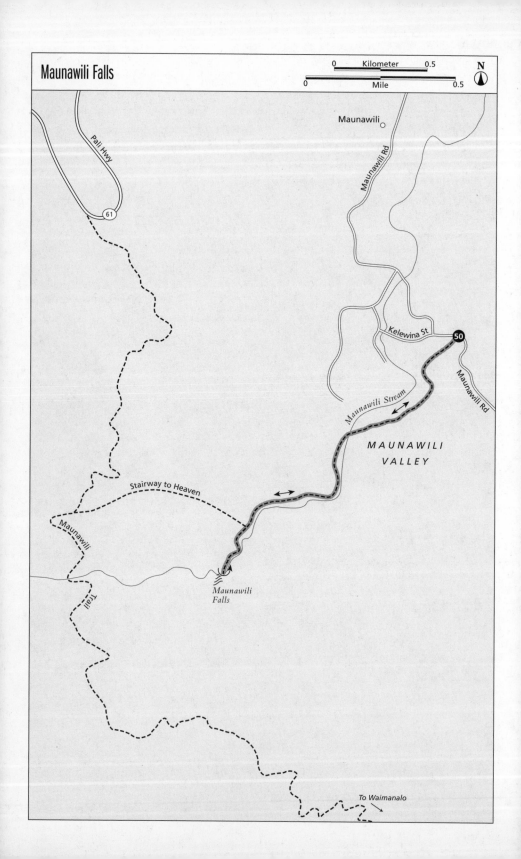

Maunawili Falls

0 — Kilometer — 0.5
0 — Mile — 0.5

N

Maunawili

Pali Hwy

61

Maunawili Rd

Kelewina St

50

Maunawili Rd

Maunawili Stream

MAUNAWILI VALLEY

Stairway to Heaven

Maunawili

Trail

Maunawili Falls

To Waimanalo

stream twice more within the next half mile, and continue to climb. There are lot..
mango trees dropping fruit all over the place in summer, but you'll have to be quic
to beat the locals to them.

After the third crossing there is an obscure junction with a narrow trail going
uphill to the right (east) and a wider one heading back toward the stream to the left
(west). Take the left fork. At streamside you'll find another MAUNAWILI FALLS TRAIL
sign. Turn right (east) and slop through a muddy piece of ground, then veer away
from the stream, climbing alternating sets of stairs and tangles of roots. The steps get
steeper and steeper until you emerge at last into the sunshine on an open ridge where
a trail sign directs you to the left (north), up the ridge.

Catch your breath, taking in the views down to Kane'ohe Bay and up toward the
imposing vertical face of the pali (cliff). At a junction at about 1 mile the trail cuts off
to the left (south) and heads steeply downhill. The other, uphill fork is the "Stairway
to Heaven," connecting this trail with the Maunawili Trail.

The descent to the stream and the falls is very steep, on big stair steps. At the
bottom, in a beautiful forest glade, hop across a smaller stream flowing in from the
right to meet the Maunawili Stream, and follow the Maunawili Stream's right bank
upward. For the first few yards there is not much trail, just streamside rocks, but the
trail soon begins to look like a trail and you climb, steeply again, another 50 yards to
the pool and the waterfalls. The falls are less than 20 feet high, but in perfect propor-
tion with the pool at its base and the surrounding valley. Have a dip in the slightly
murky pool, then retrace your steps to the trailhead.

Miles and Directions

0.0 Start (N21 21.33' / W157 45.43')

1.0 Maunawili Falls turnoff; go left (south; downhill)

1.4 Maunawili Falls (N21 20.59' / W157 46.22')

2.8 Return to trailhead

Option: The Stairway to Heaven connects the Maunawili Falls Trail with the Maunawili Trail, which runs for 10 miles along the face of the pali. From the Maunawili
Falls trail junction you climb another 0.5 mile and 400 feet very steeply up a ridge-
line, directly toward the awesome cliff. Views in the other direction, behind you, are
equally spectacular, taking in the double peaks of Olomana flanked by Kailua to the
right and Kane'ole Bay to the left. The trail is mostly shadeless, lined with uluhe ferns
and strawberry guava. There is a wonderful patchwork of greens in a variety of textures on either side. When you meet the Maunawili Trail you can head left (northeast)
to the lower Maunawili Trailhead at Waimanalo, or right (northwest) to the upper
trailhead off the Pali Highway.

... of tropical fruit to eat in summer along this trail, as well as a great variety of scenery. Best of all, there are no crowds up here on the windward coast, far from busy Honolulu. The drive up the spectacular coast, with dozens of great beaches along the way, is a bonus. You can combine this hike with the Ma'akua Ridge Trail if you want more exercise. There are no facilities and no reliable water.

Start: End of Hau'ula Homesteads Road
Distance: 2.5-mile lollipop loop
Elevation change: 800 feet
Difficulty: Easy to moderate due to a few steep, slippery sections
Approximate hiking time: 2 to 3 hours
Trail surface: Lava
Seasons: Year-round
Other trail users: Mountain bikes, hunters
Canine compatibility: Dogs permitted
Land status: Hawai'i Department of Land and Natural Resources
Nearest town: Hau'ula

Fees and permits: None
Maps: USGS Hau'ula
Trail contact: Department of Land and Natural Resources; (808) 973-9782; www.hawaiitrails.org
Special considerations: You can park down on the Kamehameha Highway if there is no space available in the trailhead parking area. It will add 1 mile round-trip to your hike, but might be a safer place to leave your car anyway. Pig hunting is permitted here on weekends and holidays, so wear colorful clothing.

Finding the trailhead: From Honolulu take HI 61 (the Pali Highway) northeast to HI 83 (the Kamehameha Highway). Turn left (north) on the Kamehameha Highway and drive along the coast for almost 25 miles to Hau'ula. Turn left (mauka/toward the mountain) onto Hau'ula Homesteads Road (just across the highway from Hau'ula Beach Park). Go about 0.5 mile to the end of the road, where there is parking space for two or three cars at the trailhead.

The Hike

Walk straight up the road past a gate (the road on your right that curves sharply uphill is a private driveway). At about 0.1 mile is the actual signed trailhead. (You will pass another, unmarked path heading uphill to the right before this, but this is also private property. Stay on the road until you see the trail sign.)

The forest floor is carpeted with the unusual laua'e fern, whose fronds are so broad you might not recognize it as a fern until you see the spores on their backs. The trail has been hacked through a dense tunnel of Brazilian pepper (Christmas berry) trees; it emerges to climb easily through a grove of ironwoods (the trees that look like pines, but aren't). The trail coming in from the right meets yours at the beginning of the Hau'ula Loop, which you can hike in either direction. The route is described in a clockwise direction; at the junction, keep left (southwest). You will return on the

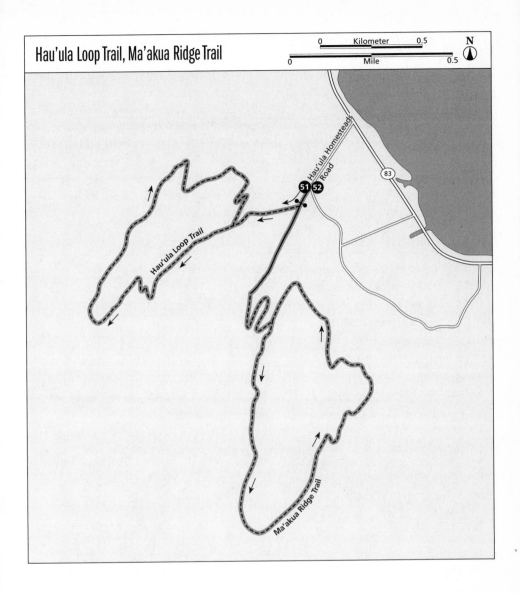

right-hand trail. To the left (south) you can look out over a long, deep gulch running up into the mountains and back down to the ocean.

The trail gradually steepens and climbs a few switchbacks to the top of a ridge at 0.7 mile, then begins to drop into the next valley to the north. Notice how the vegetation changes as you cross from the shady to the sunny side of the ridge. Now you're walking among uluhe fern, strawberry guava, and way too much of the weedy Koster's curse.

Cross a little streambed at the head of a valley and, now on the south-facing slope, you're among Christmas berry and laua'e ferns again. Climb to the next ridge at 0.9

mile, but don't drop down into this one. Instead, descend along the ridgeline, treading carefully on the slippery leaves dropped from the paperbark trees along the trail. You are heading back toward the ocean and get a bit of a view of the coast before the trail starts to drop steeply down on stair steps.

The descent becomes milder as you pass through a magically beautiful grove of Cook pines (trees that are called pines, but aren't). Cross a little creek and round the nose of the last ridge, where you get a quick peek at the marvelous irregular coastline to the north beyond the slightly funky town of Hau'ula. Several more switchbacks through ironwoods bring you back to the junction where you began the loop. If you plan to return to your car, turn sharply left and retrace your steps along the not-so-straight "stick" part of the lollipop back to the road.

Miles and Directions

- **0.0** Start where Hau'ula Homesteads Road is blocked (N21 36.35' / W157 54.52')
- **0.1** Reach the signed Hau'ula traihead
- **0.4** Hau'ula Loop begins, keep left (southwest) (N21 36.33' / W157 55.02')
- **0.7** Reach a ridgetop at 640 feet
- **2.1** Close the loop, turn left
- **2.5** Return to the trailhead

Option: If you haven't had enough, you can continue for another 2.5 miles on the Ma'akua Ridge Loop to make a sort of figure-eight-shaped hike. It begins 0.1 mile up the paved road (mauka) at a signed trailhead on the left (southeast).

Distinctive laua'e fern on the Hau'ula Loop

52 Ma'akua Ridge Trail

This is the complement to the Hau'ula Loop Trail. It is about the same distance and starts at the same trailhead but has a completely different feel to it, and hiking both routes makes an interesting half-day outing. This trail is a little less frequently used for some reason, and is not so well-maintained, but is not difficult. There are lots of fruit to eat in summertime.

See map on page 179.
Start: End of Hau'ula Homesteads Road
Distance: 2.5-mile lollipop loop
Elevation change: 800 feet
Difficulty: Moderate
Approximate hiking time: 2 to 3 hours
Trail surface: Lava
Seasons: Year-round
Other trail users: None
Canine compatibility: Dogs permitted
Land status: Hawai'i Department of Land and Natural Resources (DLNR)

Nearest town: Hau'ula
Fees and permits: None
Maps: USGS Hau'ula
Trail contact: DLNR; (808) 973-9782; www.hawaiitrails.org
Special considerations: You can park down on the Kamehameha Highway if there is no space available in the trailhead parking area. It will add 1 mile round-trip to your hike, but might be a safer place to leave your car anyway. Pig hunting is permitted here on weekends and holidays, so wear colorful clothing.

Finding the trailhead: From Honolulu drive HI 61 (the Pali Highway) northeast to HI 83 (the Kamehameha Highway). Turn left (north) on the Kamehameha Highway and drive along the coast for almost 25 miles to Hau'ula. Turn left (mauka/toward the mountain) onto Hau'ula Homesteads Road (just across the highway from Hau'ula Beach Park.) Go about 0.5 mile to the road's end. There is crowded parking for two or three cars at the trailhead.

The Hike

Walk up the road past a gate; the road on your right that curves sharply uphill is a private driveway. At about 0.1 mile pass the signed trailhead for the Hau'ula Loop Trail on the right (northwest). Continue on the road another 0.1 mile to the Ma'akua Ridge Trailhead sign on the left (southeast).

Cross the rocky creekbed through a hau thicket and begin climbing moderately steep switchbacks, sometimes squishing through ripe mangos fallen from the trees overhead. You will come to one switchback that overlooks the ocean, just past a sheltered picnic table shaded by trees. Continue climbing to the next switchback, where you will find the beginning of the loop part of the trail.

You can hike the loop in either direction; it's described here in a counterclockwise direction. Continue up along the switchbacks to the right (south). This trail is steeper, rockier, and narrower than the Hau'ula Loop Trail across the gulch to the north. Crunch through the long hala leaves on the trail, and watch for orange passion fruit hanging from vines. Their gaudy purple flowers won't necessarily make you passionate, but their various parts are said to symbolize the passion of Christ. Too bad it's an invasive weed.

You gain the high point of this hike on a ridge at 800 feet in about 1 mile. Descend from the ridge carefully on a crumbly, narrow trail to wade a gulch at its base. Be sure to pause to admire the spectacular huge red African tulip tree flowers against the silvery crowns of the kukui nut trees.

Where the trail crosses the streambed in the gulch watch for the switchback heading up to the left to stay on the trail. It's easy to miss. Follow a very narrow ridge and cross over into the next gulch to the south. You'll have to duck under lots of low branches here. Work your way around the south side of the ridge, dropping little by little, then more quickly on switchbacks. The trail becomes grassy as you go through more open places in the foliage, where you'll find a lovely patch of ulei, a shrub in the rose family with small white flowers.

Finally, turn a corner where the trail overlooks the town and the coastline. It looks like you're almost home, but first you have to negotiate one more steep, rocky stretch down into, and back up out of, a gully. Once back on the ridge, pass a scary looking black lava overhang, and shortly beyond find the bench and the junction where you began the loop.

Follow the switchbacks down the hill to the stream crossing and the road, turn right, and return to your car.

Hau'ula town and coast from Ma'akua Ridge

Miles and Directions

0.0 Start where the Hau'ula Homesteads Road is blocked (N21 36.35' / W157 54.52')

0.2 Ma'akua Ridge Trail begins

0.4 Beginning of loop; go right (uphill/south) on switchbacks (N21 36.17' / W157 54.58')

1.0 High point of hike at 800 feet

2.1 Close the loop; start downhill to the right

2.5 Return to the trailhead

53 Ka'ena Point North

Like the hike to Ka'ena Point from the south, this is an easy walk near a beautiful shoreline with tide pools to explore and endangered species of Hawaiian flowers to examine along the way. From December to May you are almost guaranteed sightings of nesting albatross and migrating humpback whales. You can sometimes spot rare Hawaiian monk seals on the rocks. This northern approach to the point is different from the southern one in that off-road vehicles can make it as far as the boundary of the protected area and have left a multitude of scars on the land. The Ka'ena Point Natural Area Reserve at the point is still unspoiled and well worth the trip.

Start: The end of the northern arm of the paved Farrington Highway

Distance: 5 miles out and back

Elevation change: None

Difficulty: Easy

Approximate hiking time: 2 to 3 hours

Trail surface: Dirt road

Seasons: Year-round, but it is best from the beginning of January to mid-April when the albatrosses are nesting and the humpback whales are migrating

Other trail users: Mountain bikers. Four-wheel-drive vehicles can go as far as the last 0.5 mile.

Canine compatibility: Dogs not permitted

Land status: State land and natural area reserve

Nearest town: Wahiawa

Fees and permits: None

Maps: USGS Ka'ena

Trail contact: Hawai'i Division of Forestry and Wildlife; (808) 973-9782; www.hawaiistateparks.org

Special considerations: There is no shade or water on the trail and it can be hot, even with the sea breeze. Take sunscreen and water. Car break-ins are not such a serious problem on the north side as they are at the south Ka'ena trailhead, but do not leave anything in your car anyway.

Finding the trailhead: From Honolulu drive HI 1 (the Lunalilo Freeway) west to HI 2. Take HI 2 toward Wahiawa. Turn west on HI 99 toward Schofield Barracks, then keep left (northwest) on HI 930 (the Farrington Highway). Follow the Farrington Highway to its end. Highway numbers are not prominently displayed, but you will pass Dillingham Airfield on the final leg to the trailhead.

The Hike

You can get to Ka'ena Point by following the terrible "main" dirt road that continues past the trailhead gate, or by following one of the many four-wheel-drive tracks that wind along the beach, or you can follow the shoreline, which is cooler and more scenic, but longer the closer you are to the sea. The distance of 5 miles is measured along the main road.

The cliffs to your left (south) are a thousand shades of green and the sea a thousand shades of blue, with patches of red Hawaiian dirt and white surf in between. There are lots of lava shelves and tide pools, but watch out for sneaky waves while exploring them. Among the tire tracks lots of tough little succulent native beach plants have managed to hang on, and at about mile 2 there is an isolated grove of sisal (agave) plants, like giant lettuces with long skinny flowering stalks sticking up 7 or 8 feet. They are not native, but escapees from cultivation.

At the 2-mile mark the road is finally blocked even to all-terrain vehicles, and especially to dogs, as this is the entrance to the natural area reserve. Please heed the signs and stay on trails. There is so little of this pristine environment left, you won't want to step on anything fragile.

Enter a zone of white sand dunes held in place by carpets of beach naupaka, little blue morning glories, apricot-colored ilima, and the beautiful and endangered 'ohai, a low shrub with outsize red pea-like flowers. There is a clearly defined trail that makes a little loop around the dunes.

Sea arch

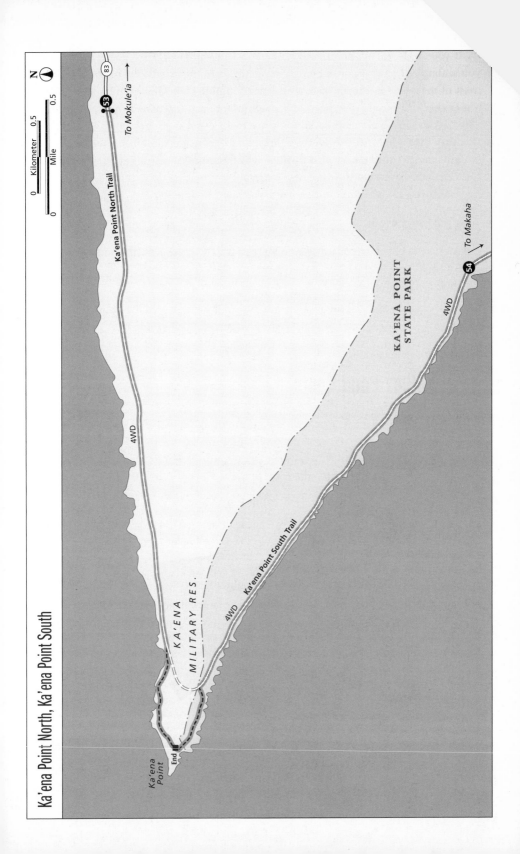

Ka'ena Point North, Ka'ena Point South

re fortunate enough to be here in late winter or early spring, all around the naupaka are nesting Laysan albatross, huge, gull-like birds that spend their lives in the air over open ocean, coming to land only to breed.

At the very point itself, beyond the lighthouse, you can sometimes spot endangered Hawaiian monk seals basking on the rocks—and if you're very lucky indeed you may catch sight of the blow or breach of migrating humpback whales. Even without the exciting fauna, it's a thrill to watch the waves coming toward you from two directions, crashing together below the point.

When you have had enough, retrace your steps to your car.

Miles and Directions

- **0.0** Start where the end of the road is blocked by a gate (N21 34.44' / W158 14.14')
- **2.5** Ka'ena Point (N21 34.30' / W158 16.52')
- **5.0** Return to the trailhead

Option: You can walk all the way around the point if you have a few more hours and a car shuttle. The trail will take you to the southern (Makaha) side of the point.

54 Ka'ena Point South

Don't miss this one. It is an easy walk on a stunning shoreline, with possible sightings of nesting albatross, rare monk seals, and humpback whales. There are endangered species of native Hawaiian flowers, tide pools, and blowholes. The point itself, in native Hawaiian belief, is where the souls of the dead leave earth for the afterworld.

See map on page 185.
Start: End of the paved Farrington Highway on the southern side of Ka'ena Point
Distance: 5 miles out and back
Elevation change: None
Difficulty: Easy
Approximate hiking time: 2 to 3 hours
Trail surface: Dirt road
Seasons: Year-round, but it's best from the beginning of Jan to Apr when the Laysan albatross are nesting and the humpback whales are migrating
Other trail users: Mountain bikers, four-wheel-drive vehicles only at the beginning and end of the trail
Canine compatibility: Dogs not permitted

Land status: Ka'ena Point State Park and Ka'ena Point Natural Area Reserve
Nearest town: Makaha
Fees and permits: None
Maps: USGS Ka'ena
Trail contact: Hawai'i Department of Land and Natural Resources; (808) 973-9782; www.hawaiistateparks.org
Special considerations: According to local police there are daily break-ins of vehicles at the trailhead, even though it is patrolled as frequently as the authorities can manage. Better to park an extra 0.5 mile farther back down the highway, near the lifeguard station. Leave nothing in your car.

Finding the trailhead: From Honolulu take HI 1 northwest all the way past Kapolei, where HI 1 becomes HI 930 (the Farrington Highway). Follow the Farrington Highway to where the pavement ends.

The Hike

Your hike begins at the foot of the cliff upon which squats a white object that looks like Paul Bunyan's golf ball—it's actually one of the domes of the nearby military satellite tracking station. There is no sign or official trailhead here, just the end of the pavement. The hillside mauka (toward the mountain) is mostly covered with koa haole and other dry scrubby plants. Makai (toward the sea) is one of the most wild and wonderful shorelines ever. Clear, turquoise water breaks into waves that thrash the rugged black lava cliffs. There are blowholes and sea arches and endless tide pools filled with sea creatures. (If you choose to explore some of these, stay alert for big waves that can sneak up on you.)

As you hike along the dirt road, a red and white lighthouse appears on the point, and you'll notice underfoot a series of railroad ties, all that's left of a railroad that used to run all the way around the point. At about 0.7 mile, you reach the rockslide that closed the road that replaced the old railroad. A sign warns that the trail is closed ahead due to hazardous conditions, though nobody pays any attention to it. A trail has been worn through the fallen rock, and at one point a couple of sturdy boards span a broken section of the cliff with good lava handholds. There's a lava tube here too, where molten rock flowed under the ground and out into the sea.

Nesting albatross and chick

When you enter Ka'ena Point Natural Area Reserve, at about 2.2 miles, please heed the signs and stay on trails. There is so little of this pristine environment left. You enter a zone of white sand dunes held in place by carpets of beach naupaka, native blue morning glories, apricot-colored ilima, and the beautiful and endangered 'ohai. A clearly defined trail makes a little loop around the dunes at the point.

If you are fortunate enough to be on the point in late winter or early spring you will see nesting Laysan albatross, huge, gull-like birds that spend most of their lives over the open ocean, coming to land only to breed. At the point itself, beyond the lighthouse, you can sometimes spot endangered Hawaiian monk seals basking on the rocks. If you're very lucky you can catch a sight of migrating humpback whales. Even without the wildlife, it's a thrill to watch the waves crashing together below the point.

When you have had enough, or more likely, run out of time, retrace your steps to your car.

Miles and Directions

0.0 Start where the pavement ends (N21 33.22' / W158 14.55')

0.7 Rockslide

2.2 Ka'ena Point Natural Area Reserve boundary

2.5 Ka'ena Point (N21 34.30' / W158 16.52')

5.0 Retrace your steps to the trailhead

Options: You can also walk all the way around the point if you have a few more hours and a car shuttle, winding up on the northern (Mokule'ia) side of the point.

Kaua'i: The Garden Island

Kaua'i, the Garden Island, is the oldest of the four major Hawaiian Islands, though at five to six million years old, it's still a baby in geologic terms. Its longer exposure to wind and rain has weathered the island's bare lava into soil, so more green things can grow. That's why it's the lushest and most garden-like of all the islands. Another reason is that the trade winds bring an average of 450 inches of rain each year to Mount Wai'ale'ale near its center, making it the wettest place on earth. Beneath Mount Wai'ale'ale is the Alaka'i Swamp. The layer upon layer of lava created by the single gigantic volcano that built Kaua'i is so dense that water does not drain away but collects in the swamp, creating an environment where only very specialized organisms can survive. Kaua'i is also unique in having several navigable rivers. On the other islands the lava is more porous so that rainwater percolates right through, and even in an environment with lots of rain, water must be carefully conserved.

The windward cliffs of the Na Pali Coast have eroded into sharp ridges and valleys where rainwater is funneled back into the sea as on other islands, but here some of the rock layers are so resistant that streams flowing down from the crest cannot cut through them and shoot out over the cliff edge in lacy waterfalls. This impervious lava on Kaua'i also explains its relatively high elevation. It is higher than its neighbor O'ahu because its hard rock makes it more resistant to erosion. Mosquitoes cannot survive in the higher and cooler mountains, so Kaua'i has lost fewer of its native bird species to the introduced mosquito-borne diseases that have been partly responsible for decimating bird populations on other islands.

The ruggedness of the cliffs and the torrential rainfall, which add so much to the beauty of this island, have also made road building and other development expensive and impractical. Thus there is more unspoiled wilderness here, more habitat for rare Hawaiian plants, insects, and birds than on the other islands.

What the rainfall means for hikers is that Kaua'i trails are often slippery and messy. Kauai's famous red dirt is used to dye the genuine "Red Dirt T-shirts" for sale all over Hawai'i. This stuff turns to slippery slimy clay when it is wet, and on the windward side of the island it is almost always wet. Puddles and slick roots and boulders are a fact of life here, so hiking poles, caution, and expendable clothing are recommended.

Kaua'i Overview

Those spectacular knife-edged ridges, cliffs, and deep canyons also mean lots of steep ups and downs for hikers, and many trails along the cliffs are narrow with lots of exposure, not for those who are afraid of heights. The rainfall and narrow canyons also make stream crossings problematic if flash floods are expected, or more likely unexpected.

Probably the most well known of Kauai's trails are the Kalalau Trail along the Na Pali Coast and Waimea Canyon, the Grand Canyon of the Pacific, places that every hiker who comes to Hawai'i hopes to experience. Both are worth all the superlatives bestowed on them, but you must be physically fit and well prepared. Neither one of them is kid stuff.

The other main center for hiking on Kaua'i is Koke'e State Park. There are trails for every age and level of conditioning, and it is cooler and less buggy here at 4,000 feet than elsewhere on the island. The park museum (open 10:00 a.m. to 4:00 p.m. daily) is one of the best sources of trail information, maps, and books on the whole island. Koke'e State Park has housekeeping cabins and camping operated by a concessionaire. For information on accommodations contact Koke'e Lodge at Koke'e State Park, P.O. Box 367, Waimea, HI 96796; (808) 335-6061; www.thelodgeatkokee.net. There is also a restaurant that serves breakfast and lunch.

There are some excellent trails near the island's capital, Lihue, as well.

The best map for getting around Kaua'i is published by the University of Hawai'i Press. For hikers, the *Recreation Map of Eastern Kaua'i* published by Hawaii's Division of Forests and Wildlife (DOFAW) is useful. Send a cashier's check or money order for $6 to the DOFAW at 3060 Eiwa Street, Room 306, Lihue, HI 96766, or pick one up in person. The *Northwest Kaua'i Recreation Map,* published by Earthwalk Press, covers the Na Pali Coast and Koke'e and Waimea State Parks, where most of the hiking on Kaua'i is concentrated. It is a good supplement to USGS topographic maps, which are often out of date. This island has experienced so much flooding, exacerbated by steep cliffs and soil denuded by goats, that trails frequently have to be rebuilt and rerouted, and the USGS can't keep up.

As on all of the Hawaiian Islands, if you do not live here, you simply must rent a car in order to access most trails. There is bus service, but it is not of much use to hikers. It is easy to rent a car in Lihue at the airport, but on weekends in summer, a reservation is a must.

Cheap lodging is hard to come by on Kaua'i too. There are several campgrounds run by the Kaua'i Department of Parks and Recreation, for which you will need a permit. You can sometimes get one from a park ranger at the site, or pick one up at the County of Kaua'i Department of Public Works, 4444 Rice Street, Room 150 Lihue, HI 96766, or send for an application by mail. The phone number is (808) 241-6671. Camping in state parks, which includes backcountry camping, also requires a permit. You can apply for one of these by mail at the Hawai'i Department of Land and Natural Resources, Division of State Parks, 3060 Eiwa Street, Room 306, Lihue, HI 96766; (808) 274-3444. Camping permits are not available online.

55 Nounou Mountain (Sleeping Giant) East

The Sleeping Giant is the distinctive mountain behind Kapa'a and Wailua. The high (southernmost) point is his forehead, the next point to the north is his chin. The trail climbs up to his thighs and torso, makes a sharp turn, and goes up to his chest, where you can end the hike at a picnic spot or scramble all the way up to the summit. It offers great views and a good steady workout. It's popular with locals and tourists because it's so convenient to the Coconut Coast. Midday is hot so it's best in the morning and late afternoon.

Start: Nounou Mountain East Trailhead
Distance: 3.6 miles out and back
Elevation change: 1,150 feet
Difficulty: Moderate
Approximate hiking time: 2 to 3 hours
Trail surface: Well-maintained lava with one or two eroded spots; the last few hundred yards are a steep scramble
Seasons: Year-round
Other trail users: None

Canine compatibility: Dogs permitted
Land status: Nounou State Forest Reserve
Nearest town: Wailua
Fees and permits: None
Maps: USGS Kapa'a, or the Kauai Recreation Map, available from the Hawai'i Division of Forestry and Wildlife
Trail contact: Hawai'i Department of Land and Natural Resources; (808) 274-3433; www.hawaiitrails.org

Finding the trailhead: From the Lihue Airport turn right (north) onto HI 51, the first street after you leave the airport. In 1.5 miles HI 51 turns into HI 56 (the Kuhio Highway). Continue north for 4 more miles, crossing the Wailua River and passing the now abandoned Coco Palms Resort, to Halelilo Road at a traffic light. Turn mauka (toward the mountain) and drive a little over 1 mile to an inconspicuous parking area on the right. It's just before the road makes a turn to the left and is marked with a trail sign.

The Hike

The trail starts to the right (east) of the parking lot. Climb up a little ridge shaded by ironwood. Before the climb gets serious, notice the small tree on the right with its succulent leaves covered in graffiti. It's called an autograph tree because writing on its leaves is more or less permanent. Begin a set of switchbacks lined with koa haole shrubs that shade the trail, but also block the cooling trade winds. The trail was originally marked every quarter mile, but only a few of these low metal markers remain.

The trail is clear and easy to follow, except for a couple of scrambles over big rocks. You'll see lots of bare spots where hikers have cut the switchbacks. In one or

Trail to the Sleeping Giant's head ▶

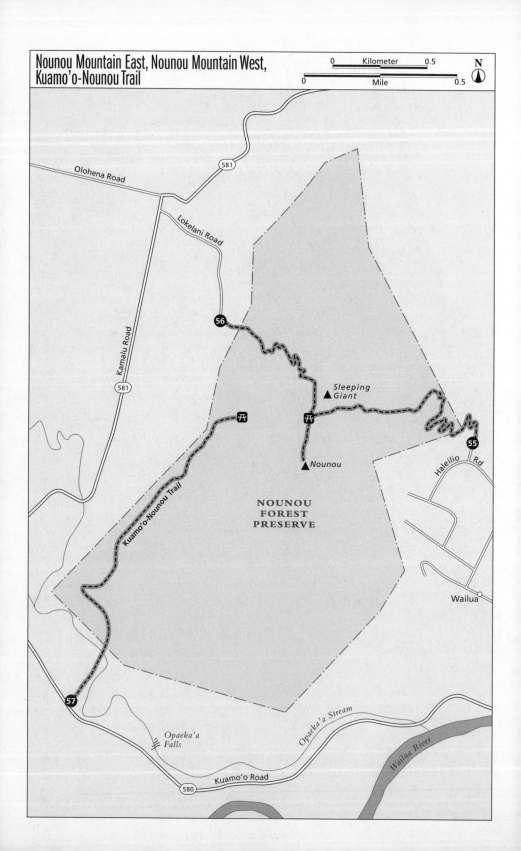

Kilometer

0   0.5

0   Mile   0.5

N

Olohena Road

581

Lokelani Road

Kamalu Road

581

56

Sleeping Giant

▲

Nounou ▲

55

Haleilio Rd

Kuamo'o-Nounou Trail

NOUNOU FOREST PRESERVE

Wailua

57

Opaeka'a Falls

Opaeka'a Stream

Wailua River

Kuamo'o Road

580

two places the trail has become so badly eroded by shortcuts that it is hard to find. Please don't add to the damage.

After about 0.5 mile the grade levels out and even drops a bit, but not for long. The switchbacks resume and the trail swings south, climbing through strawberry guava to wonderful views of the jagged Anahola Mountains to the north, then crossing to the west side of the ridge to present equally fine views of the Makaleha Mountains to the west. After a few more switchbacks you come to a badly eroded red dirt patch. Go slowly here, keeping an eye out for the spot where the trail resumes, upward and to the right, then pause to notice how you got up so you won't get confused coming back down.

At 1.5 miles reach a junction with the Nounou Trail West, which comes in from the right (north). The sign is low and easy to miss. Keep climbing and follow a few more switchbacks to a flat grassy area with shaded, much battered picnic tables. The Sleeping Giant's head is hidden from you here, as are the best views, but you can walk around the hilltop and peer through the foliage to find them.

If you have no head for heights, turn around here. The rest of the way up is steep, requiring hands and feet now and then, and is dangerously slippery when wet. If you decide to continue, follow the trail down the far side of the grassy picnic area. Go through a little dip, cross a narrow windy ridge, then scramble up a steep path . . . hardly a trail . . . to the giant's chin. Another narrow ridge and another short, steep grunt takes you to the giant's head at 1,250 feet.

Soak up the panorama of the coastline, the Wailua River, and the mountains, and return the way you came. **Option:** If you have arranged a shuttle, you can descend via the Nounou Mountain West Trail.

Miles and Directions

0.0 Start at the Nounou Mountain East Trailhead (N22 03.40' / W159 20.46')

1.5 Junction with Nounou Trail West; turn left (south) (N22 03.49' / W159 21.14')

1.6 Picnic area

1.8 Summit (N22 03.40' / W159 21.17')

3.6 Return to the trailhead the way you came

56 Nounou Mountain (Sleeping Giant) West

This is the shorter of the two routes to the top of the Sleeping Giant, the distinctive mountain overlooking Kapa'a and Wailua. His forehead is the high, southernmost point, while the next point to the north is his chin. The views on the way up the eastern side are better en route, but it's spectacular from the top no matter how you get there. You can end your hike at a picnic area on the giant's chest, or scramble on up to the summit along a steep, exposed ridge. The route is popular with both locals and tourists because it's so convenient to the Coconut Coast and to the suburbs on the inland side. Midday is hot, so it's best to hike in the morning and late afternoon. If you can arrange a ride or a car shuttle, a climb up one side of the mountain and down the other makes a perfect outing.

See map on page 194.
Start: Nounou Mountain West Trailhead
Distance: 2.4 miles out and back
Elevation change: 810 feet
Difficulty: Moderate
Approximate hiking time: 1.5 to 2.5 hours
Trail surface: Steep, sometimes slippery lava with exposed tree roots
Seasons: Year-round
Other trail users: None

Canine compatibility: Dogs permitted
Land status: Nounou State Forest Reserve
Nearest town: Wailua
Fees and permits: None
Maps: USGS Kapa'a, or the Kauai Recreation Map, available from the Hawai'i Division of Forestry and Wildlife
Trail contact: Hawai'i Department of Land and Natural Resources; (808) 274-3433; www.hawaiitrails.org

Finding the trailhead: From the Lihue Airport turn right (north) onto HI 51. In 1.5 miles HI 51 turns into HI 56 (the Kuhio Highway). Continue north another 4 miles. Just after crossing the Wailua River turn left (mauka/toward the mountain) on HI 580 (Kuamo'o Road). Drive about 3 miles on Kaumo'o Road to HI 581 (Kamalu Road), and turn right. Continue on HI 581 for a little over 2 miles until you reach Lokelani Road. Lokelani is 1 block before you reach a T intersection. Turn right (east) onto Lokelani Street and follow it for about 1 mile, through a housing tract, until it ends at the marked trailhead. There is plenty of space for parking in the lot, but no facilities.

The Hike

From the trailhead sign follow the grassy path left and uphill alongside a pasture. (At least it was still a pasture when this guide was researched. There was lots of construction going on.) The path is wide, passing first through strawberry guava, then into a stand of Cook pines that has been planted along the ridge.

At 0.2 mile meet a junction with the Kuamo'o–Nounou Trail, which rambles along the base of the hills to the southwest. Your route keeps climbing up the ridge-line, then swings right (south) and heads up the giant's torso via switchbacks. There are lots of eroded-out tree roots to negotiate. In another 0.2 mile, what appears to be another unmarked trail crosses this one. Turn left (east).

The trail becomes steeper and more deeply eroded as you climb, but you can use the excuse of admiring the views to rest. You can look out east over Kapa'a to the ocean, across a green valley toward the Makaleha Mountains, or north toward the jagged Anahola peaks.

Climb through one more dark corridor of strawberry guava before meeting the Nounou Mountain East Trail, marked by a low and inconspicuous sign. Turn right (south) and climb up a few more switchbacks to a flat grassy area with covered, somewhat battered picnic tables. The giant's head is hidden from here, but you can see the trail by walking to the other side of the grassy flat and looking south.

If you have no head for heights, enjoy a snack and turn around here. The rest of the way is steep, requiring hands and feet to ascend, and is dangerously slippery when wet. If you continue, follow the trail down the far side of the grassy picnic area through a little dip, cross a narrow windy ridge, then scramble up a steep path to the giant's chin. Another ridge and another short, steep climb takes you to the summit at 1,250 feet.

Soak up the views, then return the way you came. If you have arranged a shuttle, you can descend via the Nounou Mountain East Trail.

Miles and Directions

0.0 Start at Nounou Mountain West Trailhead (N22 04.03' / W159 21.32')

0.2 Junction with Kuamo'o-Nounou Trail; keep left (N22 03.58' / W159 21.23')

0.8 Junction with Nounou Mountain East Trail; turn right (N22 03.49' / W159 21.14')

0.9 Picnic area

1.2 Summit (N22 03.40' / W159 21.17')

2.4 Return to the trailhead

The Sleeping Giant

57 Kuamo'o-Nounou Trail

This is a pleasant ramble through forest along the western base of Nounou Mountain (the Sleeping Giant). You can stop (or turn around) at a covered picnic table overlooking the valley below the misty Makaleha Mountains. Or you can connect with the Nounou Mountain West Trail and finish with a hard push up to the head of the Sleeping Giant. There are a variety of native and introduced flowers to enjoy, and wild fruits to eat. It's a popular hike with locals.

See map on page 194.

Start: Kuamo'o-Nounou Trailhead

Distance: 2.6 miles to the picnic shelter and back; 8.8 miles to the summit of the Sleeping Giant and back

Elevation change: 300 feet to the picnic shelter; 800 feet to the summit

Difficulty: Easy to the picnic shelter; more difficult to the peak

Approximate hiking time: 1 to 3 hours

Trail surface: Fairly smooth footing to the picnic area; steep and rocky from there to the summit

Seasons: Year-round

Other trail users: Cyclists and equestrians

Canine compatibility: Dogs permitted

Land status: Nounou State Forest Reserve

Nearest town: Wailua

Fees and permits: None

Maps: USGS *Kapa'a* or the *Kaua'i Recreation Map,* available from the Hawai'i Division of Forestry and Wildlife

Trail contact: Hawai'i Department of Land and Natural Resources; (808) 274-3433; www.hawaiitrails.org

Finding the trailhead: From the Lihue Airport turn right (north) onto HI 51. In 1.5 miles HI 51 turns into HI 56 (the Kuhio Highway). Continue north for 4 more miles. Just after crossing the Wailua River turn left (mauka/toward the mountain) on HI 580 (Kuamo'o Road). Continue for 2.5 miles, passing the Opaeka'a Falls Overlook on the way. The trailhead is on the right (east) side of the road. It's easy to miss: There is only a small pullout for two to three cars, a small trailhead sign, and an open gate painted yellow at the edge of a field next to a house.

The Hike

Step over the threshold of the yellow gate and walk between private houses and a pasture on a mowed grass path. Drop down into a little gully to cross a creek on a bridge, then turn left (west) at a beautiful white-barked Albizia tree. These big shady trees, with lacy foliage and broad umbrella-shaped tops sprinkled with delicate white flowers, are especially pretty in spring and early summer. It's too bad that they have become serious pests, crowding out native species.

The native hau thicket you'll pass through next has been able to hold its own against the invading Albizia, however. Pass through another open gate, and soon the dense hau forest gives way to dark overarching strawberry guava bushes, another invading species, but one with edible fruit in summer. Climb a rise at 1.3 miles, where you will find a covered picnic table overlooking a valley. Pause to enjoy the view of the mountains beyond before going on, or turn around here.

If you want to climb Nounou Mountain, follow the trail as it swings right and rises and falls, veering right again at a slightly obscure spot to pass a lonely clump of bamboo. Continue ascending and descending gently, occasionally gaining altitude by way of a few switchbacks as you pass in and out of streambeds decorated with an assortment of ferns. Reach the highest point on the trail at 640 feet amid a grove of Cook pines, where a clearing offers another vista. After crossing a few more gullies, you meet the junction with the Nounou Mountain West Trail. You can either retrace your steps to where you began, or you can turn right (east) and head steeply uphill to the summit of Nounou Mountain. The left fork takes you back out into the suburbs and the Nounou Mountain West Trailhead.

Miles and Directions

0.0 Start at the Kuamo'o-Nounou Trailhead (N22 03.00' / W159 21.59')

1.3 Picnic shelter (**Option:** first turnaround point for a total hike of 2.6 miles)

2.2 Junction with Nounou Mountain West Trail; turn right (east) (**Option:** second turnaround point for a total hike of 4.4 miles) (N22 03.58' / W159 21.23')

2.8 Junction with Nounou Mountain East Trail; turn right (south) (N22 03.49' / W159 21.14')

4.4 Summit (N22 03.40' / W159 21.17')

8.8 Return to the trailhead

View of the mountains from the Kuamo'o Trail

58 Kuilau Ridge

The scenery on this hike is drop-dead gorgeous, and since the entire hike is on an old road, you can actually enjoy the scenery while you're walking without slipping on tree roots or falling over slimy rocks. You can combine this hike with the Moalepe Trail, as many people do, but you'll need to have a car at the other end, or time to turn around and come back the same way. If you have time to do only one of the two, this side is the more interesting. When you've finished your hike, you can have a quick dip in the stream to cool off in the Keahua Forestry Arboretum just around the corner.

Start: Kuilau Ridge Trailhead
Distance: 4 miles out and back
Elevation change: 740 feet
Difficulty: Easy
Approximate hiking time: 2 to 3 hours
Trail surface: Abandoned road
Seasons: Year-round, but muddier in winter
Other trail users: Cyclists and horses
Canine compatibility: Leashed dogs permitted
Land status: Lihue-Koloa State Forest Reserve
Nearest town: Wailua
Fees and permits: None

Maps: USGS *Waialeale* and *Kapa'a; Kaua'i Recreation Map* from the Hawai'i Division of Forestry and Wildlife
Trail contact: Hawai'i Department of Land and Natural Resources; (808) 274-3433; www.hawaiitrails.org
Special considerations: Judging from the broken glass often seen at this trailhead, this is a likely spot for your car to be broken into. Leave nothing in your vehicle—or better yet, park just around the corner at the arboretum, which is not quite so isolated.

Finding the trailhead: From the Lihue Airport drive north on HI 56 (the Kuhio Highway) to HI 580 (Kuamo'o Road) in Wailua. The intersection is just after crossing the Wailua River. Turn mauka (toward the mountain) and continue uphill for about 7 miles, through suburbs and semirural areas on narrowing road to the marked trailhead on the right. If you reach the Keahua Forestry Arboretum, you've gone too far. There is room for four or five cars at the trailhead, but no facilities of any kind.

The Hike

There is a good map posted at the trailhead, along with information about how to avoid contributing to the spread of an especially noxious weed called purple plague. There is also a place to brush off your boots before and after your hike to remove any hitchhiking seeds you might have picked up. This plant is a serious bad guy.

Walk up the smooth, well-graded road, ascending gently at first, slightly more steeply later, but never strenuously. There are mileage signs almost every 0.25 mile up. The way is lined with paperbark trees, guavas, kukui nuts, all kinds of ferns and vines and creepers. One especially beautiful vine is a wild sweet potato with perfectly heart-shaped leaves.

Kuilau Ridge, Moalepe Trail

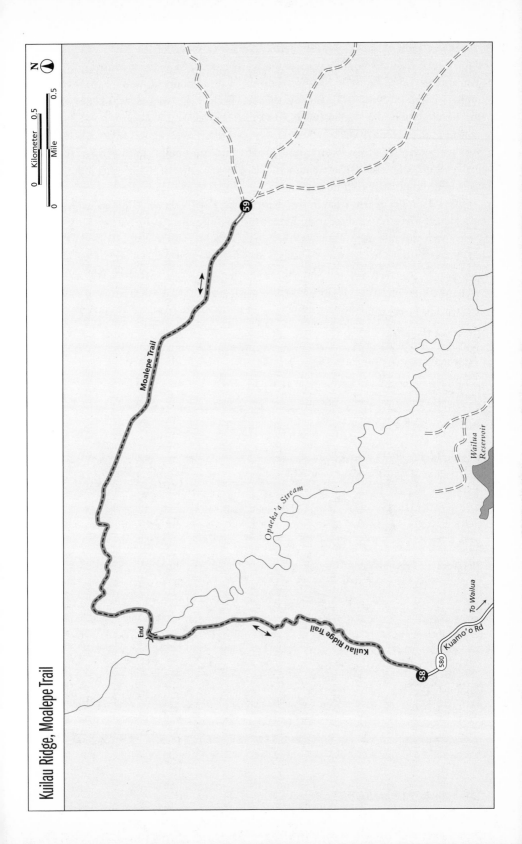

Moalepe Trail

End

Kuilau Ridge Trail

Opaeka'a Stream

Wailua Reservoir

To Wailua

Kuamo'o Rd

580

58

59

N

0 Kilometer 0.5

0 Mile 0.5

As you gain elevation you get better and better views of the Makaleha Mountains, whose tops are almost always obscured by clouds. Among the peaks are Mount Wai'ale'ale, said to be the wettest spot on earth, and Mount Kawaikini (5,243 feet), highest point on Kaua'i. You can usually see back down the valley all the way to the beach, where the Wailua River flows into the sea. You also get a good look at Nounou, the Sleeping Giant, whose slopes also offer several good hikes. All around you are patches of green in an unimaginable variety of colors and textures. As you gain elevation, you see fewer weeds and more Hawaiian natives, like ohia lehua with its bright red powder-puff flowers.

At 1.25 miles reach a flat, mowed picnic area with sheltered picnic tables and spectacular views in all directions. This is the high point of your hike at 1,140 feet. From here, the trail drops down to the northeast a bit, winds around a ridge, rises a bit, and arrives at a bridge over Opaeka'a Stream. This is the official end of the Kuilau Ridge Trail, as a sign will tell you, and is also the end of the Moalepe Trail, coming up from the other side of the mountain. You can turn around and go back to your car from here, or you can continue another 2.75 miles to the Moalepe Trailhead.

Miles and Directions

- **0.0** Start (N22 04.16' / W159 24.59')
- **1.2** High point at 1,140 feet
- **2.0** Bridge and end of trail (N22 05.30' / W159 24.44')
- **4.0** Return to trailhead

Meeting of the Kuilau Ridge and Moalepe Trails

59 Moalepe Trail

This trail meets the Kuilau Ridge Trail just below a ridgetop. Since the two trails meet at the same spot, it is a mystery why they are not considered one and the same. At any rate, you can hike this one to the end, then retrace your steps, or continue along the Kuilau Ridge Trail for a longer hike. You will need a car shuttle unless you don't mind walking all the way back, a 10-mile round-trip. If you have to choose between the two routes, the Kuilau Ridge Trail is more scenic.

See map on page 201.
Start: Moalepe Trailhead
Distance: 5.4 miles out and back
Elevation change: 680 feet
Difficulty: Moderate
Approximate hiking time: 2 to 3 hours
Trail surface: Mostly abandoned road
Seasons: Year-round, but may be muddy in winter
Other trail users: Bicyclists and horses

Canine compatibility: Leashed dogs permitted
Land status: Lihue-Koloa State Forest Reserve
Nearest town: Wailua
Fees and permits: None
Maps: *USGS Kapa'a* and *Wai'ale'ale;* the *Kaua'i Recreation Map* from the Hawai'i Division of Forestry and Wildlife
Trail contact: Hawai'i Department of Land and Natural Resources; (808) 274-3433; www.hawaiitrails.org

Finding the trailhead: From Lihue, drive north on HI 56 (the Kuhio Highway) to HI 580 (Kuamo'o Road) in Wailua. The intersection is just after crossing the Wailua River. Turn mauka (toward the mountain) on HI 580, then turn right (north) on HI 581. Go left (west) on Olohena Road and drive to where it makes a sharp right turn and becomes Waipouli Road. Park at a wide spot on the roadside. The trailhead is well marked with a brown and gold sign. Do not leave anything in your car.

The Hike

Head east through a fenced pasture on the dirt road that climbs almost imperceptibly for 1 mile. The shrubs with soft gray foliage and pink flowers beside the trail are downy rose myrtle, unfortunately invasive weeds. You will also find guavas to eat along the way.

The trail narrows and steepens a little, heading directly toward the Makaleha Mountains. There are beautiful views down into the valley to the left (southwest) as well. Pass through a tunnel of shaggy paperbark eucalyptus trees, make one last short climb to an open spot, then descend on a couple of switchbacks down into the Opaeka'a Stream valley, to the little bridge with a sign marking the ends of the Moalepe and Kuilau Ridge Trails.

Miles and Directions

0.0 Start (N22 04.59' / W159 23.03')

2.7 End at bridge (N22 05.70' / W159 24.44')

5.4 Return to trailhead

Options: From the bridge you can return the way you came or continue on the Kuilau Ridge Trail for another 2 miles. If you hike the Kuilua Ridge make sure you have a ride waiting, or you can walk all the way back. Many locals do. You also can continue on up the Kuilau Trail for few minutes to a picnic area with covered tables.

Tree tunnel on the Moalepe Trail

60 Kilauea Lighthouse

Officially named Kilauea Point National Wildlife Refuge, this is a birdwatcher's paradise, as well as a very likely place to see dolphins, turtles, rare monk seals, and even whales. The historic lighthouse on the point and the lovely views up the North Shore are irresistible to photographers. There are interpretive exhibits, docents on duty to answer questions, and, of course, a gift shop.

Start: Refuge entrance kiosk
Distance: 0.5 mile loop
Elevation change: None
Approximate hiking time: 40 minutes, but you can spend several hours in the refuge
Difficulty: Easy
Trail surface: Paved
Seasons: Year-round; whales are present Dec–Apr

Other trail users: None
Canine compatibility: Dogs not permitted
Land status: National wildlife refuge
Fees and permits: Park entrance fee; National Parks passes are accepted
Map: *USGS Anahola,* but none needed
Trail contact: Kaua'i National Wildlife Refuge Complex; (808) 828-1413; www.kilaueapoint.org
Schedule: Open daily 10:00 a.m.–4:00 p.m.

NAUPAKA

Naupaka *(Scaveola* spp.) is a succulent large-leafed shrub with peculiar white flowers that look like they have been torn in half. They are not mutants or damaged however; their lopsided shape is an adaptation for pollinators. There are several versions of the Hawaiian myth that explains how they lost their other halves.

In one account, *naupaka* flowers used to be whole, but a beautiful maiden (it's *always* a beautiful maiden) unfairly accused her lover of being unfaithful, and in her anger, tore a flower in half and told him she would not trust him or speak to him again until he brought her a new, whole one. To punish her, the gods turned all *naupaka* flowers into halves, and the boy died of a broken heart.

There are both mountain species and beach species of naupaka, and another myth has to do with a maiden on a beach being separated from her lover on a mountain, and the gods turning each into a half flower symbolizing their loneliness and grief.

Finding the trailhead: From Lihue drive HI 56 (the Kuhio Highway) for about 26 miles to Kilauea. Turn right (makai/toward the sea) onto Kalu Street at the Shell station. Turn left at the very first block onto Kilauea Road and follow it for 1 mile, passing a scenic overlook on the right. Drive through the gate (no pedestrians allowed) and downhill to a parking area. Just beyond is the entrance kiosk. **GPS:** N22 13.45' / W159 24.09'

The Hike

You'll probably be greeted in the parking lot by a nene or two, Hawaii's rare goose. Do not feed them. Pick up a brochure as you go through the entrance kiosk; the brochure shows you how to identify the birds, when to see them nesting, and when and where to watch for sea mammals.

The ironwoods on the hillside across the little bay are almost obscured by the bodies of thousands of birds, including red-footed boobies and cattle egrets, perched among the branches. Red-tailed and white-tailed tropic birds sometimes sweep past the cliff so closely you can almost touch them. Shearwaters, petrels, and black, pre-historic-looking frigate birds soar overhead, and in winter and early spring, Laysan albatross calmly nest in hollows on the hillside only a few feet away from you.

Don't forget to look for monk seals sunning themselves among the rocks in the bay. They are the same color and smooth texture as the boulders and they don't move much, so they are easy to miss. The paved path that follows the cliff edge is lined with naupaka and other Hawaiian native plants. You can examine the little lighthouse near the point up close, and check out the exhibits in the structure behind it before returning to the parking lot.

Red-tailed tropic bird

61 Hanalei-Okolehao Trail

Fabulous views of Hanalei Bay, the Makaleha Mountains, and, weather permitting, one of the longest waterfalls you've ever seen are your rewards for toiling up this muddy and precipitous path. You climb toward the Makaleha Mountains, which culminate in Mount Wai'ale'ale, the wettest place on earth—though it is very unlikely you will see it. Long, long Namolokama Fall is the source of the Wai'oli Stream on the north side of the ridge, and the Hanalei River flows down the other side into the bay. The lower part of the trail is an old road, while the upper part doesn't even show on the topo map, but it's obvious and easy to follow.

Start: The cemetery off Ohiki Road near the Hanalei River
Distance: 3.6 miles out and back
Elevation change: 1,100 feet
Difficulty: Strenuous
Approximate hiking time: 2 to 3 hours
Trail surface: Eroded, slippery lava on the upper trail; dirt road lower down
Seasons: Year-round, but avoid when it's raining
Other trail users: None
Canine compatibility: Dogs permitted
Land status: Hanalei National Wildlife Refuge/ Halelea Forest Reserve
Nearest town: Hanalei
Fees and permits: None
Maps: USGS *Hanalei* (which does not show the trail); Earthwalk Press's *Northwestern Kaua'i Recreation Map* (which does)
Trail contact: Hawai'i Department of Land and Natural Resources; (808) 274-3433; www.hawaiitrails.org
Special considerations: This trail can be slippery, narrow, and dangerous in the rain. There is no water.

Finding the trailhead: From Lihue drive HI 56 north, then west about 33 miles to where the road descends a switchbacking hill to a bridge over the Hanalei River. Immediately after crossing the bridge, turn left (mauka/toward the mountain) on an unmarked dirt road. After you've turned you'll see a sign that says DEAD END. Drive about 0.5 mile to another unmarked dirt road going right (west/uphill), and follow it to its end at a little cemetery.

The Hike

Start at what looks like the continuation of the road below the cemetery, heading eastward. Boards with wire mesh have been installed and grass seed planted to keep the road from washing away and to make hiking easier. It's a fairly steep climb on the road among a mixture of native koa trees and introduced eucalyptus and grevillea (silk oak) to a level patch with a power pole where the beautiful view is marred by power lines. Don't be discouraged, though. Photo opportunities will improve.

The road shrinks down to trail, marked by plastic ribbon, and the way gets steeper and trickier as you climb, picking your way among tree roots. You might need to use your hands on the worst parts.

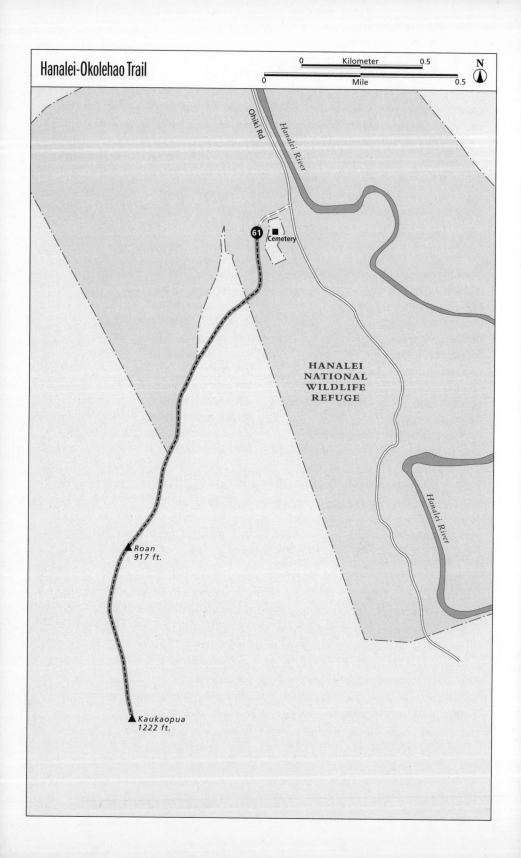

Follow the narrow ridge that runs between the Hanalei River and Wai'oli Stream, enjoying lots of places where you can get wonderful views of Hanalei Bay and river and the beautiful raggedy mountains toward the Na Pali Coast. In some places dense ferns and grasses almost obscure the trail. At 1.2 miles you come to a flat spot marked ROAN 917 on the topo, where you can catch your breath and scan the cliffs ahead for waterfalls. After a final muddy scramble, you reach the high point at Kauka'opua, 1,272 feet, where you'll find a benchmark. Don't try to go any farther as the trail disappears in the brush. Slip and slide back to your car.

Miles and Directions

0.0 Start at cemetery (N22 12.11' / W159 28.29')

1.2 Roan 917

1.8 Kauka'opua (N22 11.06' / W159 28.47')

3.6 Return to the trailhead

Hanalei Bay from Hanalei-Okolehao Trail

62 Limahuli Garden and Preserve

This wonderful garden beneath Na Pali cliffs is one of five national tropical botanical gardens in Hawai'i, chartered by Congress in 1976 to promote research and education, and preserve ecosystems and cultural knowledge. It's a good place to learn about some of the things you'll see along Kauai's trails and roadsides—not just their names, but their uses and the Hawaiian myths and legends associated with them. A loop trail winds through a beautiful setting along Limahuli Stream, with some photogenic ocean views as backdrops to the flowers. There is a collection of extremely rare species, some of which are almost extinct in the wild, the most interesting of which is the celebrated Brighamia, the wonderful "cabbage on a baseball bat."

Start: Garden visitor center
Distance: 0.8-mile loop
Approximate hiking time: 1 hour or less
Elevation change: 200 feet
Difficulty: Easy
Trail surface: Smooth easy gravel or pavement
Seasons: Year-round
Other trail users: None
Canine compatibility: Dogs not permitted
Land status: Private
Nearest town: Hanalei
Fees and permits: The fee includes a wonderful illustrated booklet, worth the price of admission alone. You can sign up for a private tour too.
Map: *USGS Haena;* map at the back of the booklet included in your admission
Trail contact: Limahuli Garden and Preserve; (808) 826-1053; www.ntbg.org
Schedule: Open 9:30 a.m.–4:00 p.m. daily except Mon and Sat
Special considerations: No food or drinks allowed on trails. Water is provided at several spots along the hike.

Finding the trailhead: From Lihue drive HI 56 (the Kuhio Highway, which becomes HI 560 in Hanalei after 39 miles) almost to its end. The garden is on the left (mauka/toward the mountain) side of the road, just before Ha'ena State Park. It has its own parking lot away from the crowds and protected from vandalism. There are bathrooms and water at the visitor center. **GPS:** N22 13.10' / W159 34.31'

The Hike

The walk starts beneath a beautiful big breadfruit tree in front of the visitor center, then wanders up along Limahuli Stream through terraces planted with taro and other plants used by the early (and some contemporary) Hawaiians. Part of the trail passes through native Hawaiian forest, and another section is devoted to threatened species, of which Hawai'i has more than its share. There is a separate section of introduced species, with information about how they got to Hawai'i. You might be surprised to learn that bananas, coconuts, mangos, guava, and sugarcane, among others, are not native Hawaiian plants at all, but were brought here for food, medicines, and tools by the early Hawaiians, or as ornamental plantings by later immigrants from Asia, Europe, and the Americas.

There is a re-creation of a typical garden from the sugar plantation era, a preserved archeological site, and a broad viewpoint with a vista of the ocean in one direction and dramatic Mount Makana in the other. This is a good spot to rest and to read about some of the local legends and traditions of the region in the little guide book.

The loop trail brings you back to the visitor center at the big breadfruit tree where you began.

Extremely rare Brighamia, the cabbage on a baseball bat

63 Hanakapi'ai Beach

This very popular hike gives you a 2-mile sample of the Kalalau Trail along the famous Na Pali Coast. The entire Kalalau Trail continues for another 9 challenging miles to its end at Kalalau Beach, but here is an opportunity to experience a bit of the route without lugging a backpack or applying for the permit that is required if you want to hike beyond Hanakapi'ai Stream. It is more challenging than you think, though it's well worth the effort. Hanakapi'ai Beach is especially fun in summer, with a natural shallow paddling pool separated from the sea by a sandbar next to where pretty Hanakapi'ai Stream flows out of the forest into the ocean.

Start: Kalalau Trailhead at Ke'e Beach
Distance: 4 miles out and back
Elevation change: 400 feet
Difficulty: Moderate
Approximate hiking time: 2 to 4 hours
Trail surface: Rough, muddy, and slippery
Seasons: Year-round
Other trail users: None
Canine compatibility: Leashed dogs are allowed on state park trails, but not on beaches
Land status: Ha'ena State Park
Nearest town: Hanalei
Fees and permits: None for a day hike
Maps: *USGS Ha'ena;* the *Northwestern Kaua'i Recreation Map* by Earthwalk Press

Trail contact: Hawai'i Division of State Parks; (808) 274-3444; www.ehawaii.gov, www.hawaiistateparks.org
Special considerations: The going is steep and slippery, and it rains a lot. Wear good shoes and old clothes. Carry plenty of water because it can be hot, even when raining, and the stream water is not potable. Hanakapi'ai Stream is subject to flash flooding. If it has been raining hard and steadily for a long time, or if the water looks muddy or you can hear rocks tumbling along the bottom, do not try to cross. Do not leave anything in your car at this trailhead. In fact, if you can manage to get a ride, don't leave your car at the trailhead at all.

Finding the trailhead: From Lihue drive HI 56 (the Kuhio Highway, which becomes HI 560 at Hanalei) for 41 miles—all the way to its end at Ha'ena State Park. The trailhead is across the street on the left (south). There is a parking lot and some space to park on the street, but it fills up very early. There are restrooms and water near the parking area.

The Hike

The trail starts at a rain shelter where muddy hikers who have just finished the trail wait for rides or for slower companions to catch up. You immediately begin a slippery, rocky climb that seems to be designed to discourage inexperienced, undercondi-tioned hikers from going any farther. (It doesn't.) It often rains here, and sometimes it pours, but you probably won't mind a cooling shower as you labor up the slope. The trail is shaded by hala, with its peculiar stilt roots and spirally arranged long leaves. These are used all over the South Pacific to make everything from floor mats to hats. You will also see ironwood, which resembles a pine, but is not related.

As you climb, be sure to look behind you back down to Ke'e Beach, which becomes more spectacular at every turn with its turquoise sea, white sand, and green tropical foliage—everybody's daydream of paradise. In about 1 mile you reach the highest point on the hike at 400 feet, where the view up the coastline to the north is probably one of the most famous in the world. It is extremely windy, so hang on to your headgear. There must be a huge pile of hats and visors at the base of the cliff, snatched away from hikers' heads by sudden gusts.

Begin the descent toward Hanakapi'ai Beach where a yellow-and-black painted pole marks the highest level a tsunami, or tidal wave, is likely to reach. Warning siren boxes all along the coast howl if a tsunami is predicted so you can get to higher ground. Another set of signs warns you about the dangers of swimming in the ocean at Hanakapi'ai Beach. The currents there are powerful and deadly. Yet another sign with notches cut in the wood keeps count of the number of people who have been killed on the beach so far. It is safe to swim in the lagoon inside the sandbar that forms during the summer months, but stay out of the surf.

Negotiate the steep rocky scramble down to the stream, which you will have to ford in order to reach the best part of the beach and the camping area. Do not cross if there is any threat of flash flooding, like brown water or rolling rocks. If you are nimble you can rock hop across the stream, but the rocks are rounded and slick with algae. Wading is safer.

Once on the west side you'll find some lovely camping and picnic sites below a jumble of round lava boulders overlooking the beautiful bay. If the tide is low you can

Lagoon and cave at Hanakapi'ai Beach

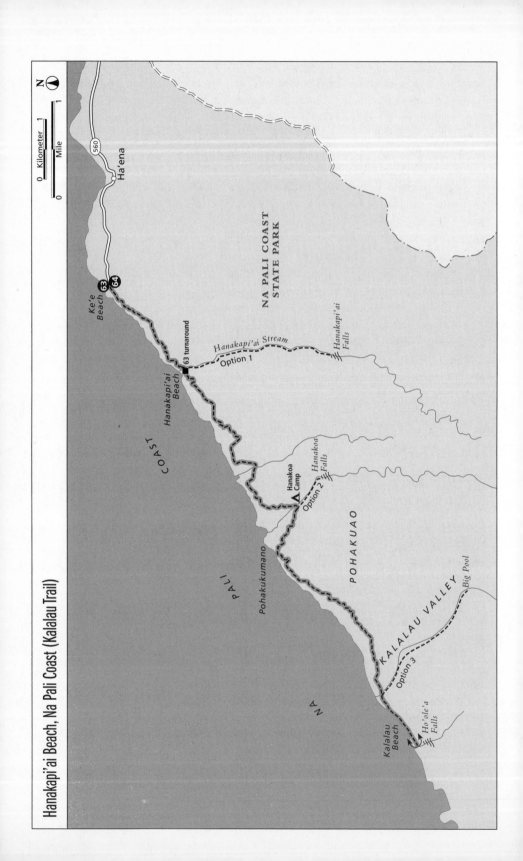

Hanakapi'ai Beach, Na Pali Coast (Kalalau Trail)

walk along the beach northward to a lava tube that cuts clear though the rock and out again into the ocean. Both big and little kids love this spot. Upstream a short distance on the west bank is a lua (toilet). Return the way you came.

Miles and Directions

0.0 Start at Kalalau Trailhead (N22 13.13' / W159 34.58')

2.0 Hanakapi'ai Beach (N21 12.30' / W159 35.51')

4.0 Return to the trailhead

Option: If you have time and energy to spare, you can add an additional 4-mile round-trip to your hike by following Hanakapi'ai Stream for 2 miles to 300-foot Hanakapi'ai Falls. The first mile along the south bank isn't too difficult, though poorly marked. You will have to cross the stream at 1 mile; the rest of the trail is vague and slippery and difficult, though there are several pretty pools along the way to cool off in.

64 Na Pali Coast (Kalalau Trail)

Probably the most famous hike in Hawai'i, this trail follows the fabled coast whose cliffs and waterfalls have been the backdrop for countless movies. For the fit and well-prepared hiker, it is the experience of a lifetime. It has beauty beyond description, tropical fruit to pluck from the trees, soft breezes, waving palms, dolphins playing offshore, all that romantic stuff. But . . . it is not an easy trail. It's strenuous and slippery and steep, and dangerously eroded in places. There can be riptides, flash floods, scorpions and centipedes, clouds of mosquitoes, broiling heat or pouring rain. You simply must be in excellent physical condition, know what to bring with you, and prepared to deal with Mother Nature on her own terms to hike the whole route. Not everybody makes it all the way. Fortunately, you can break the trip into shorter segments; there are campsites at Hanakapi'ai Beach (2 miles), at Hanakoa (6 miles), and at Kalalau Beach (11 miles at trail's end).

See map on page 214.
Start: Kalalau Trailhead
Distance: 22.4 miles out and back
Approximate hiking time: 2 to 4 days
Elevation change: Net gain is less than 1,000 feet, but the total is more like 5,000 feet, counting all the ups and downs
Difficulty: Strenuous
Trail surface: Mud, rocks, roots
Seasons: Year-round, but in winter expect more rain, wind, and mud. Winter ocean currents wash away the sandy beaches, leaving only rocky shorelines. In spring the sea and the winds change course and sand is redeposited.
Other trail users: None
Canine compatibility: Leashed dogs are allowed on state park trails, but not on beaches, so leave four-footed friends at home
Land status: Ha'ena State Park / Na Pali Coast State Wilderness Park

Nearest town: Hanalei
Fees and permits: Permits are required for overnight stays and for day hikes beyond Hanakapi'ai Beach. See sidebar.
Maps: *USGS Ha'ena; Northwestern Kaua'i Recreation Map* by Earthwalk Press
Trail contact: DLNR; (808) 274-3444; www.hawaiistateparks.org
Special considerations: Trailhead car vandalism is a serious problem. Your car might be broken into even if you have left nothing inside. You can probably park safely at the trailhead for the duration of a day hike, but don't even consider leaving your car at the trailhead overnight. Arrange to leave your vehicle wherever you are staying, with a friend, or, for a small fee, at Kayak Kauai in Hanalei, then take a cab to the trailhead. The cost is well worth it.

Finding the trailhead: From Lihue drive HI 56 (the Kuhio Highway, which becomes HI 560 at Hanalei) for 41 miles all the way to its end at Ha'ena State Park. The trailhead is across the street, on the left (south). There is a parking lot and space to park on the street, but if you're smart, you'll leave your car somewhere else and get a ride to the trailhead. Unless you get there by 9:00 a.m., there will be no parking spaces left anyway. Again, leave absolutely nothing in your car if you do park at or near the trailhead.

The Hike

The trail starts at a shelter where muddy hikers who have just returned wait out of the rain for rides or for slower companions to catch up. Begin with a slippery, rocky climb that seems to be designed to discourage inexperienced, under-conditioned hikers from going any farther. The first 2 miles, to Hanakapi'ai Beach, are very busy. You will be happy to learn that this is one of the roughest sections of the trail. It does

▶ **Be sure to stay on the trail. This is a tough hike and there is no help available if you are injured. Carry lots of water, and purify all stream water. A tent is highly recommended. It does rain and there are mosquitoes and centipedes and other creepy crawlies. Heed the warning signs about dangers like riptides and flash flooding. There are lots of injuries here, no fooling!**

get easier. The trail is shaded by hala with its peculiar stilt roots, and ironwood. The view back down to Ke'e Beach, everyone's daydream of paradise, becomes more spectacular at every turn.

It often sprinkles, and sometimes pours, on this first section of trail because of the orientation of this part of the coast, but the weather gradually improves after you leave Hanakapi'ai. By the time you have passed Hanakoa, it will probably be hot and dry. You might be thankful for a cooling shower anyway, as you puff your way up to the highest point between the trailhead and Hanakapi'ai at 400 feet. The view up the coast from this spot is one of the most famous in the world. It is also extremely windy, so hang on to your hat.

Begin the descent toward Hanakapi'ai Beach where a yellow-and-black painted pole marks the highest level a tsunami, or tidal wave, can reach. Warning siren boxes all along the coast howl if a tsunami is predicted. Another set of signs warns you about the dangers of swimming at Hanakapi'ai Beach; yet another sign with notches cut in the wood keeps count of the number of people who have been killed there so

PERMIT PROCESS

If you plan to stay overnight in Ha'ena State Park or day-hike beyond Hanakapi'ai Beach, a permit is required. You can (and should) apply one year in advance because there are quotas. You can apply for your permit by mail or call the Hawai'i Department of Land and Natural Resources (DNLR) and ask for an application form. Contact the DNLR at 3060 Eiwa Street, Room 306, Lihue, HI 96766; (808) 274-3444; www.ehawaii.gov.

The permit process is complicated, and changes in permit procedures are planned. As of 2009 you'll need to send the DLNR the dates you want; your name, address, and phone number; where you plan to spend the night (at Hanakapi'ai, Hanakoa, and/or Kalalau); and the names of everyone hiking with you. You must also send everyone's driver's license, Social Security, or passport numbers. You cannot stay more than one night at a time at Hanakapi'ai or Hanakoa. There is a nominal fee per person per night of camping; permits are limited to five consecutive nights total on the coast. Group size is limited to five.

From Memorial Day to Labor Day, one third of the permits are made available twenty-eight days or less before you plan to camp, but they go fast. You must get them in person at the DLNR's Division of State Parks office in Lihue. During the busy summer months, one third of the permits are issued on a first-come, first-served basis, but you must apply in person at the state parks office exactly twenty-eight days before your trip. If you wait until the twenty-seventh day before you want to camp, you can apply in person at any district office on any of the islands. For more information on permits, visit www.hawaiistateparks .org Na Pali park site. To check on availability of permits, call (808) 587-0300. The Kaua'i office is open 8:00 a.m.–3:30 p.m. Mon–Fri.

far. It is safe to swim in the lagoon inside the sandbar that forms during the summer months, but stay out of the surf.

Negotiate the last steep rocky scramble down to the stream, which you will have to ford in order to reach the best part of the beach and the camping area. Do not cross if the water is brown or if you can hear the sound of tumbling rocks underwater! If you are nimble you can rock hop across the stream, but the rocks are rounded and slick with algae. Wading is safer.

Once on the west side you'll find some lovely campsites overlooking the beautiful bay. If the tide is low you can walk along the beach northward to a lava tube that cuts clear through the rock and out again into the ocean. Upstream a short distance, on the west bank, is a lua (toilet). You can also visit Hanakapi'ai Falls, 2 miles mauka (toward the mountain) from the beach.

To continue on the Kalalau Trail, pass just below the pit toilet and turn right (southwest) onto the less obvious of two trails that lead up to a rocky path, beginning a steep, switchbacking climb past enormous swordlike agave plants. At 3.3 miles you reach the Kalalau Trail's highest point at 900 feet. It's marked by a huge boulder whose shade you'll probably be sharing with a few other panting hikers.

The trail winds in and out of several stream valleys, the next one with reliable water at Waiahuakua. Each of these valleys requires some steep up-and-down switchbacking, but you don't drop all the way down to the coast again until near the end at Kalalau. As you descend into Hanakoa Valley, watch your footing. The trail is very narrow and the fallen kukui nuts roll like marbles under your boots. The sight of Hanakoa Falls pouring over the cliff can easily make you forget to pay attention.

Hanakoa Valley, roughly the halfway mark to Kalalau, is sublime. You'll surely want to stay awhile. There are a couple of decrepit shelters on either side of the stream, as well as a lua (toilet). The stream splits into two forks, making the crossing easier than at Hanakapi'ai. There are lovely wading pools at the base of little cascades, big old mango trees, mountain apples, and the remains of terraces where native Hawaiians once grew taro and later haoles grew coffee. There is a sad community of mangy feral cats too, begging for handouts. You'll probably be able to hear the baa-ing of feral goats on the hillsides as well. They are breeding faster than they can be hunted, though one disgruntled native bow hunter complains, "They're too tame. The tourists feed them pizza." They are eating all the native vegetation along with the pizza, contributing to the serious erosion all over Hawai'i and damaging this trail. You can make another side trip from here up to Hanakoa Falls.

Leaving Hanakoa Valley you ascend gradually at first, then drop extremely steeply down to your lowest point on the trail before the end at Kalalau Beach. Toward the low point of this descent is a big stretch of badly eroded red earth. The narrow, slippery trail clings to the cliff side, with a long drop to the ocean below. It's not a route for the faint-hearted. The scary part is only about a 0.5-mile long, but you'll use lots of adrenaline. Here and there the path ducks into a shaded valley with a little stream, each one a great relief from the unrelenting sun.

After 8 miles, cross a pretty stream to Pohakuao, where you'll find a few old terraces and a helipad. It's a good spot for a rest and a drink, as well as for sighting your goal, Kalalau Valley, still 3 miles ahead. Watch for black, prehistoric-looking frigate birds and graceful white tropic birds soaring offshore.

Cross a second branch of Pohakuao Stream and begin another narrow section of trail under usually blistering sunshine. At 8.5 miles look seaward and downhill to two big holes worn completely through the lava cliff. (Just before this you will have passed a spectacular sea arch, but it's easier to spot going the other direction.) A final climb, partly shaded, partly through low prickly lantana bushes, will probably make you feel

◀ *Waterfall at end of Kalalau Trail*

you've had just about enough of this. Then, at last, you'll top a ridge known as Red Hill and gaze into the opening of the incomparable Kalalau Valley. The cliffs above the valley are the most spectacular yet. Concentrate on negotiating the last, bare, slippery, eroded red slope down onto a goat-chewed grassy terrace. If there are no hunters in the area, you will probably see at least twenty goats grazing there.

Descend gently through beach naupaka, then carefully cross Kalalau Stream, with slippery rocks but fairly easy to wade. The trail on the far side is a little obscure, but if you look to the right and uphill you will find it again. Shortly after the stream crossing a spur trail heads left (southeast) up the Kalalau Valley to Big Pool.

The campground is a long flat terrace that extends for almost 1 mile, separated from the sand and the sea by Java plum trees. There are lots of sites with one lua partway along and another at the far end. There are mosquitoes, as well as centipedes and scorpions hiding in the leaf litter. Shoes are advisable, as are tents. Beyond the campground is lovely Ho'ole'a Falls, where you can have a shower. Just be aware that big rocks do get washed over the cliff now and then. Beyond the falls along the perfect beach is the outlet of a big lava tube, a cave where some people like to sleep. Do this at your own risk because the lava is unstable and caves nearby have been closed by rockslides, or simply collapsed, within recent memory. Swimming is tricky because of the strong currents. Kayakers do manage to land here though.

This is your turnaround point. The land beyond Kalalau Beach is kapu.

Miles and Directions

0.0 Start (N22 13.13' / W159 34.58')

2.0 Hanakapi'ai Beach (N21 12.30' / W159 35.51')

3.3 High point of the trail

6.2 Hanakoa Valley (N22 11.27' / W159 37.12')

7.0 Lowest, narrowest, most dangerous section of trail before Kalalau

11.2 Kalalau Beach (N22 10.25' / W159 39.25')

Option 1: Hanakapi'ai Falls. From Hanakapi'ai Beach follow Hanakapi'ai Stream along its south bank for about 1 mile to a stream crossing. For the next mile, the trail is vague, slippery, and difficult, though there are several pretty pools on the way. In 2 miles you reach gorgeous Hanakapi'ai Falls, dropping 300 feet into a pool.

Option 2: Hanakoa Falls. From Hanakoa Valley, follow the left (northern) fork of the stream from its junction above the shelter, and scramble up along its south bank for about 0.3 mile to a beautiful waterfall. There is no official trail.

Option 3: Big Pool. This trail follows the south side of Kalalau Stream, heading up the valley through old Hawaiian agricultural terraces for 2 miles to a popular pool.

65 Awa'awapuhi Trail

One of the most spectacular views of the Na Pali Coast from above lies at the end of this upside-down hike. It was once a nature trail with signposts corresponding to descriptions in a guidebook published by the Division of Forestry and Wildlife, but the guide is no longer available and most of the signposts are gone. This is an easy stroll when the trail is dry, more challenging when wet. It is also one leg of a popular 9-mile semiloop connecting the Nu'alolo Cliff Trail with the Nu'alolo Trail. If it is raining hard, choose another hike. The path is steep and slippery and dangerous, and there won't be views anyway.

Start: Awa'awapuhi Trailhead
Distance: 6.2 miles out and back
Elevation change: 1,600 feet
Difficulty: Moderate
Approximate hiking time: 2 to 4 hours
Trail surface: Well-graded lava
Seasons: Year-round
Other trail users: None
Canine compatibility: Dogs not permitted
Land status: Koke'e State Park and Ku'ia

Natural Area Reserve
Nearest town: Waimea
Fees and permits: None
Maps: USGS *Ha'ena* and *Makaha Point* maps are out of date since trails have been rerouted due to storm damage. The *Northwestern Kaua'i Recreation Map* from Earthwalk Press is more current.
Trail contact: Koke'e Museum; (808) 335-9975; open daily 10:00 a.m. to 4:00 pm.

Finding the trailhead: From the Lihue Airport turn left (south) on HI 51 (the Kapule Highway) to Rice Street. Turn right (northwest) and go through town to HI 50 (the Kaumuali'i Highway). Turn left (west) and drive about 25 miles to Waimea. Turn right (north) onto HI 550 (Waimea Canyon Drive). It's not clearly marked, but if you miss it, continue on to HI 552 (the Koke'e Road), which is clearly marked with a big sign indicating Waimea Canyon and Koke'e State Park. The two roads, 550 and 552, come together after 7 miles. Continue ascending the winding road, passing Koke'e Lodge on your left, to milepost 17. The trailhead and parking area are on the left.

The Hike

The trail begins above 4,000 feet where it is often cloudy, but unless it has been raining long and hard, it usually gets drier as you descend. You begin by climbing a short way, but this doesn't last long. There is a wonderful variety of native and introduced trees and flowers, along with a few sad and battered posts that used to match a guide to this former nature trail. The way is shady and mostly smooth, beneath koa trees and the powder-puff blossoms of ohia lehua, hung with lilikoi vines.

About halfway along there is an opening in the trees affording your first really good view of the coast. Heed the warning signs and stay away from the edge as the cliff is deeply undercut. Listen for birdsong here, too. This is one of the outposts

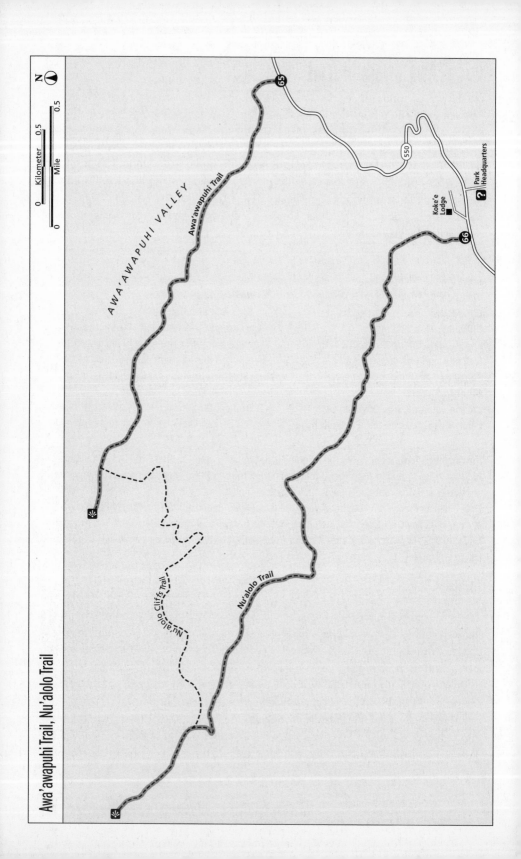
Awa'awapuhi Trail, Nu'alolo Trail

where native honeycreepers like the i'iwi and apapane still survive, since it's too high and cool for their deadliest enemies, disease-carrying mosquitoes.

As you continue to descend the vegetation becomes lower and shrubbier, and the trail gradually narrows until you drop down into a notch on switchbacks. If the trail is muddy use extra caution; dropping down might become more than a figure of speech. Once on level ground, push your way through a thicket of lantana and strawberry guava to the Nu'alolo Cliff Trail junction. An obvious, but unmarked path to the right leads less than 0.25 mile to the overlook of the Nu'alolo Valley on one side and the Awa'awapuhi Valley on the other. Return the way you came.

Miles and Directions

- **0.0** Start (N22 08.27' / W159 38.59')
- **3.1** Trail ends at Nu'alolo Cliff Trail junction (N22 09.07' / W159 40.30'). Follow the short unmarked spur to the viewpoint.
- **6.2** Return to the trailhead

Option: To complete the Nu'alolo Cliff Loop from the end of the Awa'awapuhi Trail, turn left (south) onto the narrower and more exposed Nu'alolo Cliff Trail. It drops steeply to cross Nu'alolo Stream, climbs steeply back out of the valley, then switchbacks down to Nu'alolo Flat and a covered picnic table almost hidden in head-high grass.

Glimpse of the Na Pali Coast from the Awa'awapuhi Trail

Once you leave the flat, the trail becomes very narrow and exposed, and is deadly if wet. Turn around! If it is dry, continue on to the Nu'alolo Trail in 2.2 miles. From the junction, you can turn right (northwest) and follow a spur for 0.5 mile to the Lolo Overlook—also much too dangerous to attempt when wet—or turn left (southeast) and follow the Nu'alolo Trail for 3.2 miles back up to the trailhead at the Koke'e State Park ranger station.

It usually isn't hard to get a ride 2 miles back up the road to your car at the Awa'awapuhi Trailhead. Walking back up the road is discouraged since it is narrow and winding, with blind curves and no shoulder. The entire semiloop, from the Awa'awapuhi Trailhead to the Nu'alolo Trailhead, is 9 miles.

66 Nu'alolo Trail

This popular trail leads to one of the finest views of the Na Pali Coast. It can be combined with the Awa'awapuhi Trail via the Nu'alolo Cliff Trail to make a 9-mile semiloop. It is an upside-down hike, so start early, take plenty of water, and do not overestimate your stamina. Many people find it a struggle to get back up to the trailhead before dark. If it is raining do not go past the Nu'alolo Cliff Trail junction to the viewpoint. It is on a narrow, exposed, slippery ridge, very dangerous if wet.

See map on page 222.
Start: Nu'alolo Trailhead
Distance: 7.4 miles out and back
Elevation change: 1,500 feet
Difficulty: Moderate if dry; strenuous if wet
Approximate hiking time: 3 to 4 hours
Trail surface: Sometimes slippery red dirt
Seasons: Year-round
Other trail users: None
Canine compatibility: Dogs not permitted
Land status: Koke'e State Park and Ku'ia

Natural Area Reserve
Nearest town: Waimea
Fees and permits: None
Maps: USGS Ha'ena and Makaha Point maps are out of date since trails have been rerouted due to storm damage. The Northwestern Kaua'i Recreation Map from Earthwalk Press is more current.
Trail contact: Koke'e Museum; (808) 335-9975; open daily 10:00 a.m. to 4:00 p.m.

Finding the trailhead: From the Lihue Airport turn left (south) on HI 51 (the Kapule Highway) to Rice Street. Turn right (northwest) and go through town to HI 50 (the Kaumuali'i Highway). Turn left (west) on HI 50, and drive about 25 miles to Waimea. Turn right (north) onto HI 550 (Waimea Canyon Drive). It's not clearly marked, but if you miss it, continue on to HI 552 (the Koke'e Road), which is clearly marked with a big sign indicating Waimea Canyon and Koke'e State Park. The two roads, 550 and 552, come together 7 miles farther. Continue ascending the winding road 8 miles more to Koke'e State Park headquarters, on the left (north). The trailhead begins just to the left (south) of the little ranger station, on a dirt road that separates the lawn of the restaurant and museum from the cabin area. There is a sign, clearly visible from the highway.

The Hike

From the trailhead sign, head up the service road to the trail on the left (west). The trail climbs over a hump, then begins a slippery, muddy scramble over tree roots down along a streambed (on your right) lined with a combination of native koa trees and karakanut trees, an exotic species with big dark shiny green leaves. This part of the trail is almost always wet.

Enter a valley that gradually widens as you proceed, passing through several little grassy meadows blooming with flowers that are very pretty, but unfortunately are mostly weeds. The trail follows a ridgeline over ups and downs, with the downs longer and steeper than the ups, passing through vegetation that becomes more and more dense. Among the tangle of greenery are maile vines, not spectacular in appearance but used in wedding leis for their fragrance, and the funny, 3-foot-high, upside-down mops called hahalua, endemic to Hawai'i.

The way steepens as you reach a junction with a hunter's trail that goes off to the left (northwest), then drops even more steeply down a narrow gulch where you'll probably have to use your hands, or sit down and slide. Not far beyond you arrive at Nu'alolo Cliff Trail junction at mile 3.2 miles. Ahead is a 0.5-mile spur leading out to one of the most stunning views in the world, the Lolo Overlook. The trail runs along a knifelike ridge with long, long drops on either side, and the footing is as slippery as soap when wet. Do not go out to the point unless the ground is dry. There is

Nu'alolo Valley from the trail

a nominal barrier and an END OF TRAIL sign on the barren point, along with a couple of stubborn pine trees. You can see paths going farther, but these are remnants left after the last couple of hurricanes blasted them, and they do not go anywhere you want to go. Watch and listen for feral goats on the cliffs. The view of the Nu'alolo Valley is incredible: an immense amphitheater, lined with the silvery crowns of kukui trees, opening out onto the Na Pali Coast with its green and black cliffs, white surf, and blue sea.

When you're done haul yourself back up to the trailhead, or if you have the time and stamina, hike the semiloop back up to the Awa'awapuhi Trailhead.

Miles and Directions

0.0   Trailhead at Koke'e State Park headquarters (N22 07.44' / W159 39.35')

2.8   Hunter's trail junction

3.2   Nu'alolo Cliff Trail junction (N22 08.46' / W159 40.46')

3.7   Lolo Overlook (N22 09.02' / W159 41.49')

4.2   Return to junction

7.4   Return to trailhead

Option: To complete the Nu'alolo Cliff Loop from the junction of the Nu'alolo Trail and the Nu'alolo Cliff Trail, turn left (east) onto the cliff trail. Negotiate a section of narrow, exposed trail for less than 0.25 mile, heading away from the cliff edge to follow a faint path through head-high grass to a covered picnic table at 0.4 mile. Follow switchbacks up to a ridge, drop steeply to cross Nu'alolo Stream, climb steeply back out of the stream valley, then wind your way to the junction with the Awa'awapuhi Trail (1.4 miles from the picnic table).

From this junction it is a moderate climb back up to the Awa'awapuhi Trailhead for a total hike of 9 miles. It should not be difficult to get a ride back down to Koke'e park headquarters if you have not arranged a shuttle. Walking back down the road is discouraged since it is narrow and winding, with blind curves and no shoulder.

67 Pu'uka'ohelo–Berry Flat Trail

This is a cool and lovely, often misty, walk among a crazy mixture of tropical flowers, California redwoods, Japanese cedars, and other surprises. Many were planted as experimental forests in the 1930s by the Civilian Conservation Corps (CCC). Part of the route is along dirt (mud) road winding through the back lanes of down–home Hawai'i. (Please do not trespass on private property.) It is described from Koke'e State Park headquarters, because not only is the road a beautiful walk in itself, it is not passable by ordinary passenger cars even when dry, and when wet it is tricky even for four–wheel–drive vehicles.

Start: Koke'e State Park headquarters
Distance: 5.5-mile lollipop loop
Elevation change: 400 feet
Difficulty: Easy
Approximate hiking time: 2 to 3 hours
Trail surface: Four-wheel drive road; well-graded trail
Seasons: Year-round, though it rains more in winter and there is more chance of slippery mud
Other trail users: A few four-wheel-drive vehicles and cyclists on the road portion
Canine compatibility: Dogs are permitted on the road, though dogs in nearby residences might be territorial

Land status: Koke'e State Park
Nearest town: Waimea
Fees and permits: None
Maps: USGS Ha'ena; Northwestern Kaua'i Recreation Map by Earthwalk Press
Trail contact: Koke'e Museum; (808) 335-9975; open daily 10:00 a.m. to 4:00 p.m.
Special considerations: Do not take an ordinary passenger car down the Mohihi-Camp 10 Road. Car rental agencies say you're on your own if you get stuck. Furthermore, it's slippery and dangerous when wet, and even in a four-wheel drive vehicle you'll slide off the road when mud fills the tread on your tires. Walking is safer, easier, and more fun.

Finding the trailhead: From the Lihue Airport turn left (south) on HI 51 (the Kapule Highway) to Rice Street. Turn right (northwest) and go through town to HI 50 (the Kaumuali'i Highway). Turn left (west) and drive about 25 miles to Waimea. Turn right (north) onto HI 550 (Waimea Canyon Drive). It's not clearly marked, but if you miss it, continue on to HI 552 (the Koke'e Road), which is clearly marked with a big sign indicating Waimea Canyon and Koke'e State Park. The two roads, 550 and 552, come together 7 miles farther. Continue ascending the winding road 8 miles to Koke'e Lodge and Museum on the left (north), beyond a wide grassy picnic area. There are cabins for rent, a coffee shop (open only for breakfast and lunch), and a great museum (not to mention restrooms and cold drinks, and a telephone).

The Hike

Follow the driveway out of the Koke'e Museum parking area to HI 550 and turn left (east). Almost immediately turn right (south) onto an unmarked road with a sign

PASSION FLOWERS

Banana poka is the vine you see draping itself over so many of the trees at Koke'e. It is one of several kinds of passion flower *(Passiflora* spp.) introduced to Hawai'i from South America. Its flowers are some of the most intricate and beautiful in the world, with large open blossoms, some pink, some white, some purple, and showy; exserted stamen; and pistils surrounded by a frilly structure called a corona, in addition to its petals.

Despite the prominent reproductive parts, the passion flower name does not mean what you think it does. The pious Spaniards who came to the Americas determined to convert the heathen to Christianity saw the flower as a representation of the

Passion flower

Passion of Christ. The five sepals and five petals are supposed to represent the ten apostles present at the crucifixion, the corona either a halo or a crown of thorns, the three stigmas the nails, the tendrils the scourges . . . You get the idea.

Passion fruit or lilikoi

The fruits are green to orange in color, more or less egg-shaped, about 3 inches in diameter, and delicious, if somewhat slimy in texture. The ones called lilikoi are used to flavor all kinds of pastries, snacks, and desserts in Hawai'i.

Unfortunately, beautiful and delicious as they are, two species of passion flower have escaped cultivation to become terrible pests. Their fruits are eaten by birds who then deposit the seeds in the treetops. These germinate and spread so exuberantly they sometimes form a kind of drapery over native vegetation, blocking sunlight and strangling their hosts. Feel free to pick and eat as many of the fruits as you like.

marked YWCA CAMP SLOGGETT. This becomes the Mohihi–Camp 10 Road, though you're not likely to see a street sign anywhere.

The stroll along the road is a delight to wildflower lovers, especially in spring and summer. There are fuchsias, elderberries, daisies, nasturtiums, ginger, hydrangeas, irises, orchids, and more. Unfortunately, all of these are nonnative intruders, some of which have overrun rare native Hawaiian species. The worst culprit is the very invasive banana poka.

When you reach the turnoff to Camp Sloggett on your right, keep left (northeast) on the main road. Just beyond the junction is a sign marking a parking area (for four-wheel-drive vehicles) for the Halemanu-Koke'e, Kumuwela, and Waininiua Trails. Beyond this, the road splits again; keep left (north). Continue on the main road, ignoring other spurs heading off into the bushes. Most of these are private driveways. You'll pass two chain-link encircled water treatment plants along the way.

Reach yet another unmarked Y junction. The two forks appear identical, and either will take you to one end or the other of the Berry Flat Trail. For now, take the left fork (traveling the loop in a clockwise direction) and in about 0.25 mile arrive in a clearing with a sign marking the Pu'uka'ohelo Trail on the left (north). Leave the road and follow the path into the forest.

The narrow trail winds through dense strawberry guava bushes beneath a taller canopy of native koa trees. In 0.5 mile you'll reach a junction with the Water Tank Trail that goes left (west), back toward the Koke'e Discovery Center and the Koke'e

Redwood forest

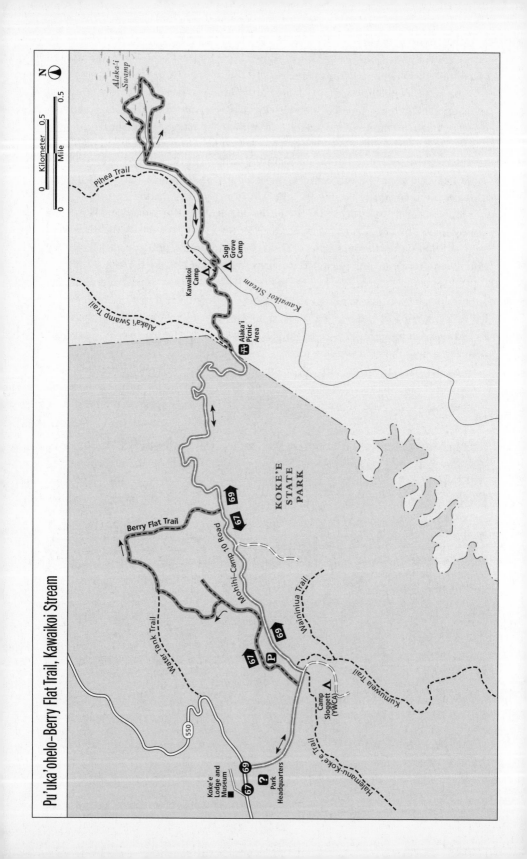

Pu'uka'ohelo–Berry Flat Trail, Kawaikoi Stream

Road. This junction is not shown on older maps. Keep right on the fork marked BERRY FLAT TRAIL and enter another world. California redwoods filter the sunlight falling on bright green ferns and mosses. Japanese sugi cedars and occasional ginger plants are all that remind you you're not in California. At what appears to be another three-way junction, keep right on the Berry Flat Trail. The unmarked third fork goes nowhere at all. Eventually, the redwoods begin to thin out a little and you find yourself among the berry bushes that give the trail its name. In just a small patch are crammed almost every kind of berry imaginable: raspberries, blackberries, elderberries, and even strawberries.

The trail abruptly ends at the Mohihi–Camp 10 Road, which you follow to the right (southwest) Turn right at a second junction and in another 0.25 mile find yourself back where the two forks of the Y converge. Go straight ahead, back to the PARK HERE sign and trailhead, turn right, and continue on back to HI 550 and Koke'e park headquarters.

Miles and Directions

0.0 Start at the Koke'e park headquarters turnoff. Turn left (east) onto HI 550 (N22 07.45' / W159 39.31')

0.2 Turn right (south) on the road marked YWCA CAMP SLOGGETT (N22 07.46' / W159 39.25')

1.3 Camp Sloggett turnoff; keep left to the PARK HERE sign, then immediately turn right

1.8 Unmarked Y junction; take the left fork (N22 07.40' / W159 38.50')

2.1 Pu'uka'ohelo Trail; turn left (north)

2.2 Berry Flat / Water Tank Trails junction; keep right (northeast) (N22 08.06' / W159 38.40')

3.2 Berry Flat/Mohihi-Camp 10 Road junction; turn right (west) onto road and right again (northwest) at first junction (N22 07.51' / W159 38.21')

3.7 Unmarked Y junction; go straight ahead

5.5 Return the same way you came to HI 550 and Koke'e park headquarters

68 Canyon Trail–Black Pipe Trail Loop

This is surely among the most exciting hikes in Koke'e State Park, offering heart-stopping views into Waimea Canyon as well as a visit to a waterfall flowing from a beautiful little pool surrounded by tropical vegetation. Most hikers walk down to the falls and pool and back up again the same way. On this hike you return via the Black Pipe Trail, making a slightly longer trip and allowing a greater variety of scenery and more solitude. You also can continue on to the end of the Canyon Trail and the Kumuwela Lookout, where you can connect with any number of other trails in the park. But this loop gives you the most scenery and variety for the least effort.

Start: Halemanu Valley Trailhead
Distance: 3.1-mile lollipop loop
Elevation change: 300 feet
Difficulty: Moderate
Approximate hiking time: 2 to 3 hours
Trail surface: Dirt road; trail
Seasons: Year-round, but likely to be wet and slippery in winter
Other trail users: None, except four-wheel-drive vehicles on the Halemanu Valley Road at the beginning and end

Canine compatibility: Dogs not permitted
Land status: Koke'e State Park
Nearest town: Waimea
Fees and permits: None
Schedule: Open daily 10:00 a.m.–4:00 p.m.
Maps: USGS Ha'ena, Makaha Point, and Waimea Canyon; the Northwestern Kaua'i Recreation Map by Earthwalk Press, available at the Koke'e Museum and elsewhere, is more up-to-date
Trail contact: Koke'e Museum; (808) 335-9975

Finding the trailhead: From the Lihue Airport turn left (south) on HI 51 (the Kapule Highway) to Rice Street. Turn right (northwest) and go through town to HI 50 (the Kaumuali'i Highway). Turn left (west) and drive about 25 miles to Waimea. Turn right (north) onto HI 550 (Waimea Canyon Drive). It's not clearly marked, but if you miss it continue on to HI 552 (the Koke'e Road), which is clearly marked with a big sign for Waimea Canyon and Koke'e State Park. The two roads, 550 and 552, come together 7 miles farther. Continue ascending the winding road (HI 550) to Milepost 14 and the boundary of Koke'e State Park. Park on the left side of the road. The trail begins on the four-wheel-drive Halemanu Valley Road, across the street.

The Hike

Walk down the Halemanu Valley Road, watching for occasional local traffic in a forest of koa, blackberries, ginger, lantana, and banana poka, to a junction marked with a trail sign. Follow the sign to the right (south) toward Waipo'o Falls, Kumuwela Road, and the Cliff Trail. A little farther on you can make a short side trip uphill to the right (south) on the Cliff Trail for a view of Waimea Canyon without cars all around you, then return to the junction. Just beyond is the "official" trailhead for the Canyon Trail. (There is another cutoff, not clearly shown on the Earthwalk map, to the

Pu'u'hinahina Lookout. This one parallels HI 550 and winds up at a parking lot off the highway.)

Switchback steeply downhill in koa forest, passing into and out of a gully with an irrigation ditch at the bottom. Soon the first fabulous Waimea Canyon vista appears. Pass the turnoff to the Black Pipe Trail on the left (east), and continue to descend on an open ridge-line of eroded red dirt, then climb to a broad knob scattered with some oddly eroded boulders. Take in the canyon, which you can see all the way to its mouth at the sea, wave at the unofficial Kaua'i State Bird, the helicopter, then follow the trail curving left down a series of steep log steps.

▶ Most of the mileage you will see on trail signs and in many guides gives you the distance from the trailhead to your destination. Remember that many of these trails have trailheads along roads that are not passable to ordinary passenger cars. You must remember to add the mileage you will walk on the road to the mileage on the trailhead signs to get a total distance.

It looks like you're about to drop off the edge of the world, but instead you swing back into foliage where you can hear running water for the first time. Wind through boulders to the most charming little pool and cascade you've ever seen, trimmed with elderberry and yellow ginger. Just downstream, 800-foot Waipo'o Falls drops straight down the cliff side. You can clamber down a very short distance to peer around the corner for a glimpse of a small section of the big falls, but be very, very careful. If you simply must get a better look, go about 0.5 mile farther along the Canyon Trail to where you can look back across the canyon.

When you have had enough, go back up to the Black Pipe Trail junction and turn right (east). This trail gets much less use than the Canyon Trail. It winds up and down along the hillside, at one point giving you a view of the big bald patch and other hikers gaping at the canyon from the Canyon Trail. At one point, when you get to a very overgrown notch where it looks like the trail ends, look to the right for a grassy patch. The trail continues across it and resumes clearly on the other side.

Ignore an unmarked trail forking off to the right (downhill, northeast), and continue uphill on switchbacks until you reach an unmarked road. Turn left (northwest) and follow the road down to the main Halemanu Valley Road and the big trail sign. Keep right and return to the main highway and your car.

Miles and Directions

0.0 Start (N22 06.56' / W159 40.11')

0.5 First road junction, turn right (south)

0.6 Second road junction with sign to falls; turn right (south)

0.7 Cliff Trail spur; main trail stays left (southeast) (N22 06.55' / W159 39.55')

1.2 Black Pipe Trail junction, go straight (south) (N22 06.47' / W159 39.56')

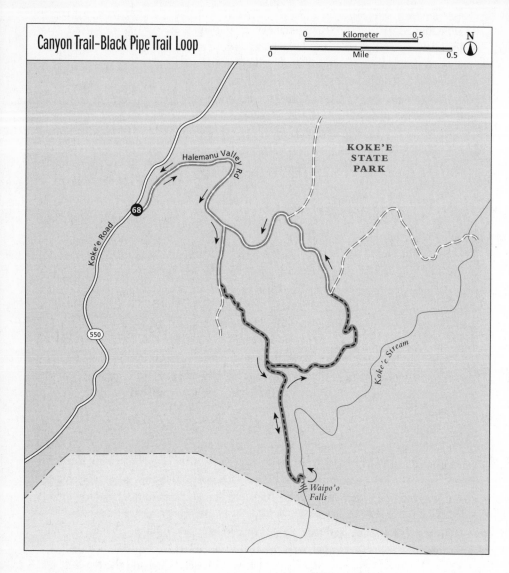

1.6 Pool and top of falls; turnaround point (N22 06.19' / W159 39.42')

2.0 Return to Black Pipe Junction, turn right (east)

2.6 Turn left (northwest) on unmarked road, then right (north) at Halemanu Road junction (N22 06.57' / W159 39.46')

3.1 Return to the trailhead

Option 1: Waipo'o Falls. For a better view of Waipo'o Falls, go downstream a few yards from the little ginger pool and watch for a narrow grassy path leading across the stream. There is a board bridge to help you cross if the water is high. The rocks are very slick. Climb steeply up the other side and wind around the cliff, ducking into and out of a couple of deep green gullies. After you emerge from the second gully, about 0.5 mile beyond the stream crossing, there is an open red-dirt viewpoint from which you can look back across to the trail at hikers moving along it like tiny ants, and below them, see most of the lower waterfall.

Option 2: Kumuwela Lookout. If you still haven't had enough, you can continue even farther, climbing all the way to the end of the Canyon Trail (2.9 miles from its beginning). At trail's end you'll find a picnic table at Kumuwela Lookout (3,515 feet). This marks the beginning of the much less traveled, and less scenic, Kumuwela Trail, which winds its way back up to HI 550. You will have this trail to yourself, except, perhaps, for a few pigs. Watch out for hunters, too.

Slippery slope on the Canyon Trail

69 Kawaikoi Stream

The Kawaikoi Stream Loop itself involves less than 3 miles of this much longer hike, but you can only get to it by crossing the entire Alaka'i Swamp, starting from the Pihea Trail or by this route, following the Mohihi–Camp 10 Road from Koke'e State Park headquarters. The latter route is described here, since it is the quicker and easier way from this side. The Kawaikoi Stream area is so exquisitely beautiful that it is worth any effort you make to get there, and the walk along the Mohihi Road is itself a joy, passing as it does through flowery gardens and making a stop at a dizzying overlook of the Po'omau Canyon from the Alaka'i picnic area. There are wonderful swimming holes along the stream and a short foray into the mysterious Alaka'i Swamp as a bonus. You can do this hike as a day hike or as a backpack since there are camping areas at Kawaikoi Camp and Sugi Grove Camp.

See map on page 230.

Start: Koke'e State Park Headquarters

Distance: 9.9-mile lollipop loop (with a very long stick)

Elevation change: About 600 feet, though you start and end at approximately the same elevation

Difficulty: Moderate

Approximate hiking time: 5 to 7 hours

Trail surface: Everything from hard, dry red dirt road to soft, mushy red mud to puddles

Seasons: Year-round, but high water is more likely to be a problem in winter

Other trail users: Four-wheel-drive vehicles on the Mohihi–Camp 10 Road

Canine compatibility: Dogs permitted on the road, but not in the swamp

Land status: Koke'e State Park

Nearest town: Waimea

Fees and permits: None for a day hike. If you plan to camp, you can apply for a permit by mail or call the Hawai'i Department of Land and Natural Resources and ask them to send you an application form. Contact information is: 3060 Eiwa Street, Room 306, Lihue, HI 96766; 808-274-3444.

Maps: USGS Ha'ena; the Northwestern Kaua'i Recreation Map by Earthwalk Press

Trail contact: Koke'e Museum; (808) 335-9975; open daily 10:00 a.m.–4:00 p.m.

Special considerations: Do not take an ordinary passenger car down the Mohihi–Camp 10 Road. Even four-wheel-drive vehicles get stuck or slide off the road when it has been raining because mud fills in the treads on their tires. If it has been raining steadily and hard, and the water in Kawaikoi Stream is running high and swift, turn around! Fording is much too dangerous. All water along the way must be purified, and if you plan to spend the night, you will need a tent and a permit.

Finding the trailhead: From the Lihue Airport turn left (south) on HI 51 (the Kapule Highway) to Rice Street. Turn right (northwest) and go through town to HI 50 (the Kaumuali'i Highway). Turn left (west) and drive about 15 miles to Waimea. Turn right (north) onto HI 550 (Waimea Canyon Drive). It's not clearly marked, but if you miss it continue to HI 552 (the Koke'e Road), which is clearly marked with a big sign for Waimea Canyon and Koke'e State Park. The two roads, 550 and 552, come together 7 miles farther. Continue ascending the winding road 8 miles to Koke'e Lodge and Museum. Park in the lot here.

The Hike

Follow the driveway out of the Koke'e Museum area to HI 550 and turn left (east). Almost immediately turn right (south) onto an unmarked road with a sign for YWCA CAMP SLOGGETT. This becomes the Mohihi–Camp 10 Road though you're not likely to see a street sign. The road is lined with wildflowers almost all the way, especially in spring and summer.

When you reach the turnoff to Camp Sloggett on your right, keep left (north) on the main road. Just beyond the junction is a sign marking a parking area for several radiating trails. Immediately to the left of the sign the road splits again; keep left (northeast). Continue on the main road, ignoring other spurs heading off into the bushes. Most of these are private driveways.

When you reach yet another unmarked Y junction, take the right fork. Pass the entrance to the Berry Flat Trail on your left (west) about 0.5 mile past the junction, continuing downhill to cross a stream on a bridge. Climb again between high banks of uluhe fern, then descend to cross the tumbling stream on another bridge.

The forest just gets prettier and prettier as you advance, with orange wild iris and purple orchids brightening the roadside. Climb to the grassy Alaka'i picnic area, where there are covered tables and a lua (pit toilet). At the southern end of the flat is a fabulous view down the impossibly deep Po'omau Canyon, running directly south.

Pool on Kawaikoi Stream

Return to the road and pass the junction with the Alaka'i Swamp Trail; a sign tells you Kawaikoi Camp is only 0.75 mile ahead. Descend gradually at first, then more steeply, to Kawaikoi Camp on its grassy flat beside the stream. There is a covered picnic table and a lua here too. You can wade the stream to camp at Sugi Grove Camp, which is just beyond the ford and to the right of the road, if you prefer. Either way, you will have to cross the stream to hike the loop, but do not try it if the water is high.

From Sugi Grove Camp, the trail cuts sharply off the road to the left (northeast) and climbs a bit through redwoods and cedars, following the trail above the stream, sometimes in shade, sometimes in the open. You are not far from the edge of the swamp here, and the ground is mossy and muddy. The trail drops to streamside just before the trail splits to begin the loop.

Take the right fork, hiking the loop in a counterclockwise direction. Wade a tributary of the stream, sometimes squishing through boggy ground. The variety of vegetation along the stream is so rich it's hard to watch your step: Jungly forest-type vegetation alternates with carpets of moss and clumps of ginger. Keep left along the main trail, ignoring any side paths, negotiating mud puddles and boggy spots, hopping over rivulets, grateful for dry stretches of ground. In about 0.5 mile ford the main Kawaikoi Stream again, closing the loop almost immediately afterward.

Retrace your steps to Sugi Grove Camp, wade the stream one last time, pass Kawaikoi Camp, and follow the Mohihi–Camp 10 Road back to the trailhead.

Miles and Directions

0.0 Start at Koke'e State Park headquarters. Turn left (east) onto HI 550 (N22 07.45' / W159 39.31')

1.3 CAMP SLOGGETT trail sign; keep left to the PARK HERE sign, then immediately turn left (northwest)

1.8 Unmarked junction; take the right fork (northeast) (N22 07.40' / W159 38.40')

3.1 Alaka'i picnic area (N22 07.44' / W159 37.30'). Make a short detour uphill for the view, then return to the road and follow the sign eastward toward Kawaikoi Camp.

3.8 Kawaikoi Camp (N22 07.54' / W159 37.21'). Cross the stream on the road. Sugi Grove Camp is just beyond. The trail cuts sharply left away from the road.

4.7 Begin the actual Kawaikoi Loop loop, keeping right (N22 08.09' / W159 36.51')

5.2 Close the loop

6.1 Return to Kawaikoi Camp

9.9 Return to Koke'e State Park headquarters

70 Pihea Trail to the Alaka'i Swamp

This is the shortest, easiest way into—and back out of—the fabulous and forbidding Alaka'i Swamp. The swamp fills the crater of the volcano that originally built the island of Kaua'i. Its floor consists of such impermeable lava that moisture does not drain away but gathers in pools and puddles and bogs . . . and there is a lot of moisture to gather. Looming over the swamp, after all, is Mount Wai'ale'ale, the wettest place on earth. There are organisms in the swamp that live nowhere else in the world. They have only managed to hang on when so many of Hawaii's other inhabitants have gone extinct because this place is too rugged and inhospitable for anything to disturb them, including mosquitoes. The catch is that it is not very hospitable to hikers either. Trails are rough and steep and muddy, and often so obscured by clouds that there are no vistas. Don't let that deter you from this hike, though. It gives you a taste of an absolutely unique environment that is truly beautiful, and the first mile or so along the ridge overlooks the Kalalau Valley, where you are much more likely to have fantastic views.

Start: Pihea Trailhead at the Pu'u O Kila Lookout

Distance: 3.5 miles out and back

Elevation change: 600 feet

Difficulty: Moderate

Approximate hiking time: 3 to 4 hours

Trail surface: Eroded road; rough, muddy trail; boardwalk

Seasons: Year-round, but likely to be wetter in winter

Other trail users: None

Canine compatibility: Dogs not permitted

Land status: Napali-Kona Forest Reserve

Nearest town: Waimea

Fees and permits: None for a day hike

Maps: USGS Ha'ena; the Northwestern Kaua'i Recreation Map by Earthwalk Press

Trail contact: Koke'e Museum; (808) 335-9975, open daily 10:00 a.m. to 4:00 p.m.

Finding the trailhead: From the Lihue Airport turn left (south) on HI 51 (the Kapule Highway) to Rice Street. Turn right (northwest), and go through town to HI 50 (the Kaumuali'i Highway). Turn left (west), and drive about 25 miles to Waimea. Turn right (north) onto HI 550 (Waimea Canyon Drive). It's not clearly marked, but if you miss it continue on to HI 552 (the Koke'e Road), which is clearly marked with a big sign for Waimea Canyon and Koke'e State Park. The two roads, 550 and 552, come together 7 miles farther. Ascend past Koke'e State Park headquarters, beyond which the road becomes more narrow, winding, potholed, and patched, up to the Kalalau Lookout (your last chance for a bathroom) at mile 18. Beyond, the road becomes miraculously smooth and perfect again. The road ends in less than 1 mile at the Pihea trailhead and Pu'u O Kila Lookout. There is a large parking lot, but no facilities.

The Hike

From the lookout at the trailhead the view is spectacular, with the Kalalau Valley makai (toward the sea), and the Alaka'i Swamp mauka (toward the mountain). A sign points to Mount Wai'ale'ale, but the sign is most likely all you will ever see of it. The clouds that swirl around the Kalalau Valley and the Na Pali Coast are not nearly so dense, and if you willing to wait a few minutes, they might blow away.

Na Pali Coast from the Pihea Trail

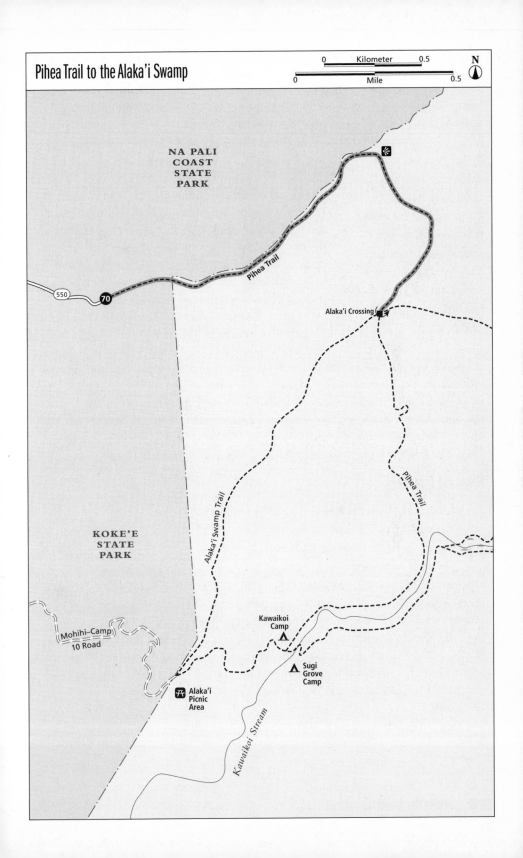

Pihea Trail to the Alaka'i Swamp

NA PALI
COAST
STATE
PARK

Pihea Trail

550

70

Alaka'i Crossing

Pihea Trail

Alaka'i Swamp Trail

KOKE'E
STATE
PARK

Kawaikoi
Camp

Mohihi–Camp
10 Road

Sugi
Grove
Camp

Alaka'i
Picnic
Area

Kawaikoi Stream

Kilometer

0   0.5

Mile

0   0.5

N

The trail first descends along a broad ridgetop, following all that remains of a misguided attempt to build a road connecting Koke'e with Ha'ena, making a highway all the way around the island. It was originally planned to follow this ridge down into and across part of the swamp! It will only take you a few minutes of travel along this route to understand why that plan had to be abandoned.

▶ Take lots and lots of water, even though it looks like a soggy place. The hike back up out of the swamp is hot work. Also take a windbreaker or something more substantial than a T-shirt. You are above 4,000 feet and it can get breezy on the ridge.

The trail flattens out and becomes narrower and more overgrown as you progress. At 0.8 mile a short spur heads uphill to the left (northwest) to the Pihea viewpoint, providing another vista into the Kalalau Valley. It is a muddy scramble involving loose handholds and precarious balancing on slimy tree roots. Return to the main trail, which almost immediately turns sharply right (south) and descends steeply into the swamp. A boardwalk keeps you from sinking beyond your knees in mud and protects the trail from erosion.

Stop frequently to listen for the native birds that still flourish here because the weather is too cool for mosquitoes, carriers of the diseases that killed so many birds elsewhere on the islands. Some of the most interesting of these birds have long curved bills that are exactly the length and shape of the unusual flowers you can find here if you look carefully. The blooms are likely to be clustered at the base of the leaves of tall plants that look like upside-down mops, or cabbages on sticks, the famous lobelioids of Hawai'i. There are showy wild hydrangeas, big fuzzy tree ferns, and bizarre mosses and fungi. The trail levels out at the signed Alaka'i Crossing, your turn-around point.

Miles and Directions

0.0 Start at the Pu'u O Kila Lookout (N22 08.51' / W159 37.52')
0.7 Spur trail to Pihea overlook (N22 09.15' / W159 37.06')
1.7 Alaka'i Crossing (N22 08.48' / W159 07.04')
3.5 Return to the trailhead

Options: If you would like more swamp, the Pihea Trail continues for another 2 miles to Kawaikoi Camp, which is on Kawaikoi Stream, which you will have to ford. You can camp here or at nearby Sugi Grove Camp if you have a permit, available from the Department of Land and Natural Resources. There is much more to see, but the going is tough and muddy and slow. If you have a shuttle you can follow the Mohihi–Camp 10 Road from the camp all the way back to Koke'e park headquarters. In fact, you can enter the swamp from that direction and finish at the Pu'u O Kila Lookout.

71 Iliau Nature Trail

The trail through this Alice in Wonderland grove, part of Waimea Canyon State Park, has recently been given a thorough renovation, with shiny new signs identifying the plants and adding fascinating bits of lore about each. You don't need signs to tell you that the things growing around you are no ordinary roses and petunias, but weird and rare organisms utterly unlike anything you have ever seen. The stars of the show are the pompons-on-sticks, the iliau that grow only here on Kaua'i. This is also a good place to enjoy breathtaking views down into Waimea Canyon without cars whizzing along a highway just behind you.

Start: Trailhead sign on HI 550 in Waimea Canyon State Park
Distance: 0.5-mile loop (or less)
Elevation change: Negligible
Approximate hiking time: 20 to 30 minutes
Difficulty: Easy
Trail surface: Fairly smooth lava
Seasons: Year-round

Other trail users: None
Canine compatibility: Dogs not permitted
Land status: Waimea Canyon State Park
Nearest town: Waimea
Fees and permits: None
Maps: USGS *Waimea Canyon;* none needed
Trail contact: Koke'e Museum; (808) 335-9975; open daily 10:00 a.m. to 4:00 p.m.

Finding the trailhead: From the Lihue Airport turn left (south) on HI 51 (the Kapule Highway) to Rice Street. Turn right (northwest) and go through town to HI 50 (the Kaumuali'i Highway) Turn left (west) and drive about 25 miles to Waimea. Turn right (north) onto HI 550 (Waimea Canyon Drive). It's not clearly marked, but if you miss it continue to HI 552 (the Koke'e Road), which is clearly marked for Waimea Canyon and Koke'e State Park. The two roads, 550 and 552, come together after 7 miles. The trailhead is between mileposts 8 and 9 on HI 550, on the right (east) side of the road. There is a not-very-obvious brown-and-gold trail sign right next to an emergency call box. Park along the road on the opposite side and lock your car. GPS: N27 05.26' / W159 66.09'

The Hike

Climb up the bank to a bench beneath a shady tree. Turn to the right (east) and descend a few steps to find yourself in a grove of, among other things, upside-down mops, some with big bouquets of little flowers erupting from their tops. These are the iliau (*Wilkesia sp.*), whose ancestor was a small member of the sunflower family that was transported, most likely by a bird, 2,500 miles over the sea from the Americas to the Hawaiian Islands. Here it evolved into oddities like the silversword that grows in the barren red cinders on Haleakala on Maui, the greensword of the Maui bogs, and the iliau. It retains its pompon-on-a-stick form for two to ten years, after which it shoots a 4-foot stalk right out of the center of the leaves, along which are slender, drooping stems tipped with yellowish puff-ball flowers. Then it dies.

Iliau Nature Trail, Kukui Trail and Waimea Canyon

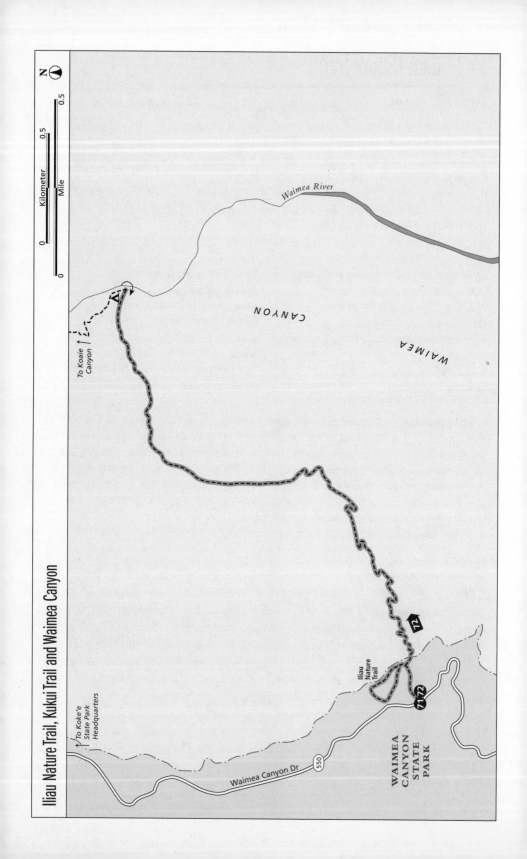

Almost at once you come to a signed junction with the Kukui Trail, which goes straight ahead down into Waimea Canyon. Your trail keeps left (east) and continues to describe a more or less oval path, part of which runs near the edge of the cliff where the views out over Waimea Canyon are the best.

Among the other inhabitants of this garden is the a'ali'i, a shrub with clustered, reddish, winged fruits. These are hops, related to the ones used to make beer. Another is pukiawe, with small short leaves that remind you of a conifer. It has lots of very small pink and white berries, a favorite of nenes (Hawaiian geese). These were used by the Hawaiian ali'i, or chiefs, who had so much power that they could not mix with common people without polluting themselves or injuring their subjects. A bath in the smoke from burning pukiawe would temporarily dissolve this barrier so that the chief could behave like a normal human now and then.

When you have closed the loop at the Kukui Trail junction, turn right and go back uphill to the trailhead. If you are not ready to go back yet, you can walk a few hundred yards along the Kukui Trail to a grassy area with a covered picnic table.

Iliau plants on the Iliau Nature Trail

72 Kukui Trail and Waimea Canyon

Waimea Canyon, the "Grand Canyon of the Pacific," is more than 13 miles long and over 2,500 feet deep, depending on where you take your measurements. The scale is smaller than that of the Grand Canyon, of course, but the nearly vertical red-dirt cliffs really do resemble those of the mainland's southwest canyon country. This hike takes you from the rim to the river in only 2.5 miles on very steep, seriously eroded trail that can be treacherous when rainy and wet and cruelly hot when the sun is out. Still, for physically fit hikers, this one is worth the sweat and the mud. The Waimea River at the bottom forms cool and pleasant pools where you can have a dip, and if you want to stay longer, you can spend the night at Wiliwili Camp.

See map on page 244.
Start: Kukui Trailhead in Waimea Canyon State Park
Distance: 5 miles out and back
Elevation change: 2,200 feet
Approximate hiking time: 4 to 6 hours
Difficulty: Strenuous
Trail surface: Red dirt, badly eroded in places and slippery when wet
Seasons: Year-round; best in dry season
Other trail users: None
Canine compatibility: No dogs permitted
Land status: Napali-Kona Forest Reserve

Nearest town: Waimea
Fees and permits: None for a day hike. A permit is required if you plan to camp. You can apply for one by mail or call the Department of Land and Natural Resources and ask for an application form. Contact the DLNR at 3060 Eiwa Street, Room 306, Lihue, HI 96766; 808-274-3444.
Maps: USGS Waimea Canyon; Northwestern Kaua'i Recreation Map by Earthwalk Press
Trail contact: Koke'e Museum; (808) 335-9975, open daily 10:00 a.m.–4:00 p.m.

Finding the trailhead: From the Lihue Airport turn left (south) on HI 51 (the Kapule Highway) to Rice Street. Turn right (northwest) and go through town to HI 50 (the Kaumuali'i Highway). Turn left (west) and drive about 25 miles to Waimea. Turn right (north) onto HI 550 (Waimea Canyon Drive). It's not clearly marked, but if you miss it continue to HI 552 (the Koke'e Road), which is clearly marked for Waimea Canyon and Koke'e State Park. The two roads, 550 and 552, come together 7 miles farther. The trailhead is between mileposts 8 and 9 on HI 550, on the right (east) side of the road. There is a not-too-obvious brown-and-gold trail sign next to an emergency call box. Park along the road on the opposite side of the street and lock your car.

The Hike

Climb up the bank to a bench beneath a shady tree, turn right (east), and skirt the Iliau Nature Loop and its rare, endemic, upside-down mop forest. At the signed junction with the Kukui Trail keep right (east), and just a few yards beyond find a grassy area with covered picnic tables. The trail has been marked with posts every 0.25 mile, though some of these have disappeared. Other signs will remind you (again and again) that hunting is permitted here (to control the flourishing population of goats).

After a misleadingly easy couple of switchbacks, the trail begins its precipitous drop, first in the shade of native koa and introduced silk oak trees from Australia, later in the open. It has eroded into narrow trenches in some places, slippery slopes in others. You must stay alert to keep to the main trail, since there are places where you might find you have arrived at what seems to be an impossible drop-off. You might have missed a switchback, so check behind you and beside you as you descend, and don't rush.

> **Take much more water than you think you will need. Treat the river water before drinking. Do not try to cross the river when the water is high, and watch out for hunters. You will want a tent if you plan to spend the night. Expect rain and mosquitoes. If you are at all acrophobic, you will want to avoid this one.**

There is a bench at the 1-mile marker. It should remind you to stop and enjoy the view now and then instead of focusing entirely on your feet. Scan the cliffs across the gorge for waterfalls and listen for the bleating of goats on the cliffs.

Sometimes you teeter along the very top of a narrow ridge, at others the trail takes you just below the crest on one side or the other, as you descend to a fairly narrow saddle heading directly toward a bare hill (marked 2209 on the topo). At the very base of the hill make a sharp left at an inconspicuous sign, and slip and slide down another very hot, but broader, exposed ridgeline.

Where the trail swings east (right), it re-enters the forest. Switchback steeply down through a muggy, buggy, dense growth of silk oak trees, kukui, and eucalyptus. The shade is welcome, but now you have no breeze, and there are rocks hiding in the underbrush to trip you up. The appearance of huge agaves (century plants) along the trail means you have almost reached your goal. Wiliwili Camp is a wide flat spot at a junction with a dirt road shaded by eponymous wiliwili trees. These have beautiful orange flowers that bloom in the winter before the leaves appear, and carpet the ground with their pealike pods and seeds in summer. Except for the trees, the camp does not have much to recommend it, just a sheltered picnic table and a lua (pit toilet). The Waimea River is just the other side of the dirt road. Remember that this is dry country, so fires are prohibited, and be sure to purify the water before drinking. When you are ready to tackle the climb, labor back up the cliff the same way you came.

Miles and Directions

0.0   Start (N22 03.01' / W159 39.35')
2.5   Wiliwili Camp (N22 03.48' / W159 38.33')
5.0   Return to the trailhead

Option: You can explore the Waimea River in both directions from Wiliwili Camp. There is another camp about 0.5 mile upstream on the Waimea River, and two more up Koaie Canyon, a tributary that cuts off to the right. This is mostly a wet, overgrown scramble following plastic tags attached to the trees. If you have a car shuttle, you can hike 8 miles downstream to the town of Waimea. Much of this is on four-wheel-drive road that runs through private property. There are many river crossings, so do not try it at high water.

View into Waimea Canyon from the Kukui Trail

Bibliography

Carlquist, Sherwin. *Hawaii: A Natural History.* Lauai, Hawaii: Pacific Tropical Botanical Garden, 1980.

Culliney, John L. *Islands in a Far Sea: Nature and Man in Hawaii.* San Francisco: Sierra Club Books, 1988.

Daws, Gavan. *Shoal of Time: A History of the Hawaiian Islands.* Honolulu: University of Hawai'i Press, 1968.

Hawai'i Audubon Society. *Hawaii's Birds.* Honolulu: Hawai'i Audubon Society, 5th ed. 1997.

Kirch, Patrick V. *Feathered Gods and Fishhooks: An Introduction to Hawaiian Archeology and Prehistory.* Honolulu: University of Hawai'i Press, 1998.

Kyselka, Will, and Ray Lanterman. *Maui: How It Came To Be.* Honolulu: University of Hawai'i Press, 1980.

Lamb, Samuel H. *Trees and Shrubs of the Hawaiian Islands.* Santa Fe: Sunstone Press, 1981.

Morey, Kathy. *Kauai Trails: Walks, Strolls and Treks on the Garden Island.* Berkeley: Wilderness Press, 2002.

———. *Hawaii Trails: Walks, Strolls and Treks on the Big Island.* Berkeley: Wilderness Press, 2002.

———. *Oahu Trails: Walks, Strolls and Treks on the Capital Isle.* Berkeley: Wilderness Press, 2005.

———. *Maui Trails: Walks, Strolls and Treks on the Valley Island.* Berkeley: Wilderness Press, 2003.

Pratt, Douglas. *A Pocket Guide to Hawaii's Trees and Shrubs.* Baton Rouge, Mutual Publishing, 1998.

Smith, Robert. *Hiking Kauai: The Garden Isle.* Kula, Maui: Hawaii Outdoor Adventures, 2002.

———. *Hiking Maui: The Valley Isle.* Kula, Maui: Hawaii Outdoor Adventures, 2003.

———. *Hiking Hawaii.* Kula, Maui: Hawaii Outdoor Adventures, 2002.

Index

Akaka Falls State Park 74

'Aiea Loop 144

'Aihualama Trail 152

Awa'awapuhi Trail 221

Canyon Trail–Black Pipe Trail Loop 232

Diamond Head 147

Free Tropical Edibles 130

Haleakala Silversword (In Addition) 102

Haleakala Trails 89

Halemau'u Trail to Holua Cabin 94

Hanakapi'ai Beach 212

Hanalei–Okolehao Trail 207

Hau'ula Loop Trail 178

Hawai'i Tropical Botanical Garden 71

Holua Cabin to Paliku Cabin 98

Hosmer Grove 87

'Iao Needle 103

Iliau Nature Trail 243

Judd–Jackass Ginger Pool 162

Ka Iwi (Makapu'u Point) 171

Ka'ena Point North 183

Ka'ena Point South 186

Kalopa Native Forest Trail 75

Kawaikoi Stream 236

Ke'anae Arboretum 115

Kilauea Iki 42

Kilauea Lighthouse 205

Kipuka Puaulu (Bird Park) 44

Koko Crater Botanical Garden 169

Kuamo'o–Nounou Trail 198

Kuilau Ridge 200

Kukui Trail and Waimea Canyon 246

Kuli'ou'ou Ridge Trail 167

Kuli'ou'ou Valley Trail 164

La Perouse Bay (Hoapili Trail) 132

Limahuli Garden and Preserve 210

Ma'akua Ridge Trail 181

Makiki Valley Loop 159

Manoa Cliff Trail 156

Manoa Falls 149

Manuka Nature Trail 80

Mauna Loa Trail to Red Hill 51

Mauna Loa Trails 49

Maunawili Falls 174

Moalepe Trail 203

Na Pali Coast (Kalalau Trail) 215

Nakalele Blowhole 108

Naupaka 205

North Pit Junction to Mauna Loa Cabin 59

North Pit Junction to Mauna Loa Summit 63

Nounou Mountain (Sleeping Giant) East 192

Nounou Mountain (Sleeping Giant) West 196

Nu'alolo Trail 224

Observatory Trail to North Pit Junction 65

'Ohe'o Gulch and the Seven Pools 126

Olowalu Petroglyphs 135

Passion Flowers 228

Permit Process 217

Pihea Trail to the Alaka'i Swamp 239

Pipiwai Trail 129
Pololu Valley 68
Pu'u Pia 154
Pu'uhonua o Honaunau (Place of
    Refuge) 82
Pu'uka'ohelo–Berry Flat Trail 227
Pu'uloa Petroglyphs 47

Red Hill Cabin to North Pit Junction 55

Sandalwood Trade 40
Sandalwood Trail 37
Sea Caves and Black Sand Beach 118
Sliding Sands Trail to Kapala'oa Cabin 90
Sulphur Bank Trail 35

Thurston Lava Tube 33
Twin Falls 110

Wai'anapanapa Coast Trail North 121
Wai'anapanapa Coast Trail South to
    Hana 123
Waihe'e Ridge Trail 104
Waihe'e Valley (Swinging Bridges) 106
Waikamoi Ridge Nature Trail 113
Waimano Loop 141
Waipio Valley 77

About the Author

Suzanne Swedo, director of W.I.L.D., has back-packed the mountains of every continent. She has led groups into the wilderness for more than twenty-five years and teaches wilderness survival and natural sciences for individuals, schools, universities, museums, and organizations such as the Yosemite Association and the Sierra Club. She is author of *Best Easy Day Hikes Yosemite National Park, Hiking Yosemite, Hiking California's Golden Trout Wilderness,* and *Adventure Travel Tips,* all FalconGuides. She lectures and consults about backpacking, botany, and survival on radio and television, as well as in print. While she lives in Los Angeles, California, she has been leading hiking groups in Hawai'i for more than twenty-five years.